Performance
Without
Compromise

Performance
Without
Compromise

HOW EMERSON
CONSISTENTLY ACHIEVES
WINNING RESULTS

Charles F. Knight
with Davis Dyer

HARVARD BUSINESS SCHOOL PRESS
Boston, Massachusetts

The following are trademarks of Emerson or its subsidiaries: ClosetMaid™, Emerson™, InterMetro™, Knaack™, Liebert™, PlantWeb™, Ridgid™, Rosemount™, and Stack A Shelf™.

The following trademarks are owned by third parties: Craftsman™, Dremel™, Louisville Ladder™, Poulan™, Skil™, and Weed Eater™. All except Craftsman were formerly owned by Emerson or its subsidiaries.

Library of Congress Cataloging-in-Publication Data
Knight, Charles F.
    Performance without compromise : how Emerson consistently achieves winning results / Charles F. Knight with Davis Dyer.
        p. cm.
    ISBN 1-59139-777-4
    1. Emerson Electric (Firm)—Management. 2. Electric industries—United States—Management—Case studies. 3. Electronic industries—United States—Management—Case studies. 4. Corporations—United States—Case studies.
I. Dyer, Davis. II. Title.
    HD9697.A3U5455 2005
    658.4—dc22

                                                                2005002392

The paper used in this publication meets the minimum requirements of the American National Standard for Information Sciences—Permanence of Paper for Printed Library Materials, ANSI Z39.48-1992.

To the memory of

W. R. "Buck" Persons (1909–1999),

who as chairman and chief executive officer of

Emerson between 1954 and 1973

set the company on the path to greatness

Contents

Preface   ix

1   The Secret of Emerson's Success   1
    The Management Process

2   Planning, Execution, and Control   15

3   Getting Things Done   53
    Organization Approach and Leadership

4   Operational Excellence   87

5   From Technology Follower to Technology Leader   121

6   Acquisitions and the Management Process   143

7   The Globalization of Markets and Competition   161

8   Growth   183
    The Ultimate Challenge

9   Leadership Succession   207

    Epilogue, by David N. Farr   221

    Appendix A   233
    Emerson Business Segments and Divisions

    Appendix B   237
    The President's Operating Report—Page 5

    Acknowledgments   241
    Index   245
    About the Authors   255

Preface

In 1973, when I became CEO of Emerson, I was thirty-seven years old and had a tough act to follow. My predecessor, W. R. "Buck" Persons, had led the company for nineteen years and initiated its continuing transformation from a medium-sized producer of electric motors and fans with a defense contracting business into a strong, diversified manufacturing corporation. The Persons era was a time of great prosperity for the company, its employees, and its stockholders. Between 1954 and 1973, sales increased from $50 million to $938 million, and total return to shareholders averaged more than 20 percent per year.

I had begun consulting with Emerson in the 1960s and was eventually exposed to most of the company's operations. As a consultant, I served on the boards of two divisions and worked closely with Buck on a broad range of organization issues. In the early 1970s, I participated in a major study of Emerson's international position. I had lived and worked in Europe for four years, and although Emerson had little international business, was comfortable working on this topic.

Early in 1972 Buck asked me if I would be interested in succeeding him at Emerson. I was flattered by his offer, but at that time I had just acquired control of the family consulting business, Lester B. Knight & Associates in Chicago, and turned him down. Buck asked me to help him in the CEO recruiting process—which I did, although as time passed he didn't find a candidate he considered ideal.

As the process continued I changed my mind and told Buck I would like very much to be considered. He met with the board and got positive support for me to succeed him as CEO in a phased transition. I started as vice chairman in January 1973 and became CEO the following October. Buck remained chairman until his retirement in July 1974, and he and I remained close friends until his death.

When Buck tapped me to succeed him, I didn't realize at the time how intent he was on refocusing management on the challenges facing the company. Emerson was profitable and growing, but there are no guarantees in business. Our portfolio of businesses was in mature industries that were not likely to outpace the U.S. economy. Because only 12 percent of our sales originated outside the United States and much of that was in Canada, it was important to make international growth a top priority. Our technology was weak. We were fast followers, but we needed to change the game to build leadership and transform our technology base from mechanical and electromechanical technologies to electronics. Meanwhile, our acquisition activity had slowed because of antitrust considerations, and we needed to get back into the game.

Finally, I didn't know we were about to enter a very tough recession triggered by war in the Middle East and soaring energy prices and inflation. This was a sign that the robust growth enjoyed by nearly all American manufacturers after World War II was about to end, and success in the future would require new strategies and new ways of doing business.

In sum, there was a lot to do, right away, on multiple fronts. It wasn't a crisis, but Buck was right when he said that the company needed energetic leadership and intensified commitment. But Emerson's biggest need, I learned, was what I came to call the "management process." Nearing $1 billion in sales, the company was still organized and managed much as it had been when it was one-tenth the size.

I admired and wanted to keep the lean organization and small-company informality but also recognized the need for more rigor, discipline, and professionalism at all levels of management. We had to find and develop new management talent and keep the pipeline filled. To get the kind of performance we were looking for—above-average profitability sustained consistently, year after year, performance without compromise—we needed to engrain new ways of working.

During the next twenty-seven years, with the help of many thousands of energetic, committed employees, we instituted and refined the Emerson management process, and it delivered. Between 1973 and 2000, when I stepped down as CEO, the company's sales rose more than fifteen-fold, to more than $15 billion in fiscal 2000, and net earnings increased eighteen-fold, to more than $1.4 billion. Emerson's record of increased earnings per share and dividends each year for these twenty-seven consecutive years is among the longest for consistent performance in American business. During this period, total return to shareholders averaged 15 percent per year.

Meanwhile, we transformed the company under the guidance of an outstanding group of managers. We sustained strong growth, and the company is positioned to grow even faster. We revamped our portfolio, building strong business platforms that are world leaders in technology. We took the company global and established leadership positions in every major region as well as an international manufacturing base that is the world standard for efficient, best-cost operations. We forged deep relationships with our customers; we no longer provide them simply with good products at attractive prices but with high-value services and solutions that enable them to compete more effectively on a global scale.

It is important to recognize the contribution of our board to these accomplishments, because its long-term involvement, commitment, and patience have been critical to our success. During my thirty years as chairman and twenty-seven years as CEO, we had twenty-seven outside directors, including ten today, with an average tenure of sixteen years. I note this because the long-term continuity of board involvement facilitated our ability to transform Emerson into a technology leader and to expand abroad. With this consistent board participation and commitment, we had exceptional involvement in the major strategies vital to our success. During this period, we also had several inside directors at any given time. These arrangements provided an important avenue of communication, enabling our outside directors to interact with key people in the company.

The contributions of a committed, long-tenured board and only two CEOs in forty-six years gave the company the stability of leadership necessary to guide the process and achieve our results. The election of David N. Farr as CEO in 2000 positions the company for another two decades of board and executive leadership continuity and long-term success. Meanwhile, like David, most of our top executives have at least two decades of service with the company. Unlike some other companies, we have a succession process that concentrates on keeping our top management team intact during the transition. I am proud to acknowledge the commitment of our top management to the company; not one top manager left after David took over.

This book explains how we accomplished these things while simultaneously delivering consistent, strong performance without compromise through good times and bad. It offers the first detailed description of the Emerson management process, the principles we observe and the policies and practices we follow.* Of course, many of these techniques resemble those typical of other big, successful companies. What makes them unusually effective at Emerson is not only their inherent logic and utility but also the spirit in which we carry them out. We are a relentless, tenacious company. The management process channels that spirit and keeps us focused on things that are important. It works for us and it's how we work.

---

*For a brief overview of Emerson's management process, see Charles F. Knight, "Consistent Profits, Consistently," *Harvard Business Review*, January–February 1992, 57–72.

Performance
Without
Compromise

1

The Secret of Emerson's Success

The Management Process

This is the best game you will ever play—winning is key.

—Emerson axiom

At Emerson, management is about performance without compromise—achieving superior financial results consistently over the long term. For decades, we've organized and operated the company to deliver winning results. Between the mid-1950s and 2000, Emerson reported annual increases in earnings, earnings per share, and dividends per share. This record is matched by only a handful of manufacturing companies in the world and is unmatched by any that make products or provide services comparable to ours (see exhibit 1-1).

At the same time, total return to Emerson shareholders increased at a compounded annual growth rate of more than 16 percent, with $1 invested in 1956 worth $638 by 2000. And although the record string was broken in the early 2000s, Emerson continued to make money and gain market share despite an exceptionally tough economic environment.

Although Emerson does not have a high profile among the general public, our performance is well known in the business community.

EXHIBIT 1-1

Earnings and dividends performance, 1956–2000

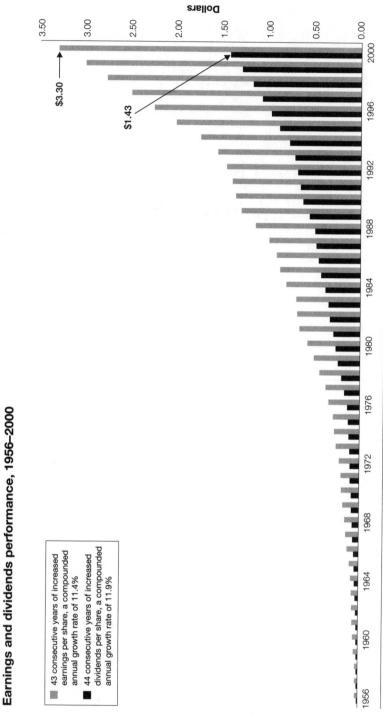

Investors have long recognized Emerson as a stock that almost always bests general economic and industrial indicators. Professors, students, suppliers, customers, and employees of other business organizations often visit to ask the secret of our success.

How do we do it? Actually, there's no mystery. We have a dynamic approach to running the company that emerged in the 1950s and continues to evolve. We call it "the management process," and it is the key to performance without compromise. The management process helps us develop superior strategies at all levels of the company and keeps us on track as we execute them with discipline and intensity. In this way, we avoid one of the most common troubles of corporations, which often struggle because they don't execute their strategies. For us, the

ABOUT EMERSON

Emerson, based in St. Louis, Missouri, is a global leader in bringing together technology and engineering to provide solutions to customers through its several businesses: Network Power, Process Management, Industrial Automation, Climate Technologies, and Appliance and Tools. Emerson holds leading global market positions in all of these businesses. In FY2004 the company earned $1.2 billion on sales of $15.6 billion and employed 107,800 people in more than 60 division and 245 worldwide manufacturing locations.

Emerson is widely recognized as one of the best-managed industrial corporations in the world. It perennially ranks at or near the top of lists of most admired or most innovative companies and best corporate citizens. In 2004, Emerson was ranked second overall in the electronics industry in the America's Most Admired survey by *Fortune* magazine. The company ranked first in five of the eight key measurements: quality of products and services, innovation, long-term investment value, use of corporate assets, and social responsibility. Also in 2004, Emerson was ranked second in the *Information Week 500* survey as one of the most innovative users of technology and a leader in e-business. And once again, Emerson is the only electronics company recognized by *Business Ethics Magazine* on its list of 100 Best Corporate Citizens.

process provides the link between strategy and action. It establishes a common set of values. It provides a structure for setting priorities, evaluating results, and solving problems. And it establishes shared ways of thinking and communicating for ease and speed of execution.

THE MANAGEMENT PROCESS

The term *management process* may seem strange and awkward. Management is usually thought of as an activity, a practice, or a profession, but seldom as a process.* Yet I believe that management is a process—a series of steps intended to deliver a result, which, in a company like Emerson, is sustained profitability. As a process, management can be broken into key steps and components, and each can be engineered, optimized, and controlled to work smoothly and reliably over time. That's what we've sought to do.

The key to making the management process work lies not only in understanding it but also in having the discipline to carry it out. The process contains six key elements (discussed later) that boil down to a simple formula. It is effective at Emerson because it rests on a foundation of core beliefs and values that are mutually consistent and reinforcing. We don't spend a lot of time talking about these beliefs, although they are widely shared and enacted in the company.

Core Beliefs and Values

During the past half-century, Emerson has had only three CEOs—the third is still near the beginning of his tenure—and all of us have held basic beliefs about how to win in business. Some of these beliefs are characteristic of any high-quality, high-performing organization, and

---

*Peter F. Drucker, *The Practice of Management* (New York: Harper Business, reissue ed., 1993); and Drucker, *Management: Tasks, Responsibilities, Practices*, rev. ed. (1973; repr., New York: Harper Perennial, 1993). Note that Emerson began describing management as a process long before the reengineering movement of the early 1990s broke business organizations into component processes—for new product development, order fulfillment, and so on. We at Emerson take a more holistic view of management as a process, as will become clear.

others are more particular to us. We sometimes express these beliefs and values simply in shorthand or axioms, such as those appearing at the beginning of each chapter in this book.

Emerson's values and beliefs begin with integrity: *We insist on integrity in everything we do.* Emerson's reputation is priceless, and we have zero tolerance for misconduct or malfeasance. Not only is this ethically the right thing to do, but also we save time and expense by operating on the basis of trust—among managers, between managers and employees, and between the company, its board, and its investors, customers, suppliers, and partners.

Our board, investors, customers, and employees all want the same thing: consistent high performance. Everyone appreciates a long-term winner. Experience tells us that when we concentrate on the fundamentals and constantly follow up, there is no reason we can't do well consistently. The basis of consistent performance is effective management—day to day, week to week, quarter to quarter, year to year.

Profitability is a state of mind. To achieve winning results over the long term, we must consistently generate high profits. We believe we can do this if our people are fully committed, focused, disciplined, and willing to work hard. As Emerson has grown, diversified, and expanded around the globe, only rarely do we encounter circumstances that prevent us from reaching our target margins.

Finding new ways to add value for customers is the path to success. Everything we do is organized to upgrade our products and services constantly while we work to control and contain costs. The only way we can stay ahead over time is to add value for customers by offering them attractive product features, outstanding service and support, and an agreeable price.

We must be the industry leader in our key markets. As number one, we are in the best position to leverage our scale, manage costs, and invest for continued growth and profitability. So, if we are not number one, we have plans to get there; and if we are the market leader, we intend to stay there.

The key to market leadership is technology leadership. Technology leadership is the only sustainable competitive advantage, and it requires a long-term commitment to investing in engineering and development.

Maintaining a strong balance sheet is a powerful competitive advantage. When we see an opportunity that we can finance only by borrowing, we have the capacity to do so.

Long-term success requires a committed organization. We can deliver all-out performance only when everyone is committed to achieving the goal and recognizes how each person's efforts contribute. We plan and manage our organization with the same intensity that we plan and manage our business.

Key managers must have autonomy to perform at their best. The key decision that leadership makes is the level at which it plans and controls profits. At Emerson, this is as close to customers and markets as possible. Observing this principle results in the best decisions made by managers closest to the sources of information, and it is a powerful motivational tool for developing the next generation of managers.

We can improve productivity only through people. Their contributions of ideas, energy, and enthusiasm—their commitment—are essential to our ability to achieve constant improvement in everything we do. It is management's responsibility to create an environment where people can make a difference.

Management's Job

We start to create this environment by sharing an understanding of management's job, which we define as *identifying and successfully implementing business investment opportunities that support the company's targets for growth and profitability.* This definition is the foundation of our approach to management, and every word is carefully chosen. The job begins with setting financial targets, which must be sufficiently ambitious

DEFINING MANAGEMENT'S JOB

As Emerson grew and diversified in the 1970s, it became apparent that our management needed a clear and widely shared understanding of priorities. We did not set out to craft an original statement of management's job. Surprisingly, when we looked in the literature, we saw nothing that crystallized our approach or fit our situation. We found interesting descriptions of what managers do, but no short, clear, direct statement about what they should do. So we crafted our own definition. After a few iterations, we got it.

We refer to the definition constantly and apply it in training and development as well as in everyday business situations.

to set us apart from competitors but also realistic and achievable. We re-examine our financial targets every year to see whether they remain valid, and we have recalibrated them when circumstances warrant.

After we fix our goals, everything else we do is geared toward achieving them. The targets drive our strategy: which kinds of businesses we're in, how we organize and manage them, and how we pay management. This means that our planning focuses on specific opportunities that will meet our criteria for growth and returns and that will create value for our stockholders. At Emerson, the people who plan are the people who execute. They have ownership and involvement, and that makes all the difference.

SIX KEY ELEMENTS OF
THE MANAGEMENT PROCESS

With this foundation of beliefs and values and our shared understanding of management's job in place, the next step is to spell out how management performs its job through the management process. The process includes six key elements, which are rooted in management theory and, more to the point, reflect Emerson's learning and experience about the essentials of successful management.

1. **Keep It Simple.** We begin with an overarching principle: Keep it simple. Peter Drucker said it well a generation ago when he explained management simply in terms of the five functions it performs: (1) setting objectives; (2) organizing work (which includes planning and assigning responsibility); (3) motivating and communicating; (4) measuring (and following up); and (5) developing people.* Despite the vast literature on management written in the intervening years, there really isn't more to add.

Although "keep it simple" is familiar advice in many aspects of life, it is much more than a platitude in management. Keeping things simple is one of the hardest management principles to observe. Growth

---

*Peter Drucker, *Management: Tasks, Responsibilities, Practices*, rev. ed. (1973; repr., New York: Harper Perennial, 1993), 400.

and success bring complexity—bigger organizations, more responsibilities, competing demands. Good management screens out the distractions and concentrates on essential tasks. It requires intense focus, discipline, energy, and commitment on the part of leaders.

The ability to keep things simple has profound implications for management. It forces us to set a few clear priorities and communicate them in ways that all employees understand and support. It also helps us overcome inertia and bureaucracy and fights the common organizational tendency to add nonessential capacity and pursue unnecessary initiatives.

2. Commitment to Planning. Management cannot do its job without deep personal involvement in planning. At Emerson, planning is a contact sport—a rigorous, intense activity performed by the people in each of our divisions engaging the top leaders of the company.

Some people have said that Emerson spends too much time on planning. We believe, however, that planning delivers a wealth of benefits. It sets the company's direction, identifying the sources of growth and profit that will carry us forward. It identifies and ranks the specific investment opportunities that will create the most value for shareholders. Because those who plan are the people who execute, planning results in a better, more uniform understanding of corporate and divisional priorities and the link between them. It also results in decision making and action that are more closely aligned from the top to the bottom of the organization.

Planning also assists in the development and assessment of management talent. Moreover, because we do it every year in every division, it helps us to ensure that we're on the right track and alerts us to the necessity of changing course. Finally, because we take a hard look every year at our customers and markets and at technology and competition, planning helps us identify major trends and inflection points that demand a companywide response.

3. Strong System of Follow-Up and Control. A recent quote in the business press declared "Vision without execution is hallucination." Many failing companies break down on just this point: they have reasonable strategies but fall short in execution. They know what to do but for some reason don't do it.

Our success in implementation is not the result of our having better systems than do other companies. Rather, it's because we take implementation seriously, are organized to follow up on our plans, and do so rigorously and routinely. We believe that our plans, once approved, are achievable if management makes the right choices and works hard enough to implement them. This is not to say that external events have no impact or that we've never been surprised. When those things happen, our system of follow-up and control enables us to detect them at an early stage and make adjustments. The very fact that we replan every year gives us the flexibility to make timely modifications to our plans to ensure successful implementation.

4. Action-Oriented Organization. Problems never disappear of their own accord. Effective leaders instill a sense of urgency in their organizations, and effective organizations take timely action to remove barriers. We have a visceral aversion to bureaucracy. We operate at the corporate level without a published organization chart because we want people to communicate quickly in terms of plans, projects, and problems, and not along organizational lines.

We plan our organization with the same intensity as we plan our businesses. Annual organization planning sessions in every business and division ensure that we have the right management in place to implement our plans.

5. Operational Excellence. As a manufacturer competing globally, Emerson defines operational excellence in terms of the standards to which it must adhere to excel in a fast-changing, highly competitive business. We must develop the best products, services, and solutions and produce them at the best cost. This requires a deep understanding of customer needs and priorities. If customers have a reason to look elsewhere, they will: plenty of alternatives are available.

Achieving operational excellence also requires rigorous analysis of the best global competitors—not comparing ourselves to ourself. It means having a global competition plan that spells out the actions we will take, as well as their priority and sequence, to ensure that we remain our customers' favored partner. It means communicating the company's objectives so that all employees understand them and the part they play in helping to reach them. Finally, achieving operational excellence requires that we effectively manage assets and ensure that they remain productive over the long term.

6. Creating an Environment in Which People Can and Do Make a Difference. The final element of the management process is leadership, which we define as creating an environment in which people can and do make a difference. Leadership is a subjective matter, and there is no single correct view of what makes a good leader. My own definition of what works best in an organization is listed in the box "Ten Keys to Business Leadership."

Summing Up the Management Process

Although we necessarily describe the management process in a linear sequence, it operates as a system. Good planning has no value without a strong system of follow-up and control, and a strong system of follow-up and control has no value without good planning. Neither can be effective if it isn't simple in the sense of being understood clearly. A

TEN KEYS TO BUSINESS LEADERSHIP

1. Be committed to success.

2. Set proper priorities.

3. Set and demand high standards of excellence.

4. Be tough but fair in dealing with people.

5. Concentrate on positives and possibilities.

6. Develop and maintain a strong sense of urgency.

7. Pay attention to detail.

8. Provide for the ability to fail.

9. Be personally involved.

10. Have fun.

complicated plan has too many working parts and is more likely to break down in execution.

Moreover, the process is not static but dynamic. The management process began at Emerson in the 1950s, with annual planning conferences, divisional autonomy, strong financial controls, and other key features. Over the years we've added organizational planning, presidents' councils, business strategy reviews, and other practices. We also step back from time to time to reexamine the process and, when appropriate, make changes.

In the early 1990s, we began to recognize that the process was essential to producing consistent profitability but was somewhat limited in its ability to generate growth (as discussed in chapter 8). So we adjusted the process. We separated planning for growth from planning for profit, and we identified and pursued our most promising growth programs and projects. It was the process that enabled us to see the need for this change while also giving us the discipline to make it.

The way Emerson operates under its management process reflects the company's particular context: its history, its products and markets, and its leadership and manner of operating. But the essentials of the management process are not particular to time and place. They are exportable, and they work in other contexts. We see this every time Emerson makes an acquisition. Our Asian, Latin American, and European employees have embraced the process as readily as our North American employees, to equally good effect.

THE MANAGEMENT PROCESS AT WORK:
CONSISTENCY AND CHANGE
OVER THREE DECADES

In sum, the management process is the secret of Emerson's success. It is how we perform without compromise, year after year. Yet for all the consistency it brings about, the process also generates significant change—as evidenced by a quick review of the company's achievements during the past three decades.

When I joined Emerson in 1973, our planning process showed that a technological revolution was sweeping over our business; electronics

were being used to enhance traditional electrical and electromechanical products, and sometimes to replace them. It was one thing to see
this trend unfolding, and quite another to take advantage of it. Emerson
was a relatively small company with limited technological capability.

Approaching the electronics revolution as a long-term challenge,
we launched an ambitious program to develop new products having
increasing electronic content. We increased spending on engineering
and development, quickened the pace of new product introductions,
and developed new metrics to track our progress. We then used our
management process and disciplines to make the program work. Such
steps enabled us to collapse a ten- to fifteen-year cycle for completely
renewing our product line into one that does it every five to six years.

At about the same time that we stepped up new product introductions, planning revealed that we could not sustain historic growth
rates without making acquisitions (something we had stopped doing
in the late 1960s because of antitrust concerns. As a result, we became more focused and disciplined about doing deals. This strategy
helped us in numerous ways: by allowing us to enter faster-growth industries and diversify our portfolio, by increasing critical mass in our
core businesses, by speeding up our learning about new technologies
and markets, and by helping us gain new management talent.

In the 1980s, as we continued to make progress in these areas,
we began to see a revolution under way in manufacturing. In a host of
industries—autos, steel, machine tools, shipbuilding, and consumer
electronics—Japanese manufacturers were radically redefining global
standards of quality and cost. So we developed our Best Cost Producer
strategy, which made us globally competitive. This strategy required
nothing less than a reinvention of the way we operated. We adopted
and adapted techniques to reach much higher standards of quality
while redesigning operations to lower costs and increase throughput.
We also moved fast to set up new operations in low-cost areas such as
Mexico and, later, the Asia-Pacific region. As a result, at a time when
many U.S.-based manufacturers struggled or went out of business, we
more than held our own.

Meanwhile we focused on serving our global customers with global
support operations and worked to contain a wide range of cost factors,
including design and engineering services and purchased inputs. We

now operate increasing numbers of facilities in Europe (including Eastern Europe), Latin America, and Asia (especially China). We also employ increasing numbers of knowledge workers—engineers, customer service reps, and administrative personnel—around the world to support our global operations.

And we continued to transform the company as new challenges appeared. In the late 1980s and early 1990s, we noticed two important trends that affected how we were organized and how we operated. First, we recognized that our long-standing and deeply held traditions of divisional autonomy and division-level planning came at a cost: we were missing opportunities to collaborate and also were not systematic about adding complementary pieces via acquisition. Second, customer expectations and behavior were changing in important ways: customers were becoming more demanding, and they also wanted stronger relationships with their key suppliers. Sensing these trends, we began to restructure Emerson, gathering the divisions into business platforms so that we could identify and pursue new growth opportunities and work more closely with our major customers.

In the 1990s, we recognized that sustaining a premium price for our stock would require that we generate faster growth. Thus we launched and cultivated new programs that focused our attention on the greatest opportunities for growth. We repositioned our portfolio to include high-growth businesses such as Process Management and Network Power. We created the Emerson brand platforms to gain better leverage of corporate resources and further strengthen relationships with our key customers. Finally, we began to bundle our components into higher-value systems and solutions for our customers.

In each of these instances, our management process enabled us to identify the need to change, focused our attention on how to do it, and guided us through the transition. Meanwhile, we never skipped a beat in delivering increased earnings, earnings per share, and dividends per share every year. We succeeded in combining impressive consistency *and* fundamental change. The management process is the way we did it.

2

Planning, Execution, and Control

Planning isn't perfect.
That's why we do it every year.

—Emerson axiom

E merson's consistently strong performance is planned. Luck—good or bad—and unexpected circumstances play roles, but we deliver on our promises because we plan in detail what to do and then execute the plan, following up diligently to ensure that we stay on target. Our process is pretty basic, but the trick is having the discipline to keep at it month by month, quarter by quarter, year by year. Our commitment to planning and control keeps us on track.

It's no coincidence that our long record of improved annual earnings began in the mid-1950s, when we began to take planning seriously. Now it has become a way of life that permeates the organization. Planning is truly at the heart of what we do. It is how we deepen our understanding of our business. It is an activity that occurs at multiple levels of the corporation, in multiple events, on an annual cycle. And it leaves no aspect of our business untouched.

At the most basic level, planning is a critical step in enabling us to perform management's job by identifying the investment opportunities that make us grow the top and bottom lines and outperform our competition. Then our systems for follow-up and control make sure we stay on course.

Beyond their impact on our financial and competitive performance and business mix, planning and control are central to the way Emerson works. Our annual cycle of meetings provides a direct channel of communication between corporate, business-level, and division managers, without intermediaries and summary reviews. It aligns management at all levels behind what we are doing and intend to do. It takes the politics out of decision making and creates a blameless organization in which responsibility for major decisions is shared—although, of course, our general managers are held accountable for proper execution. Thus if we have chosen the wrong plan, we don't waste time fixing the blame; rather, we rally together to find the best solution.

Because line managers do the planning, it removes the artificial gap between strategy and operations. The preparation, discussion, and reworking that go into our plans are important factors in building strong, cohesive management teams. Planning instills rigor and discipline. It trains new generations of leadership in our policies and culture, and it exposes them to senior corporate management at an early stage in their careers. It also gives senior corporate managers valuable insights into the thinking and performance of managers at the lower levels of the company. Planning is a source of learning as we compare current and projected performance to past performance and to competitive benchmarks, and as we transfer new ideas and techniques from one part of the business to another.

Finally, we have a dynamic approach to planning; that's why we plan every year and meet regularly to track our plans and ensure we stay on target. Planning helps us to avoid surprises but also to deal with them swiftly when they occur. It gets us ready to respond quickly to new opportunities when they emerge unexpectedly. It helps us to sustain momentum and alerts us to the need to make midcourse corrections. And it helps us identify the times for important, discontinuous change. Because we are constantly revisiting and updating our plans, we gather a tremendous amount of information about significant trends in our markets and about our competition. Planning tells us when we must change and in what direction.

As potent a management tool as planning is, it has no value if it cannot or will not be executed. At Emerson, we take execution just as seriously as we take planning, and our annual cycle of follow-up and control helps ensure that we put our plans into effect and track our progress against them.

We invest a lot of time in planning and control; more than half of the CEO's calendar is consumed in planning, and the COO and other top executives are even more engaged in our control cycle. We believe that this is time well spent. This level of detail, along with the continuous repetition and iteration in the process, is a distinguishing feature of Emerson's management process. The results bear us out.

THE PURPOSE OF PLANNING

Emerson's ultimate responsibility is to our shareholders, who invest because they expect us to deliver consistently strong results. Our financial model (see exhibit 2-1) lays out targets for earnings growth

EXHIBIT 2-1

Emerson financial model

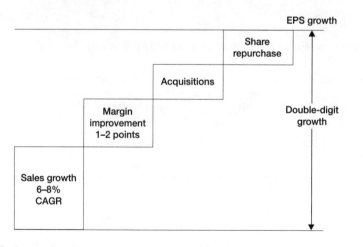

EPS: Earnings per share
CAGR: Compounded annual growth rate

that exceed the averages of the industries in which we compete. To meet these targets, we must grow faster than our markets, continue to operate at high levels of profitability, and use acquisitions and a share repurchase program to drive our performance and create value for our investors. We get there through planning.

Because Emerson is a diversified global company, we understand that our corporate performance is the cumulative result of the achievements of each of our units. We do not ask each unit to aim at the same or even similar targets for growth and earnings. Rather, we recognize that each plays a distinct role in creating value for our shareowners and customers, and we assess it accordingly. Exhibit 2-2 shows our portfolio of units according to the type of performance we expect. In the upper-left quadrant, "growers" lead the way in outpacing the organic growth of their markets. In the upper right, "cash flow, ROTC funders" generate the cash and high returns necessary to support growth and achieve our target margin. (ROTC stands for return on total capital.) The lower-right quadrant consists of units with significant potential to become funders at high levels of ROTC for the corporation. The lower-left quadrant includes a small number of units that are no longer critical to our future, and we are likely to dispose of them. In the center lie a still smaller number of units that struggle. We will fix these and move

EXHIBIT 2-2

Everyone has a role in creating value for Emerson

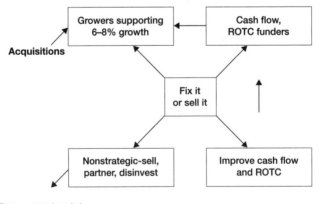

ROTC: Return on total capital

them into one of the upper- or lower-right groupings, or they will slide
into the lower-left grouping earmarked for divestiture or disinvestment.

Note that this model is dynamic. It identifies roles and aspirations
for the units, showing how each adds value to shareholders. We expect
units with below-average results to improve cash flow and returns,
whereas funders are driven to evolve into growers. Units that cannot
meet our targets or do not fit our long-term strategy will be sold. Acquisitions constantly add to the mix.

THE EMERSON PLANNING CYCLE

Now let's take a brief look at Emerson's organization, which is essential
to understanding our management process. We have a multidivisional
structure, which now includes more than sixty divisions. For reporting
purposes, we group these into five business segments under the corporate brand: Process Management, Climate Technologies, Industrial Automation, Network Power, and Appliance and Tools (see appendix A).
Historically, the divisions were relatively autonomous units, and most
came to us via acquisition. We still plan and control profits at this level.

In the late 1980s and early 1990s, for reasons that will become
clear, we began gathering divisions within the same industry or those
having common customers into entities we call *businesses* under a *business leader*. More recently, we've called these entities *business platforms*,
a term we use synonymously with *businesses*. Most of these correspond
to the business segments we report, but the Appliance and Tools segment includes several smaller business platforms.

Note that the business platforms do not represent a distinct layer
of organization comparable to the group layer in many large corporations. For example, we do not generally have staff at this level.

Within this organization structure, we rely on a comprehensive, integrated annual planning cycle to guide our decisions. (See exhibit 2-3,
focusing for the moment on the information below the monthly calendar.) Beginning each November, the cycle begins at the division level,
where we plan separately for profitability and growth as well as for organization. During the ensuing months we support the divisions with
reviews of international markets and with functional conferences on
technology and other corporate areas.

EXHIBIT 2-3

Emerson's planning and control cycle

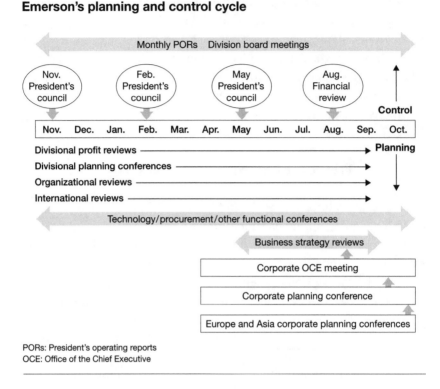

PORs: President's operating reports
OCE: Office of the Chief Executive

During the following summer, we conduct strategy reviews of our business platforms. We use this opportunity to identify and extract synergies among the divisions and leverage our capabilities. Finally, in late summer, we pull together the corporate plan. This plan is presented first to the Office of the Chief Executive (OCE) and then to our annual corporate planning conference each October at our headquarters in St. Louis. We also hold corporate planning conferences in Europe and Asia to communicate the corporate strategy to wider audiences of managers.

Profit and Growth Planning in the Divisions

In my view, management's most important decision is to determine the level at which it plans and controls profit. This should be at the lowest level possible so that decisions are made as close as possible to customers and the market. For us, this is the division level, where each division president has global responsibility for his or her unit.

From a planning perspective, the key events at the division level are the profit review, the planning conference, and the organization review, which are held in sequence. In the profit review we start by ensuring that we have a stable division that will deliver on its profit commitments. Next, in the planning conference, we look at the division's growth plans to evaluate its prospects for the next five years. Finally, we examine the division's organization structure and management team to ensure that it can execute the agreed-upon strategy (organization reviews are discussed in chapter 3).

Divisional Profit Reviews

Most big companies have planning processes for their strategic business units as well as plans for meeting targets for growth and profitability. Emerson may be unique in the emphasis we put on profit planning. As discussed in detail in chapters 4 and 8, in the early 1990s we separated profit planning from growth planning; growth had become a major corporate priority, and we sought to avoid having our planning conferences highly focused on operating margin. At the same time, we needed reliable profit forecasts in light of the intensely competitive environment in global manufacturing. So we decided to hold separate conferences for profit planning and growth planning. In the former, we required that profit plans be based on conservative assumptions about pricing and volume growth; we want to be sure that we'll continue to make money even in tough times.

At the *profit review*, division management—the division president and his or her top reports—meets with the corporate *profit czar*, a top executive whose major responsibility is to ensure that the divisions and the corporation as a whole deliver their target margins on an annual basis. Also present is the executive in charge of the appropriate business platform.

The profit review examines five years of history as well as the current year and projections five years out. Thus we open an eleven-year window into the business—a view long enough to spot significant trends and provide context for evaluating proposed actions. The session is structured on a profit model that takes into account price changes and inflation factors along with productivity improvements, including cost reduction and containment programs, methods of leveraging fixed costs, and changes in the business mix (see chapter 4). As noted, we make conservative assumptions in all of these areas to ensure that we will not inflate our estimates and that we can deliver results even in tough times. This approach forces us to identify and discuss in detail specific programs to meet our margin objectives. This includes necessary job moves (both salaried and hourly), plant relocation, outsourcing, and other actions to improve asset management.

Following the profit review, the profit czar prepares a summary memo that is available for the planning conference, the next event in the cycle, which typically is held several months later.

Divisional Planning Conferences

With near-term operating issues addressed and profitability established through the profit review, the planning process shifts to growth strategy at the *divisional planning conference*. This one- or two-day meeting includes division management, Emerson's CEO, and selected corporate officers. Each division has a full-fledged conference every other year, or more frequently if market conditions dictate. Some divisions have a scaled-down update meeting in the alternate years. In this meeting the CEO visits the division for an update on key initiatives from the prior conference.

The ultimate objective of the divisional planning conference is to determine the best way to create value for the corporation. Division management sets the agenda and demonstrates exactly how value will be created. We do not require specified exhibits, but we expect to see informed discussion of financial and competitive performance—sales, profit, return on capital, market size, penetration, and pricing trends—as well as customer and competitor analysis.

As with the profit reviews, we use an eleven-year time horizon, looking five years back and five years out on both the P&L and the balance sheet. A common tendency in planning is the "hockey stick" forecast: revenues or profits (or both) that are projected to inch up during the near term but will rocket upward after several years of sustained investment. Put another way, a hockey stick projection invites a company to make low-yield investments while waiting for the eventual payday, which may or may not materialize. The eleven-year window puts hockey stick projections into perspective. In general, we have greater confidence in investments that yield constant, steady improvements.

Division management's presentation includes a quick description of the strategy for generating growth and improving margin. Achieving that, however, requires systematic and detailed analysis of customers, markets, competitors, and channels, and this analysis is the heart of the meeting. It takes substantial planning and backup data to produce this information. Division managers must develop and demonstrate a deep understanding of the division's business. Senior division managers work together on the plan for months before the conference. They often tell us that the greatest value of the planning cycle lies in the teamwork and discipline required in the preparation phase.

Although the planning conference belongs to the division president and his or her team, our role is to engage in a dialogue to help division managers improve their plans and results. We look at the quality of the research and analysis and at the integration and consistency of the overall plan. We challenge the management team to define the key issues and challenges facing the business and to spell out the corresponding actions to address them. We want to discuss the top three to five initiatives in detail and consider issues that support and challenge them.

Incidentally, the repeated nature of the exercise from year to year helps us to distinguish what is truly changing, evaluate its significance, and measure appropriate responses. It is easy to focus on the positives and history in these meetings, but we constantly push management to discuss what keeps them up at night. The point is to develop strategies to succeed, regardless of the market conditions.

Finally, we look for management's conviction that the plan is right and actionable and that it will be implemented enthusiastically and well. It is important for division managers to show their capacity for leadership and their willingness to make tough decisions, such as redeploying assets and fixing or discontinuing underperforming operations.

By design, the mood in a divisional planning conference is confrontational. The burden of proof is on division managers to convince us that the plan is well thought out and is backed up by thorough research and rigorous analysis. Although we're not trying to put anyone on the spot, we want to challenge assumptions and conventional thinking and give enough time to every significant issue. Corporate attendees typically have been at Emerson more than twenty years and have experienced many of the same issues faced by the division. We are there to impart knowledge. We also want proof that a division is stretching to reach its goals, and we want to get into the details of the actions that division managers believe will yield improved results. Our expectations are high, and a division officer who comes poorly prepared has made a serious mistake.

Note that the CEO's role—carried out in much the same way today by David Farr as during my tenure—makes this process work. In preparation for the conferences, we review all the inputs from the previous planning cycle—profit, growth, and organization plans—and draw on corporate staff as a resource. Over the years, though, I became pretty familiar with each division's issues, organization, and people. I also recognized patterns of similar circumstances across divisions and tried to bring this insight to bear. The conference itself invariably demanded intense involvement and concentration. When I attended a planning conference, I was there working for the division; I was concentrating every ounce of energy on understanding the issues the division faced. I was trying to help management get to a plan that would yield better results, and I didn't view a planning conference as successful unless we agreed on what we were going to do.

Although we are confrontational, the challenges offered by corporate leaders to the divisions are never personal. Voices may rise and tempers flare, but only in the spirit of getting to a better answer for the division. We conclude the conference with a dinner that is primarily a social occasion where everyone can relax and share in our common enterprise, no matter how heated the day's debate. If I had a difficult exchange with someone, I took care to spend time with that person at dinner.

The output of the divisional planning conferences is a set of action items and priorities that are mutually accepted. Emerson's CEO also writes a letter to the division president summarizing the plan, action items and other commitments, and any other important issues. The letter then becomes part of the next planning conference's agenda, and the contents are followed up in the meetings in our control cycle. There may also be a brief post-planning conference, meeting, or phone call if a particular topic requires further analysis. The president or business leader frequently responds to the CEO's letter by describing the tactical steps the organization will take to address the action items or issues.

The divisional planning conference is also an occasion for corporate executives to assess division management. We look for knowledge of and belief in the plan, quality of thinking under pressure, leadership skills, and performance as a team. A single conference will not make or break a career, but it will get someone noticed. A good performance can accelerate career development.

The divisional planning conference clearly benefits the division. But it is also a critical element in developing the strategy at the level of the business platform and the corporation. The interaction between the division managers and the leaders of the company—and the education that comes from it—is invaluable. It is here that we discover new information about our customers, competitors, and markets and see the impact of new technologies. It is here that we spot trends that require us to respond or adapt. Corporate leaders spend between one-third and one-half of their time engaged in these discussions, and it pays off in the understanding and insight we gain into our business and the knowledge transfer that occurs throughout Emerson.

Strategy Reviews: Planning at the Business Level

We build plans from the bottom up, but we do not just sum up the division plans; we also plan at the level of the business platforms to ensure that we leverage resources and integrate the whole while identifying opportunities that transcend the existing divisions. At this higher level, we make choices and trade-offs about which opportunities to pursue most aggressively, which businesses to bolster, and which, perhaps, to deemphasize or even exit.

The business platforms hold annual reviews each summer. The *strategy review* is an occasion for the business leader and key reports to meet with the CEO, president, and other corporate officers to review and discuss major strategic and operational challenges and critical actions. These sessions, which typically take about half a day, deal with big picture issues.

Note that we do not plan and control profits at this level; those are responsibilities of the divisions. Nor do we evaluate or reconsider any division's strategy; those are tasks for other times and places. In fact, one of our ground rules for strategy reviews is that we are forbidden even to mention the divisions by name. Rather, we focus on growth and marketing strategy to establish and sustain industry leadership. We also consider the financial outlook for the business platform. We believe that the businesses have greater potential than the sum of their parts. In these strategy reviews it is up to the business leaders to show how they will maximize this potential, whether by organic growth or acquisitions.

As with the divisional planning conferences, we take a long view in the strategy reviews, looking back and forward from the current year in five-year horizons. The corporate officers play the same role they play in the divisional planning conferences: challenging, probing, and working as hard as we can to ensure that we develop an outstanding, actionable plan. Similarly, we follow up strategy reviews with letters documenting commitments and agreements, and we revisit the strategy every year.

We talk about acquisitions to bolster weaker areas of our current served markets, and, more important, we look for acquisition candidates that can take us into adjacent markets and increase our overall served market size. We always want to be number one in our markets. As we succeed in gaining share, however, we need constantly to expand our available markets to continue to grow as a corporation.

Corporate Planning

Information generated for and during the divisional planning conferences, profit reviews, and business platform strategy reviews becomes raw material for the *corporate planning conference* (CPC) we hold each fall; the CPC is attended by the top three hundred officers of the corporation and the divisions. But planning at the corporate level extends far beyond preparing for the annual planning conference. From this vantage point, we view the whole as being different than the sum of its parts. Our divisions and business platforms are part of a portfolio, and we constantly measure and evaluate the growth, profitability, and cash flow profiles of each of them.

Before the conference, we identify key themes emerging from the division conferences and strategy reviews and combine them with an analysis of the macroeconomic environment. We incorporate this information into the *corporate plan*: an integrated, focused statement of corporate objectives and our plans for meeting them. The plan is considered first by the Office of the Chief Executive, which contributes its thoughts and insights before presentation at the CPC and regional corporate planning conferences.

We approach the building of our plan in a highly disciplined manner. We maintain a small, highly skilled planning staff at headquarters to assist with corporate planning, as well as to work with the divisions in preparing their plans. This staff assembles materials for the OCE's review and helps with identification and assessment of opportunities and challenges primarily at the division and corporate levels. Working on the staff is an important developmental assignment for many of our best young managers. Several planning department heads, including David Farr and Charlie Peters, have subsequently moved to top executive positions (Farr is Emerson's current chairman and CEO).

As valuable as is this staff resource, however, it does not screen plans and programs generated by the divisions and businesses before their presentation to senior corporate executives, including the CEO, at planning conferences and strategy reviews. The active involvement of top division executives in developing their plans, and top corporate executives in reviewing them, are significant factors in the effectiveness of Emerson's planning process.

Corporate Planning Conferences

After the corporate plan is assembled and approved in the early fall each year, the corporate planning conference serves primarily as a vehicle of communication to our managers. The CPC is an ideal setting for sharing success stories and for challenging conventional wisdom. Corporate officers share overall results and communicate the financial plan for the coming year as well as the strategic plan for the next five years.

The conference may also include outside speakers, discussions of economic forecasts, and reviews of best practices at one of the divisions or businesses. It is a great occasion for recognizing areas of accomplishment as well as areas that require additional attention. As in the division planning conferences, we not only compare ourselves to our historical performance but also compare ourselves to a peer group of high-performance companies to ensure that we match up well in the metrics most important to our shareholders.

Messages communicated in the corporate planning conference

(and identical conferences we hold for senior managers in Europe and Asia) are crucial because the participants go back to their divisions and relay our goals, aspirations, and targets to thousands of employees. We take care, therefore, that the messages we send are clear, concise, and received as intended. We distribute a package containing the key corporate or regional priorities for the next fiscal year and five years out, along with other supporting exhibits. The conferences are occasions for us to motivate and inspire the key managers who carry out the work of the corporation every day, and we expect participants to integrate these broad objectives into their divisional objectives and plans as they go through the year.

The Role of the Board of Directors

We routinely involve Emerson's board of directors in reviewing business-level and corporate strategy, and our board members take these responsibilities seriously. Commitment and involvement, from top to bottom, from the boardroom to the shop floor, drive the Emerson management process.

Emerson's board typically meets eight times per year, and virtually every meeting includes a detailed examination of the strategy of one of the businesses. Each fall the board reviews and considers the annual corporate plan. It also reviews our organization structure and top executive talent every year. Periodically, we hold an off-site meeting with the board to review our corporate strategy in detail.

All these reviews represent the ultimate assessments and endorsements of our plans, and they add high value. The board's insights and contributions frequently result in better, more compelling corporate plans. Senior managers are pushed to identify new growth opportunities and platforms, and our assumptions are probed, clarified, and sometimes challenged. We are obliged to think rigorously about investments, staffing, and other key concerns.

Beyond their role as a group, individual board members routinely push management to consider new approaches to our business and management process—a welcome practice that goes back decades. In the 1970s, for example, Gerry Lodge, who was about to become a director, introduced us to Joel Stern, then of Chase Manhattan Bank, who was beginning to develop an approach to valuation that would eventually sweep across corporate America. Stern argued that long-term stock prices correlated more closely with certain economic measures, such as free cash flow and return on total capital (ROTC), than with traditional indicators such as earnings per share (EPS) and dividend payouts. We didn't subscribe completely to Stern's views, but we embraced some of them, with resulting changes in how we measured division performance.

In the 1980s, several board members, including Dick Loynd (a former Emerson executive) and Gen. Bernard Schriever, USAF (Ret.), urged us to increase our investments in engineering and development. Loynd was particularly vocal about getting us to move beyond talking about annual cost reductions to emphasize new products, new markets, and new customers. Later, he played a key role in prompting us to bolster our capabilities in strategic marketing. We mention these among many possible examples to emphasize the value of an active, committed board of directors whose members regularly contribute new ideas to our plans and follow up on them.

So from November through October, the wheel turns full circle, and we start the process all over again. This process may sound repetitive and boring. But redoing or revisiting the plans every year creates tremendous momentum and excitement, and paying attention to detail helps us deliver consistent, constantly improving results.

SUMMING UP: THE PAYOFF OF PLANNING

Emerson relies on planning for much more than its textbook role of describing how corporate objectives will be achieved. For us, planning serves these purposes:

- Sets the company's direction, identifying the sources of growth and profit that will carry it forward.

- Identifies and ranks the specific investment opportunities that will create the most value for shareholders.

- Removes the artificial distinction between those who plan and those who execute so that those responsible for implementing the plan understand it, believe in it, and are prepared to act on it without hesitation.

- Stimulates productive tension in the organization as corporate, business, and division managers agree on targets that require actions beyond the routine.

- Results in better, more uniform understanding of corporate, business-level, and divisional priorities and the links between them. It also results in decision making and action that are more closely aligned from the top to the bottom of the organization.

- Assists in the development and assessment of management talent. The planning process is an intensive learning experience for managers, and corporate executives get to see young division managers on stage and in action at a much earlier point than happens in many companies.

- Takes politics out of the company. The planning process creates a blameless organization because everyone signs off on the plan. The divisions, the businesses, and the corporation are joint owners of the plan; we're all in it together. If something goes awry, it is no one's fault. We all pitch in to make the correction.

- Helps to build *momentum*—one of the most important and least understood factors in a company's growth. The power of momentum—the result of cumulative positive change—fueled by the tremendous number of initiatives approved in planning conferences, reinforces advantages of scale and helps us overcome the tendency of big organizations to get bogged down as they grow.

- Prepares us to respond swiftly when new opportunities emerge; in effect, planning enables us to make at least some of our luck.

- Enables us to identify important trends and inflection points in our business environment and prepare to make significant changes throughout the company.

This latter approach alerted us to significant challenges and steered us to the right response in a number of key areas, as indicated by exhibit 2-4. In particular, we did the following:

- Built a comprehensive new product development program that now accounts for more than one-third of annual sales, and invested to transform a technology follower into a technology leader (chapter 5).

- Completed more than two hundred acquisitions, representing a total investment of more than $10 billion, with more than 80 percent of this investment paying returns exceeding the cost of capital (chapter 6).

- Responded successfully to the globalization of our markets and competition by implementing our Best Cost Producer and operational excellence strategies. This approach allowed us to be globally competitive and accelerated our expansion into international markets (chapters 4 and 7).

- Gathered dozens of autonomous divisions focused on the U.S. market into strong business platforms that are global leaders, with nearly half of corporate revenues originating overseas (chapters 7 and 8).

- Launched new growth programs and expanded the scope of our business from manufacturing discrete components to developing systems and related services and solutions for our customers worldwide (chapters 7 and 8).

- Repositioned our portfolio toward high-growth businesses such as Process Management, Climate Technologies, and Network Power.

EXHIBIT 2-4

Foundation for growth

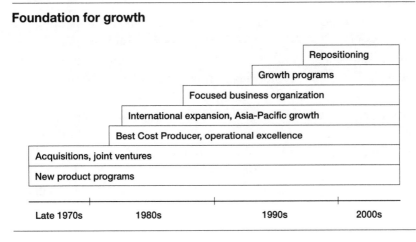

As important as planning is to Emerson, it is only one key component of the management process. As noted, even the best plan has no value if it is not well executed. A strong system of control and follow-up is the essential complement to rigorous, intense planning.

EXECUTING THE PLAN

As noted, we believe that when companies struggle, the reason is not because they don't know what to do but because, for whatever reason, the organization doesn't do it. Based on Emerson's experience— as well as my personal experience as a director of other large organizations and an interested observer of business generally—such failures have four main causes.

The first problem is that the people who make the plans don't have the responsibility for making the plans work. Plans go to the bottom of an operating manager's desk drawer, and that's the end of them. Second, goals and incentives may be misaligned. People may be rewarded for doing something different from what is needed. A third problem is a lack of continuity in key management positions: people who should follow through on a matter at a critical juncture have been promoted or have moved on, and their successors lack the knowledge, commitment, and passion to do what is necessary. Finally, the problem may be poor communications. The people who must make something happen may not know what to do, or they may have received confusing or conflicting directions.

To avoid these problems and ensure that a good plan is executed well, an organization must have a strong system of follow-up and control. At Emerson, several factors enable us to implement our plans effectively. First, the people who plan are the people who execute the plan. They have ownership and involvement; it's their plan, and not a corporate plan. Second, we pay for results. Our managers get paid for delivering on the commitments they make in planning, and thus there is no conflict between what they need to do and what they earn. The third factor is a matter of attitude: we believe that if the plan is solid and the context doesn't shift and we work hard enough, we can and will execute the plan. We don't ask for the impossible. We succeed through focus, discipline, intensity, and sheer persistence—qualities that cumulatively add up to commitment. A fourth factor is our significant investment in internal communications. As noted, the planning process itself is an important channel of communication, and we use the meetings in our annual control cycle to keep the channel open and active.

Finally, this cycle, which includes both short- and long-term reviews, keeps our operating managers focused on important matters. There is no time for things to get out of whack; we'll quickly catch and get on top of a deteriorating situation. Thus we avoid surprises and can see at an early stage when we're veering off course or when the plan itself might need revision.

Doing five things helps to ensure that a good plan is executed effectively and that a vision is a blueprint for success:

1. Eliminate the gap between planners and doers.

2. Pay for results.

3. Support and ensure continued involvement of leaders and managers.

4. Communicate clearly and constantly.

5. Adopt processes and systems to measure, track, review, and evaluate progress.

THE EMERSON CONTROL CYCLE

We track execution through a multilayered control cycle designed to assess performance and identify potential problems from multiple perspectives: short-term and long-term, bottom-up, and top-down. (See exhibit 2-3 presented earlier, focusing now on the information above the monthly calendar and in the boxed insert, "Emerson's Control Cycle," below.) With the CEO involved heavily in planning, the corporate responsibility for tracking performance and meeting commitments falls to the chief operating officer and chief financial officer. Ed Monser, our current COO, took over in 2002 as the latest in a line of outstanding operating executives that stretches back for many years, with signal contributions from Larry Keyes, Bill Rutledge, Jim Hardymon, Al Suter, and David Farr. Our Senior EVP and CFO, Walter Galvin, has been on the job for more than a decade after following in the footsteps of John Wilson. Galvin possesses deep knowledge of Emerson's financial performance, as well as a rare gift of being able to penetrate to the heart of complex issues to find and communicate clearly the right answers. Because Emerson is staffed by talented executives, the control cycle reduces the likelihood of our encountering unforeseen operating problems that could cause us to miss our financial commitments.

Everything starts at the division level, where we plan and control profits. The cycle begins each year with the financial review, in which each division president, along with appropriate staff, meets with the COO, the CFO, and other senior corporate officials. Like the president's council, the financial review has a one-year time horizon, as opposed to the five-year horizons of planning conferences and profit reviews. The financial review occurs late in the fiscal year and considers performance against financial plan, with a detailed financial forecast of the coming year.

The output of the financial review becomes the baseline against which we measure our progress. In addition, we push the divisions to think through various scenarios and to plan actions that may be required. As a result, our managers have a prepared set of actions they can take if the environment changes. This contingency planning is particularly helpful in an economic downturn; we are not paralyzed by bad news because we've planned for it.

During the fiscal year, the division presidents submit presidents' operating reports (PORs) every month. The reports summarize the divisions' results and immediate prospects, focusing on the current month and the three months ahead, and they also update expectations for the remaining quarters and fiscal year. The most important exhibit in the package, "the Page 5" (see appendix B), tracks historical planned and actual results by quarter for the prior and current years and looks forward to the remaining quarters and the year.

In most companies, budgets are a static tool prepared once a year, and performance during the year is tracked against them. We don't follow this practice because it doesn't allow for circumstances to change, sometimes in unanticipated ways. Our PORs, unlike traditional budgets, are a dynamic tool: we update expected annual results each month

EMERSON'S CONTROL CYCLE

Financial review—Annual budget meeting

- Prior year review and fiscal year close
- Future year forecast

Presidents' operating reports (PORs)—Monthly reporting format

- Updates expectations for
  - next 3 months individually
  - each quarter and fiscal year

President's Council—Once per quarter meeting in St. Louis

- COO, business leader, division president, and financial officer
- Reviews quarter close, expectations, and opportunities
- Monitors four to five fiscal-year strategic imperatives

Monthly board meeting

- Business leader at division with five to ten key managers
- Reviews financials and actions from division plans

and make rolling comparisons against historical and projected performance. The forecast we make at the start of the year becomes a reference point, but not the standard to which we manage. In fact, the life of a budget at Emerson is one month. As the year unfolds, we make constant adjustments, focusing on the difference between expected and actual results. Thus in, say, May, we're not managing to an obsolete number established the previous August.

The PORs give us a good sense of how the business is evolving month to month and prompt us to make changes in a timely manner. For example, if we see a revenue problem in a division or business, we revise our plans and make up the shortfall elsewhere so that we deliver on our corporate EPS commitment. Note that the PORs, along with other aspects of our control cycle, do not focus only on financial progress. The reports also give us an opportunity to review progress against major initiatives the divisions are undertaking.

Each division has its own management board, with the business leader serving as chair. Other members of the board include the division president and the top five to ten division officers. In part, these boards are a legacy of Emerson's growth through acquisition and commitment to divisional autonomy, but, more important, they reflect our insistence on planning and controlling profits at this level. We don't want the performance of these units aggregated with the results of other divisions so that trends, deviations, problems, and opportunities become difficult to detect. The division boards meet six to eight times per year to review financial performance and monitor actions and programs approved in the annual planning conference. They also track how performance will affect management compensation so that division managers are aware of the risks and rewards of meeting their commitments.

Looking farther out, the president and chief financial officer of each division meet quarterly in St. Louis with the business leader, the COO, the CFO, and other corporate officers to discuss short-term operating results and lock in on the current quarter. We call these sessions *presidents' councils* (see exhibit 2-3). The sessions review performance during the current quarter as well as expectations and opportunities in the quarter ahead. We pay particular attention to how the top four or five strategic initiatives for the fiscal year are playing out.

Another key exhibit we use in presidents' councils is the waterfall chart, which lists all the components of cost for a division (see chapter 4). The waterfall chart requires division managers to understand what is happening to each cost component, to provide a good explanation for any upward trend, and to ensure that progress in other areas will offset any problems and enable the division as a whole to reach its target margin. This chart is the heart and soul of the president's council because it both identifies problem areas and indicates where actions must be taken to protect margins.

Meanwhile, top corporate officers routinely keep a close watch on the divisions and businesses. The office of the chief executive—which currently consists of the CEO, the president, the COO, the CFO, and a senior executive vice president—meets ten to twelve times each year to review and discuss issues facing the divisions, businesses, and corporation as a whole. At these meetings, the PORs, summary letters, and memoranda from the presidents' councils, along with other inputs from the divisions and businesses, are typically on the agenda. The process gives the OCE intimate familiarity with the details of all the businesses.

The OCE also holds regular conference calls that are open to all divisions. The calls emphasize two-way communications. Division managers have opportunities to update progress, discuss current problems, or raise questions or concerns, while corporate management informs the divisions of broader corporate matters.

Regular meetings of senior operating executives in Europe and Asia serve a similar purpose. These regional general managers' meetings devote ample time to reviewing operating results and provide opportunities for division management to discuss particular issues and challenges.

The ultimate review of Emerson's performance occurs at the level of the corporate board of directors, which is well informed, active, and hardworking. The approval threshold for capital expenditures, for example, is $10 million, a relatively low level for a company of our size. We do this both because we want to keep the board involved in important business decisions and because we want our operating managers to

THE VOICE OF A BUSINESS LEADER

According to John Berra, head of Emerson's Process Management business, the time commitments to the planning and control cycle are significant. "Just when you finish one meeting, there's another to get ready for," he says. "It does take a lot of time. In fact, it can seem an unbelievable gauntlet. But it doesn't get in the way of our work, nor is it above and beyond our work. It *is* the way we work, how we get our job done. The process forces us to focus on the important things and tracks how we're doing on them. You can't run open loop for long. It's not for the faint of heart, and people who can't handle it don't stay. But if you trust and follow the process, it definitely works."

interact with—to present to and be seen by—the board. This policy helps ensure that our operating managers are fully committed to their plans and proposals. Meanwhile, as noted, the board undertakes a detailed review of our corporate or business-level strategies every year, and it closely tracks our performance against the plan. Board members have access to detailed operating reports, and they raise pointed questions when they have any concerns. In this respect, the board serves as yet another check on performance and spurs us to execute our plans successfully.

And so the cycle continues, as monthly PORs feed into quarterly presidents' councils and annual financial reviews. Emerson's steady focus on short-term performance and on achieving short-term objectives reinforces the discipline and consistency we seek. In turn, our success in meeting our targets, month by month, quarter by quarter, and year by year serves as an important motivational tool to stimulate still better performance.

Like our planning cycle, our cycle for follow-up and control is sometimes benchmarked. Typically, observers come away impressed but also somewhat intimidated by the rigor and intensity of what we do. Some people believe that we invest too much time in meetings and reviews. This underscores the reason that management processes and systems cannot be lifted whole cloth from one organization and installed elsewhere without modifications. What works for Emerson cannot be expected to work exactly in the same way elsewhere. But Emerson's systems and processes are only part of its success. Equally important are the development and ownership of the plans by the people who will implement them, our conviction that we can carry out the plans, and our investment in communications. The spirit in which we follow up on our plans and control our businesses is as important as the mechanisms through which we do these tasks.

Like our planning cycle, our control cycle generates many benefits in addition to tight controls. It drives us to stay close to our customers and to monitor our competitors' moves. It fosters improved management skills, teamwork, communications, and focus on fundamentals. It serves as an ongoing mechanism to identify and assess management talent, and it helps assimilate acquisitions into the company.

Our control cycle and the management philosophy it embodies ensure that we will do what we say we will do. They reinforce a sense of urgency when we confront problems and challenges. The problems with accuracy and transparency of financial information that cropped up recently at several American companies are not likely to happen at Emerson; we have too many reviews and checks and balances, and our most senior executives stay informed and involved. Decades before the Sarbanes-Oxley Act, our managers were signing off on their results every quarter.

Ultimately, the best way to ensure performance is to promote and retain smart, hardworking people and give them the latitude and incentives to do their jobs well. That is the essence of Emerson's organization approach and the subject of the next chapter.

PLANNING, EXECUTION, AND EMERSON'S EVOLVING STRATEGY

The cumulative impact of Emerson's commitment to planning and execution is shown not only in our consistently strong results but also in dramatic changes in our portfolio of businesses. Since the 1970s Emerson has become vastly larger, stronger, and more diverse, and this growth and transformation were facilitated by planning. The magnitude of the change is evident in the contrast between the Emerson of 1973, when we had about a dozen divisions generating revenues of approximately $940 million (primarily in the United States), and today's corporation, which has achieved global leadership in eight business platforms through approximately sixty divisions and generates revenues of $16 billion. We achieved this growth and transformation, of course, while attaining consistent increases in earnings and dividends—in other words, through disciplined execution.

It is important to explain how following our planning and control cycle enabled us to build our strong business platforms. It did so in several ways. First, as noted in exhibit 2-4, it alerted us to challenges that affected all of our units: the imperative to upgrade our technology base and develop more new products faster; the need to resume making acquisitions; the drive to become a global Best Cost Producer, and so on. As we encountered these trends and issues throughout the company, we launched corporate initiatives to address them—topics treated in later chapters.

Our planning and control cycle also helped us within each division and, as they took shape in the late 1980s and early 1990s, within each business platform. Our approach yielded insights and significant actions as we worked to build global leadership. Finally, in a few instances, our emphasis on planning led us to exit some businesses that had historically been strong contributors but, we came to believe, no longer fit with our future. Several factors drove exit decisions: failure of growth to materialize, our inability to put together a portfolio of leading divisions, and other conditions that limited profitability or return.

The role of our planning and control cycle in shaping and reshaping our businesses and corporate portfolio is evident in the evolution of our major business platforms and in decisions and actions we took to enter or exit certain businesses.

Emerson Process Management

During the past three decades we built a global leadership position in process management essentially from scratch, relying on acquisitions and a bold strategy crafted in our planning process. Back in 1973, only one Emerson division, Brooks Instrument, participated in process control. It was a bit player in a field then dominated by Honeywell, Foxboro, and Yokogawa. At the time, we were looking for diversification opportunities in industries that featured faster growth and higher technology than we experienced in our core businesses (motors, construction products, tools, and industrial drives and controls), and we recognized the promise of process control. In addition to its attractive growth and technology prospects, the industry was compatible with our strength in manufacturing components for industrial customers.

Brooks Instrument was too small and too specialized a foundation, however, so Joe Adorjan, who led our corporate planning staff, launched a search for a significant acquisition candidate. In 1976, we found it: Rosemount Inc., a leader in pressure sensors. Rosemount gave us a strong position in measurement, one of the three main segments in the process control industry.

We improved Rosemount's performance through our operating disciplines and, in division planning conferences, also identified further opportunities to bolster our position. We made several acquisitions, including Micro Motion, a leader in next-generation flow measurement instruments acquired in 1984. As we became a major factor in measurement, we also planned to enter the other major industry segments: actuation and control systems. In the latter area, Rosemount had a system in development based on smart components, but our plans indicated that we could get where we needed to be much faster through more acquisitions. In 1992, we spotted an ideal opportunity. Monsanto was restructuring its portfolio and looking to sell its Fisher unit, a global leader in actuation that had a control system under development that was complementary to ours. With the strategic advantages clear from our planning, we moved fast to close the deal.

Fisher made us immediately competitive across all segments with the industry leaders. We soon vaulted past these rivals, however, by capitalizing on a deep understanding of evolving trends in process control observed over time in our planning cycle. We combined Fisher and Rosemount, and, under John Berra's leadership, we recognized an opportunity to reshape the industry through a bold new approach. New information technology—microcomputers and smart devices for measurement and control in the field—meant that control systems could be redesigned to operate more efficiently. Expensive central processing stations could be downsized, with significant savings to customers.

Armed with this insight, which was refined and sharpened in several planning conferences, Berra led an industrywide effort, working with customers, competitors, and suppliers to develop new standards and a new open systems architecture. Meanwhile, Emerson pioneered the first server-based distributed control system based on the new specifications. The new system, PlantWeb, proved a resounding success, putting Emerson at the forefront of technology across all segments of the process control industry. We also built a major business in services and solutions. Today we are widely recognized as the global industry leader in all segments.

Emerson Climate Technologies

Similarly, planning played a key role in the creation of an industry-leadership position in climate technologies by preparing us to move quickly with changing circumstances. In the 1970s, we already had a foundation in heating, ventilating, and air conditioning (HVAC) and were a supplier of hermetic motors to compressor manufacturers. We also had several divisions that made HVAC controls. From division planning conferences, however, it was clear that we were vulnerable to powerful customers. In the mid-1980s, one of our customers in compressors, with which we had a sole-source agreement, suddenly announced that it would seek multiple suppliers of hermetic motors. This event could have created problems, but the opportunity to purchase the privately held Copeland Corporation—a leading maker of compressors with an intriguing and potentially revolutionary technology (the scroll compressor) in development—opened up a new strategy that more than offset the impact of this development. When the owner put Copeland up for sale, we hastened to close the deal.

Copeland proved an ideal foundation for growth. Not only did it provide a ready market for our hermetic motors, but it also enabled us to integrate forward into a higher-value-added product, the compressor. Better yet, Copeland offered the potential to reshape the industry through the scroll compressor. This device promised significantly better performance—higher energy efficiency, greater reliability, less noise, the ability to operate with a wider range of refrigerants, and, ultimately, lower cost—than traditional reciprocating units. It was no small challenge, however, to manufacture the device cost-effectively. In fact, it had never been done commercially; it required unique machining and tooling capabilities, and we would have to build capacity from scratch.

Emerson's planning process, operational disciplines, and deep pockets proved pivotal in commercializing the scroll. During the 1990s, we developed and executed a successful preemptive strategy for the scroll technology, both from the development and the capacity perspective. Generation after generation of designs flowed from the Copeland development teams, each passing difficult hurdles for performance and cost improvements. In concert, the desire for operating savings by end users and increasing energy regulations drove the demand for higher-efficiency approaches. With the best product in hand, Copeland carefully coordinated the application of the scroll compressor with the broad array of original equipment manufacturers (OEMs) while also carefully adding capacity in anticipation of demand. Copeland blended successful and consistent performance in delivering new products, managing customer relationships, and maximizing the opportunity to achieve larger production scale and meaningful cost advantages, and this combination made Copeland the global leader in compressors by the end of the decade.

A key element of our success was also hammered out in planning conferences. We developed a *franchise strategy* that enabled operations in North America, Europe, and Asia to add manufacturing capacity simultaneously based on common configurations of equipment and processes. This approach offset the investment risk, because units of capacity were interchangeable regardless of their location. Next, management in the business and the divisions worked together to bundle our HVAC products and services into packages and systems for customers. We developed, for example, complete, modular refrigeration systems designed for heavy-use applications such as supermarkets and convenience stores. From that point, we've been working on next-generation digital and communications technologies to link on-site refrigeration equipment and systems with central monitoring. We are thus able to provide retail customers with a comprehensive energy-efficient and cost-effective solution to their refrigeration needs.

In sum, through planning and execution, we transformed an interesting but vulnerable business from generating a few hundred million dollars of revenue to producing more than $3 billion by the end of the 1990s. The acquisition of Copeland was a key step, but the real success came from our effectively developing the new scroll technology, the franchise strategy to add capacity and preempt the competition, and the services and solutions thrust that significantly increases the value we offer to customers.

Emerson Network Power

Emerson Network Power evolved from several small divisions and independent acquisitions in the 1970s and 1980s that eventually developed into an intriguing business. Our Industrial Controls division, for example, made uninterruptible power supplies for industrial customers. Another division, AC/DC Electronics, produced small power supplies for conversion from alternating to direct current for makers of electronic equipment. In 1987, we acquired Liebert, the industry leader in systems to control temperature, humidity, and other environmental factors in computer and data rooms. Liebert also produced uninterruptible power supply capabilities for certain related applications. With this deal, we recognized that we had interesting connections among some of our divisions as well as a foundation for an attractive business in power management. The opportunities became increasingly apparent as we repeatedly met with these divisions in our annual planning cycle.

In 1989, we made a major advance, forming a joint venture with Hong Kong–based BSR International PLC. Among other businesses, BSR had a unit called Astec, a world leader in high-volume power switching supplies. It was a complicated deal that resulted in the consolidation of several Emerson units under Astec's umbrella, with options for us eventually to acquire Astec outright—something we did over a ten-year period (for additional details, see chapters 3 and 5). In addition to giving us high-volume manufacturing and technology development capability in Asia, the deal opened new markets in the region.

During the 1990s, these businesses strengthened and grew on the foundation of increasing global demand for information and therefore for computing and communications capacity. Emerson's knowledge of Asia and electronic production increased rapidly based on Astec's aggressive involvement in China. This entity gave us the capability to compete with any global player in both design and production.

With accelerating demand for global communications reach and bandwidth, the need for expanding reliable telecommunications and data networks arose in every country. This created exponential growth markets for hardware to supply power and ensure reliability in the systems. Although most major manufacturers of telecommunications systems produced their own power supplies, the main competitors decided in the late 1990s to outsource this component and, as a corollary, to divest their internal capacity. Emerson began a series of acquisitions intended to consolidate these entities. This process started with the purchase of Nortel's power supply assets focused on North America, followed by the acquisition of a similar business from Ericsson in Sweden. Combining these two companies with Astec's assets deployed in these markets, Emerson created an entity that had the scale and geographic scope to support system suppliers, installing and then rapidly adding capacity all over the world.

The most important step, however, was acquiring the third major spin-off, this time from Huawei, a Chinese system producer, which sold us Avansys in 2000. In making this deal, Emerson added coverage of all regions in China as well as a strong relationship with Huawei. This arrangement gave us access not only to Huawei in China but also to its aggressive export organization, which sold throughout the developing world.

Beyond creating this portfolio of capabilities, the Network Power platform managers moved to rationalize our global organization. This required that we (1) migrate the backbone of product design and production to the world-class Asian organization and (2) merge selling entities in individual countries to best leverage our customer relationships. Emerson Network Power became a $3 billion platform with great promise—a world-class organization supported by broad, Asian-based product development and production capabilities and global coverage of one of the world's most promising growth industries. Although the global recession of the early 2000s had a negative impact on our Network Power business, its long-term growth prospects remain bright.

Emerson Professional Tools and Emerson Storage Solutions

Among the platforms with deep roots in Emerson's past, the story of Professional Tools and its offshoot, Storage Solutions, is the most complex. It involved an ongoing, thorough reevaluation of our business—work that prepared us, in turn, to seize significant opportunities when they emerged. The result is not only a restructured business and a highly promising new platform but also the creation of significant value for our shareholders.

In the early 1970s, we owned several premier assets in tools, including Ridge Tool, the leading plumbing tool manufacturer, and In-Sink-Erator, America's top producer of household waste disposers. At the same time, we had a long-standing, mature relationship with Sears, which marketed many Emerson-produced consumer tools under the Craftsman brand. This was the dawn of the do-it-yourself era, and Emerson was eager to capitalize on the promise of growth in these consumer markets. During the 1970s we added to this foundation by acquiring significant consumer brands such as Poulan chainsaws, Weed Eater cord-line trimmers, Skil portable power tools, and Dremel hobby tools. We also bought some related businesses with important but less well known brands such as Louisville Ladder and Harris Calorific.

Although many of these products had high potential to grow, we learned in the annual planning and control cycle that we were playing catch-up. We were positioned generally as a secondary or tertiary player in markets that were rapidly becoming fiercely competitive, especially with the emergence of low-cost producers in Asia. Our plans revealed that from these starting positions, Emerson was too weak to prevail in the long term. However, our planning also showed us that our assets could be valuable to others who were more viable global competitors. This insight led to a series of creative actions to sell or establish joint ventures (JVs) in the full range of our consumer tool businesses.

First, chainsaws and trimmers were consolidated in the 1980s and sold to Electrolux, where they had more value in that company's portfolio. Meanwhile, Robert Bosch GmbH, one of the global leaders in consumer power tools (with a particularly strong position in Europe), was interested in our Skil and Dremel brands, which were popular in North America, although Bosch was not ready to acquire them outright. So we found a way to work together, starting in 1989 with a 50-50 JV to acquire Vermont American, a power tools accessory company. As our relationship proved productive, Bosch became eager to invest directly in Skil. After two years, we formed a second JV, Skil-Bosch, which included Dremel and enabled Bosch to gain intimate familiarity with the North American consumer market. The value created by the combined entity was significant, and finally, in 1996, Bosch bought out our 50 percent interest in Skil-Bosch. Thus we got out of a business in which our long-term prospects were at best uncertain, with a substantial return on our investment.

Other creative actions enhanced the value of our tools business. While maintaining a strong relationship as a supplier to Sears, we also responded to the emergence of home centers, eventually establishing a strong presence at both The Home Depot and Lowe's. Our relationship with The Home Depot evolved along a particularly interesting path as the retailer expanded its product lines and dependence on Emerson as a supplier. The Home Depot's management developed a strong desire to build a tool brand that would be unique to its retail environment and would rise to the top of the hardware industry. To accomplish this, it licensed the Ridgid brand from Emerson and applied it to a range of tools and adjacent products, some procured from us and others from third parties. The deal added yet another dimension of value creation for our shareholders.

The next step was the disposition of Vermont American, our remaining JV with Bosch. In 2000, we sold our interest to Bosch. We retained only an accessories unit, Clairson, the American leader in wire shelving products, a business we understood from our planning process to hold high potential. During the mid to late 1990s we complemented Clairson and its ClosetMaid brand with other acquisitions in storage products, including InterMetro, Stack-A-Shelf, and Knaack. The result is a strong global position and a new business in storage solutions. Emerson Storage Solutions has revenues approaching $1 billion and, if current growth rates continue, could emerge as a significant business platform.

Meanwhile, our professional tools divisions—especially Ridge and In-Sink-Erator—continue to grow and generate cash. Our plans and operating disciplines keep these units at the forefront of their industry, where they far outpace the competition.

In sum, the Emerson tools story exemplifies the value of our approach to planning and control. It illustrates not only that strong, consistent performance is possible but also that it can be maintained during a prolonged, profound period of restructuring. I doubt that this story would have had such a happy ending without the insights and disciplines developed during our annual planning and control cycle.

Emerson Industrial Automation

Creating value in the tool business involved retaining high margins and growing assets while deemphasizing and divesting other portfolio elements lacking the necessary market position or potential. We followed a similar approach in industrial automation, which historically had been strong for us, although focused principally on North America through divisions such as Emerson Power Transmission, ASCO Valve, and Branson. Given our interest in technology-based businesses and increasingly global scope, we find technical applications and products for industrial settings attractive. This principle lay behind another significant acquisition in 1990 to broaden our base in industrial automation and expand outside North America.

Our new partner was Leroy-Somer, the leading French and European motor company. The deal delivered multiple benefits. It bolstered our position in Europe, it enhanced our technology capabilities, and it gave us an intriguing business in alternators. We understood these benefits from the process leading to the deal, but as we got inside the company and brought our planning and control disciplines to bear, we saw particular opportunities to create value in alternators. The product could be combined with diesel and natural gas engines to form generator sets (called "gen sets" in the industry) of all sizes, including those used and sold by Caterpillar and other heavy equipment manufacturers. In our planning process we took a hard look at the market for gen sets and spotted a significant opportunity. In 1994 we purchased F. G. Wilson, a leading global assembler of gen sets and thus a potentially significant customer for our alternators. We bought it with the idea that we could ultimately sell this systems capability to a bigger player in the industry while preserving the capability to supply alternators to the ultimate entity.

Our strategy unfolded as planned. After running F. G. Wilson for two years, we formed a joint venture with Caterpillar, the unit's biggest customer. The JV included the gen set assembly business; we retained the alternator business on a sole-source basis. Then, in 1999, we sold our interest in the JV to Caterpillar, still retaining the exclusive supply agreement for alternators and other electrical components. We thus gained more business with a major customer. Meanwhile, we complemented our global alternators business with other acquisitions, including MagneTek Alternators and Kato.

The market for industrial automation is large and diverse, and the links between the divisions are less significant than in other businesses; for example, there is no core of common customers. As a result, strategies and initiatives largely occur independently from one division to the next, although there is an interesting capability to combine variable-speed drives with both motor and power transmission products. To build this business platform effectively, we must manage the portfolio aggressively, divesting underperforming and low-potential assets to ensure that our attention remains on the best opportunities. Our annual cycle of planning and control is essential to our success in eliminating assets we no longer need and investing where the returns will be greatest. Today, Emerson Industrial Automation is a $2 billion-plus business platform with high profitability.

Emerson Motor Technologies and Emerson Appliance Solutions

Emerson has been manufacturing electric motors since the nineteenth century, with electric appliances a major market for our motors since the early twentieth century. As with our other businesses over the years, we've added new capabilities and related product lines through acquisitions and other investments. Today we are one of the world's leading motor manufacturers and a vital supplier of technology and innovations to the global appliance industry. We got there by planning and execution.

Our history in motors and appliance components has deep roots, but our modern success was not guaranteed—although it was planned diligently. In the early 1950s, for example, we were the third-largest motor manufacturer in St. Louis and a distant also-ran on the national scene, ranking far below GE and Westinghouse. Through acquisition and continual focus on excellence in design and production—capabilities addressed and nurtured in our annual planning and control cycle—we steadily gained market share and customers. This was basic blocking and tackling: continuous cost reduction along with steady investment to develop new product features and improve quality. As the business grew, we formed strong relationships with major appliance manufacturers such as Whirlpool and Maytag, and these relationships proved to be good for us; these companies are demanding customers—tough on pricing and sticklers for quality. Our approach and discipline enabled us to meet their needs, and, as we gained share, our relationships have evolved to become global in scope. In the 1980s, we began to set up operations in Europe and Asia through acquisitions and start-ups. Today we are well positioned in all major regions, and we are especially strong in Asia based on technology and supply relationships with Haier in China.

Our move to the business platforms in the 1990s opened up the next era of opportunity in our oldest business: to provide solutions and add still more value to our customers. The continual need to improve functionality and lower costs favors a supplier like Emerson, which leads in technology development and can produce multiple components that can be combined to form a system. Systems with coordinated designs offer cost reduction capability, faster time to market between generations, and the possibility of diagnostic applications in which multiple elements of an appliance interact to affect performance.

By now the refrain should be familiar: through the planning process we recognized this opportunity and positioned ourselves to become the systems—and therefore solutions—provider for the industry. The key step was to supplement the motor product lines with control elements. This entailed the acquisition of leading electromechanical control elements such as timers and switches, along with the developers of innovative electronic versions of these devices. These new units, in combination with purchases of revolutionary switched reluctance motor technology, gave us the capability to meet our customers' needs.

Today, Emerson has more than $2 billion in annual revenues in this business. We have globally deployed business platforms that have valued positions with all the key appliance makers. As with Emerson Process Management, big customers are a distinguishing feature of our business, and we've designed new interfaces to deal with them. Instead of organizing ourselves around our products, we've organized ourselves around distinct solutions for appliances such as washers and water heaters, an approach that benefits our customers as well as Emerson.

Exit Decisions

Although our annual cycle of planning and control has been essential and instrumental to building strong business platforms, it has also helped to keep us focused as a corporation on our best opportunities. A corollary of this focus is the continual need to reevaluate our portfolio and to exit divisions and businesses that will not contribute enough to reaching our overall objectives. Over the years, for example, we've abandoned several attempts to create industry leadership groups. Some involved long-standing businesses such as government and defense contracting and construction products, and others represented more recent initiatives to pursue growing markets (we thought) such as consumer electronics and electrical power distribution. Several factors lay behind our decisions to exit: our inability to put together a portfolio of leading divisions, the failure of growth to materialize, or other conditions that limited profitability or return.

In the 1970s, for example, our portfolio included several divisions that provided products such as exhaust fans, lighting fixtures, smoke detectors, and baseboard heaters for the construction trades—a set of units we called builder products. Many were traditional Emerson products that depended on our expertise in manufacturing and cost reduction. We did OK with most of these, but we had no sustainable technology advantage, and we lacked scale. None of our units was close to being a market leader. Planning uncovered these problems and also indicated that competition was not only intense but also about to become global. There was simply no way to build a secure position in builder products that would meet our threshold of profitability. As a result, we exited through a series of transactions over several years that collectively garnered a positive return. In this instance, planning enabled us to get out early, before more serious trouble arrived.

Our exit from consumer electronics—a division called Fisher Electronics—was a similar story. Avery Fisher had been one of the pioneers of the American consumer electronics industry, and his company had carved out a premium niche when we acquired it in the 1960s. Within a few years, though, it was abundantly clear from our planning conferences that the U.S. consumer electronics industry was in irreversible decline in the face of Japanese competition, and Fisher, as a minor niche player, had an especially tenuous future. So, again, we got out, arranging a sale that yielded a positive return—an outcome that would not have been possible had we waited much longer.

In another instance, planning helped us to get in and out of a business that at first seemed attractive but then turned south. The business was electrical power distribution. Following the first energy crisis of the 1970s, this business had seemed headed for a bright future. We acquired A. B. Chance, a maker of components for the industry, in 1976. As we dug into the business in planning conferences and followed up in the control cycle, we began to see problems that we hadn't anticipated. Chance's product line was targeted to a declining segment. After a few years we saw that we could not differentiate Chance's products through technology or create value in other ways. So we sold it, again fetching a positive return, to management in a leveraged buyout. It was a learning experience for us, with the lessons pointedly sharpened in the planning and control cycle.

A more significant change was our exit in the early 1990s from the government and defense business, which had been a key part of Emerson since the early days of World War II. This business possessed many characteristics that appealed to our evolving strategy: fast, counter-cyclical growth, high-technology content, and a global footprint. For these reasons, we made it an area of emphasis and completed several important acquisitions as recently as the mid-1980s. However, the end of the cold war in the late 1980s and early 1990s portended declining demand for these technologies, and the need to restructure our defense business loomed as a major undertaking.

In the face of better opportunities emerging in our industrial businesses, we decided to exit government and defense. We accomplished this in two steps. We spun off most of the affected divisions under the umbrella of a separate public company, ESCO, with the equity distributed to Emerson shareholders. This avoided the need to restructure the defense business in an era when many other high-potential opportunities were rife. At the same time, we found a separate buyer for another division, Rosemount Aerospace, and sold it at a substantial premium to book value.

In sum, Emerson's commitment to planning and execution has led to profound changes—a transformation—in our business over time. Our consistent high performance may have obscured the magnitude of these changes. Outwardly, we seem to evolve incrementally; on the inside, though, we deal with constant change, continually. We're always looking intently at new opportunities and better ways of creating value. The key to what we've accomplished is our commitment to planning and control.

3

Getting Things Done

Organization Approach
and Leadership

*What leaders accomplish is the result
of what other people do.*

—Emerson axiom

The design of our organization and the development of leaders—
putting the right people in the right positions—ranked among my
top priorities as CEO. Our planning cycle enabled me to get to
know hundreds of managers throughout the company and to communicate our strategy and explain our decisions and actions face-to-face.

But that wasn't—isn't—enough. We've designed our organization
with a bias toward action, where communications flow around problems,
programs, and projects, where decisions are made at the level where the
best information is available, and where a small, talented corporate staff
adds high value but doesn't slow down or get in the way of operating
management. We plan our organization with the same intensity as we
plan our operations. Finally, we've developed a shared understanding of

leadership that works for us and reinforces everything we do. An action-oriented organization is the key to getting things done.

THE VALUE OF AN
ACTION-ORIENTED ORGANIZATION

Effective management is about effective action. Often, though, organizations get in the way of effective action. They breed bureaucracy, rules, protocols, and differences in status. They generate and multiply nonessential tasks and personnel, especially at the staff level. They reroute and block normal flows of information and communication, they foster politics, and they fight against positive change.

Countering these tendencies begins with an understanding of how and why organizations get bogged down. Then it takes discipline, planning, and a big investment in communication. It also takes a compensation system that is easy to understand and designed to reward effective action.

My experience at Emerson and on boards of directors has convinced me that organizations get in trouble when they can't pass three tests (see "Three Tests of an Action-Oriented Organization"). If they don't plan and control profits and make decisions at the level closest to customers and markets, if they load up on staff, if they communicate primarily through official reporting channels, then watch out. These tests measure an organization's bias toward action, and we apply them constantly to ourselves and other organizations such as competitors or potential partners we need to understand.

Chapter 2 talked about the level at which Emerson plans and controls profits. As for headquarters staffs, we want them to be small, talented, and oriented around their functions. Emerson maintains relatively few staff functions at headquarters and insists that they operate as efficiently as possible. The biggest departments are finance (including treasury, planning, and acquisitions) and purchasing (see chapter 4), but we watch headcount closely and keep it to a minimum.

As explained later, we divide human resources into three offices: global employee relations, organization planning, and executive compensation. Each office is staffed by an executive reporting to the CEO.

THREE TESTS OF AN
ACTION-ORIENTED ORGANIZATION

1. At what level does the organization plan and control profits?
   If an organization does not do both of these at the same level,
   and if that level is not as close as possible to customers and
   markets, then raise the warning flag. Needless reviews are taking place, and the information that makes it to the top may not
   be timely or accurate.

2. How big is the corporate staff?
   Large staffs tend to foster a political environment in which the
   objective is to stymie positive change. At the same time, bur-
   dening good staff people with responsibilities to supervise large
   departments and manage big budgets misuses their talents.

3. What is the flow of communication within the organization?
   If information runs primarily through official reporting channels, beware. Organizations should communicate around
   plans, programs, problems, and opportunities. Communication should flow directly between and among the people who
   need to know and can execute plans.

Similarly, our chief legal officer, chief technical officer, chief information officer, and chief marketing officer have a few direct reports and
spend most of their time working closely with operating management.
We also have an executive, supported by an assistant, who spearheads
a major corporate initiative in lean manufacturing.

Note that we do not have a corporate public relations department.
Since the 1950s we've found it cost-effective to outsource this function
to an agency, Fleishman-Hillard. A senior account rep works directly
with our executives, coordinating with our vice president and chief
marketing officer and an assistant treasurer in charge of shareholder
communications.

SIMPLE ORGANIZATION AND
IMPORTANT PRIORITIES

A number of years ago, one of the best staff executives Emerson ever had came to me with a list of programs that Emerson's operating managers wanted to implement. The list included the names of seven people the executive would need to hire to help carry out these initiatives.

I sat down with him, grabbed a pair of scissors, and cut the list in half. "How many people do we need to hire now?" I asked. "Three," the executive answered. I cut the list in half again. "Now how many people do we need to hire?" The reply: "None." As it turned out, we were able to complete all the important programs that the divisions wanted with no additions to corporate staff. The important things always get done.

Occasionally, we hear proposals to add staff, but the presumption is that the answer will be no. We avoid loading up on staff because a large staff creates work and adds expense. For every person we hire at corporate headquarters, we often must hire others in the divisions; consider the personnel multiplier effect in a company with more than sixty divisions.

So, whenever someone wants to hire additional staff, they understand the need to build a very strong case. The best measure of containing our corporate staff is the charge to divisions for corporate operations. From 1975 until 1998 this charge was 0.67 percent of sales, one of the lowest corporate charges we were aware of. The fact that the percentage didn't change for more than two decades indicates the level of control we have on staff positions. In 1998 we increased the charge to 0.70 percent (an increase of 0.03 percentage points, or approximately $5 million per year) to fund an expanded purchasing function (see chapter 4). We believe that 0.70 percent is still a relatively small charge for corporate operations among major corporations. Two of the largest cost centers at the corporate level are purchasing and compliance, the latter necessitated by expanding government regulations and evolving accounting standards.

Emerson also works hard to keep communications open, candid, efficient, and flowing through channels necessary to conduct our business. This is the reason we don't publish our corporate organization chart: we don't need artificial barriers to communications on matters that demand timely discussion and action. We do, however, have organization charts for the businesses and divisions for planning purposes. As noted, our annual planning and control cycle provides ample opportunity to communicate the most important business issues. Our policies and processes also tend to strip away politics. Finally, we don't burden our system with nonessential communications and information.

Our emphasis on communications pays dividends not only in the management ranks but also with our front-line employees.

Communicative Management

At the operating level, preserving our flexibility to act depends on effective two-way communications and on treating people fairly—two long-standing Emerson principles. The best way to motivate people is to keep them informed and to address problems and concerns quickly and equitably. We do not have unions in most of our plants, and we prefer to keep it that way. This is not because we're anti-union—we work effectively with unions where they exist in acquired operations—but because dealing with a third party adds costs and distractions that can erode our competitive advantage in the global economy. And dealing with a third party is unnecessary if management does its job well.

Phil Hutchison, senior vice president, human resources, uses the term *communicative management* to describe our approach at the operating level. This is distinct from *participative management*, which to some observers implies a kind of workplace democracy that, taken to an extreme, can paralyze an organization. As the term implies, communicative management is about two-way communications—explaining what we're doing and why and listening to and acting on employee ideas and concerns. Doing this effectively requires a decentralized approach.

We invest heavily in two-way communications, including requiring our managers at all levels to hold frequent face-to-face meetings with the people working for them. This arrangement starts at the top, where we expect every division president to meet with all division employees, as individuals or in small groups, at least once a year. The top manager is the chief communicator, and the job entails communicating the what and why of Emerson's plans and actions as well as good and bad news. Our managers also listen closely to what employees have to say. This critical information helps us constantly improve our operations.

Every division develops and implements an annual communications plan that features a clear message about the economics of the business and its prospects for the coming year. Division managers roll out this message through an annual state-of-the-business presentation, quarterly meetings at plants between the plant manager and employees, monthly roundtables between managers and small groups of employees chosen at random, and frequent meetings of departments and workgroups. Managers at all levels in the plants are expected to "manage by walking around" daily to let people know what's going on and to take the pulse of the organization.

We also conduct confidential opinion surveys of every employee at every location around the world routinely—generally every other year. This practice was begun in 1954 in the aftermath of a bitter strike in the government and defense business, when we needed a better understanding of employee motivation. We want employees to grade us on how well we are doing with our management, supervision, and communications. A *climate profile score* gives each location a single-point measurement of how well the positive employee climate is being maintained. For instance, exhibit 3-1 shows scores in each employee group improving. The exempt group went from good to excellent, the nonexempt group from satisfactory to good, and the hourly group remained satisfactory with a modest increase in score.

The results are analyzed for what they tell us about an operation at a particular moment as well as for long-term trends. Thus they are a valuable metric that enables us to manage and monitor continuous improvement. The surveys are also a metric for HR accountability. After each survey, we write up a five- to ten-page analysis and report that is reviewed by division management, business leaders, and the CEO, all of whom take the results very seriously. The results are also a component of management incentives, and a sustained trend (up or down) has a significant impact (positive or negative) on compensation.

Two-way communication is important not only in its frequency but also in its content, which is focused on important information about

EXHIBIT 3-1

Climate profile score comparison

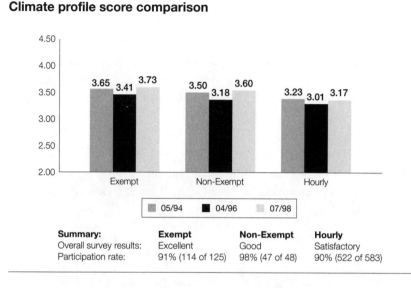

Summary:	Exempt	Non-Exempt	Hourly
Overall survey results:	Excellent	Good	Satisfactory
Participation rate:	91% (114 of 125)	98% (47 of 48)	90% (522 of 583)

the business. Employees can maximize their contributions to Emerson only if they fully understand the strategy, plans, opportunities, challenges, and economic realities of the plant and division. We claim, for example, that every Emerson employee can answer four essential questions about his or her job:

1. What cost reduction are you currently working on?

2. Who is the "enemy"—who is the competition?

3. Have you met with your management in the past six months?

4. Do you understand the economics of your job?

A reporter from *Business Week* once sought spontaneously to check this claim during a plant visit. He wanted to ask the four questions of a random set of employees, and we let him do it. When all the employees provided clear and direct answers, they passed both the reporter's test and ours.

Planning for Action-Oriented Management

An action-oriented organization also depends on action-oriented managers. Thus we also invest heavily in identifying, training, and developing the managers and leaders of the company. This is a major priority that engages the CEO and other top officers. The commitment is so strong that Paul McKnight, vice president of organization planning, points out that Emerson's CEO is also the company's chief human resources officer.

Our approach is founded on four principles that highlight the give-and-take between the individual and the organization in a high-performance company like ours. (See "An Outside View of Emerson's Culture and Personality.") We believe in the following four principles:

1. Talented managers are assets of the corporation—not of the divisions or other units in which they happen to work.

2. The corporation has the obligation to create opportunities for these managers.

3. These opportunities will involve job rotation and stretch assignments. We don't move people based on their credentials and experience but rather on their success in prior jobs.

4. Our managers have the obligation to create their own careers. We provide the opportunities; it's up to our people to take advantage of them.

The intensive effort we pour into planning our organization and human resources reflects our strong belief in these principles. We do not use standard, off-the-shelf systems for organization development. Rather, we rely on two techniques we've developed ourselves.

The first is the organization review, which is part of the annual planning and control cycle for each division. The length of this review varies depending on the size of the division; it involves the division president and HR executive along with the business leader, Emerson's CEO, and Paul McKnight. We review the status and performance of all managers, their potential to move to more challenging assignments, and specific responsibilities they might assume. We also discuss the management needs of the division, including the status of initiatives continuing from the previous year and updates on diversity. Finally, we

AN OUTSIDE VIEW OF EMERSON'S
CULTURE AND PERSONALITY

In 2003, as part of an assignment related to external communication, ad agency DDB Worldwide Communications Group undertook an evaluation of Emerson's institutional culture and provided an outsider's perspective on what makes Emerson an action-oriented organization.

Culture: What Makes Emerson's Culture Unique
What we are

- Financially focused and performance driven
- Direct in everything we do and say
- Passionate about our commitment to excellence
- Competitive: an ongoing state of wanting to win
- Forward-looking
- Engineers at heart
- Strong leaders
- Cooperative

What we would like to be

- Collaborative
  - Work in an integrated path with customers and cross-divisionally with each other to create better solutions for our customers
- Customer-focused
  - Make it easier for our customers to understand us and do business with us

Personality: The key components of Emerson's character
Dynamic: we energetically pursue answers

Smart: intelligent and savvy

Confident: strength that doesn't boast

Real: what you see is what you get

Decisive: we know what we need to do

review major issues projected for the coming year. If a division is planning to expand in Asia, for example, we want to make certain it will have the management resources to succeed. As with planning conferences and profit reviews, we prepare a summary report of each organization review, and it becomes a document of record on these issues for the coming year and the baseline for the next organization review.

In preparing for the organization reviews, division managers evaluate all managers who are department heads or higher, assessing them according to specific performance criteria. Each manager's status is summarized on a simple chart that indicates the current position, length of service, and total compensation, with similar information about potential replacements. The chart also includes color-coded evaluations of the manager's performance, potential, and cooperation, or willingness to work with corporate and other divisions on matters important to shareholders. Each division also brings its list of high-potential managers.* Exhibit 3-2 shows an example.

The second organization planning technique is adapted from a practice I once saw at a major engineering construction firm. The firm's business consisted of many large projects in different stages of completion. Most went on for years, but at any given moment some were starting up while others were winding down. To help plan assignments for key managerial and technical personnel in ever-changing circumstances, the firm developed a visual tracking system using color-coded cards displayed on a large wall. The codes identified an individual's expertise and experience and indicated when his or her involvement on a project would end. Whenever openings arose in a current project or a new project needed to be staffed, project planners looked at the wall and quickly spotted suitable candidates.

In 1980, we established a similar system in an organization room at headquarters, where we keep charts on every management team in the company. We update this information every year on the basis of the organization reviews, tracking our management employees. The charts include each manager's picture and are color-coded by expertise and experience. Thus a finance manager's chart looks different from that of a plant manager. As displayed on a wall, these charts provide a

---

*Emerson defines a high-potential manager as someone considered promotable to plant manager, division officer, or corporate director or officer.

EXHIBIT 3-2

"Color me green" example

1. Position title		
2. Name		
3. Years of service	4. Total compensation	
5. ◤	6. ▲	7. ◥

Performance rating

Potential rating

8. ▲ 9. ▲ 10. ◥ 11. ◥

Replacement's years of service

Cooperation rating

Replacement's total compensation

Replacement's name

Degree of readiness

Color codes

Gold	Outstanding	Yellow	Needs improvement
Green	Exceeds expectations	Red	Unacceptable
Blue	Meets expectations	White	New in position

ORGANIZATION PLANNING:
A VIEW FROM THE FIELD

"You can't imagine how valuable organization planning is to us," says a business leader. "Every year, I get to talk with the CEO about my people—who's doing a great job, who's struggling, who could benefit from a new assignment, who would be a great addition to help with this or that initiative. In thinking about these things, I get the benefit of the CEO's experience and wisdom as well as his assessment of my people and others whom I don't know very well.

"The discussion and the discipline are great. We don't follow the charts slavishly, though. Once, we had an opening at a division in Asia, and Chuck suggested that I offer the position to a young executive in corporate planning. I had seen the guy and liked what I saw but hadn't thought of him for this assignment. We talked it over, and the more we talked the more sense it made. We did it and it's turned out to be a great appointment. Meanwhile, we also found a good spot for the candidate I had thought would get the Asia job when the meeting opened."

wealth of information and a powerful visual aid to human resource planning. When a position opens, we know quickly which candidates are most qualified and which people might succeed the candidates who move up.

Both of these organization planning techniques—the organization review and the color-coded charts—also support our focus on follow-up and execution by letting us know when people should not be moved because they are in the middle of important assignments.

Our principles and techniques also help us deal with the sometimes tense conversations about moving individuals between divisions or from a division to a business-level or corporate job. Division managers naturally are reluctant to part with key members of their management teams. On the other hand, they understand the benefits and ultimate fairness of the system. However painful a loss may be in the short run, the division manager can be assured that the replacement will be another strong contributor.

Management Development, Emerson-Style

At Emerson, management development—including executive and MBA recruiting and leadership development—complements organization planning in creating an action-oriented organization.

In the first place, management at the company is self-selected. People are drawn to us by our culture and reputation for success. If they don't fit here, they find out pretty fast. Beyond the self-selection, our management personnel come from four sources. The first, and by far the largest, group consists of long-term employees. We believe that successful operation requires management continuity. The typical Emerson division or corporate officer is forty-five to fifty years old and has at least fifteen years of service, and more than 85 percent of promotions come from within the company. We believe that this approach contributes to strong morale and helps our culture remain cohesive. This policy also holds for Emerson's activities overseas, where we use limited numbers of expatriates. Local residents run most of our operations.

A second source of personnel is acquisitions, which account for about 40 percent of our current executives. They include our chief operating officer, the senior executives in charge of two of our major businesses, several corporate officers, and many division presidents. If the top managers at an acquisition stay—and in most cases, they do—they tend to thrive.

Third, every year we recruit twenty to thirty high-potential MBAs and put them in jobs for which they are not yet qualified. We assign them mentors and support them with leadership development programs during their first two years at the company. After that, their success is in their own hands. The best make it; the others don't. It's that simple. Most of them in fact stay. Success stories from this group include three members of the Office of the Chief Executive—Chairman and CEO David Farr, Senior EVP and CFO Walter Galvin, and Senior EVP Charlie Peters—as well as many other top corporate, business, and division executives.

Finally, we hire experienced people for certain jobs because it's important to bring in new thinking. We also hire from the outside when we need specialized experience that we do not have internally. For example, when we decided to bolster corporate marketing and develop the Emerson brand, we hired Kathy Button Bell, a seasoned marketing consultant, as our chief marketing officer. Similarly, we brought in our chief technology officer, PhD physicist Randall Ledford, from the outside after a distinguished career at Texas Instruments; Larry Kremer, head of purchasing, from Whirlpool, and Ray Keefe, our corporate champion of lean manufacturing, from Eaton Corporation. About 10–15 percent of our top executives come from the outside.

However they come to Emerson, high-performing managers get noticed through our management processes and systems, which, among other purposes, serve as vehicles for both training and assessment. Outstanding managers with more than five years of service are considered for the Emerson Leadership Program, an intensive, one-week program that twice a year draws together people from every business and every part of the world. The program is focused on the Emerson management process, and top officers constitute the faculty. The program thus provides a forum where young managers from throughout the company get to know each other and to see—and be seen by—the senior leaders of the company. Participants also receive individual feedback that helps advance their careers.

Pay for Results

Emerson's compensation policies pay for results using simple principles that haven't changed much in more than thirty years. Like many other big companies, we offer executives a compensation package mixing salary with short- and long-term incentives. Emerson's approach, however, puts a significant portion of compensation at risk—more so than is typical in most other large companies. But it also reinforces the behaviors and drives the results we seek.

Each executive in a division earns a base salary and is eligible for a year-end *extra salary*, or bonus, based on the division's performance according to measurable objectives. Extra compensation is calculated as a multiple of an extra salary *centerpoint*, which we establish as part of the total compensation target at the beginning of each year in the annual financial review. Depending on how well the division performs, the multiplier applied to the centerpoint can be as low as 0.35 at the bottom end, with the upside uncapped. If the division hits its forecast target for performance—numbers based on commitments that were mutually agreed on—the multiplier is 1, and members of the management team will receive their centerpoint extra salary. Doing better increases the multiplier, and doing worse lowers it.

The matrix in exhibit 3-3 illustrates the concept in action for the portion of management compensation based on sales and earnings. A division that hits its forecast for the period of 13.7 percent EBIT (earnings before interest and taxes) on sales of $21.2 million will see its managers rewarded with a centerpoint of 1.0. The managers could double this amount by delivering about 10 percent more sales and two additional margin points.

The formula for computing compensation targets is set by the CEO. Given our emphasis on continuity and consistency, we do not alter the formula much over time, although we do adapt it to the evolving needs of the business. At present, sales and earnings have a 60 percent weighting, with inventory turnover, days' sales outstanding (DSOs—a measure of accounts receivable), and capital turnover accounting for most of the rest. Other factors include the results of the employee opinion surveys and metrics tied to the economics of a particular division.

Long-term incentives include three types of stock compensation. These are designed to reinforce performance targets, build equity through real stock ownership, retain key executives, and reward performance. About three thousand managers are eligible for stock options, which are discretionary awards made every two to three years. Three hundred to three hundred and fifty senior-level executives who can

EXHIBIT 3-3

Extra salary program sales/profit matrix

Sales ($ or local currency, 000s)

	18,693	19,330	19,967	20,605	21,242	21,879	22,517	23,154	23,791
15.6%	1.0								2.0
15.1%		1.0							
14.6%			1.0						
14.1%				1.0					
13.7%	0.75				1.0				1.6
13.3%						1.0			
12.9%							1.0		
12.6%								1.0	
12.3%	0.35				0.65				1.0

EBIT profit

Increased sales and profit versus target yields greatest potential payout

Decreased sales and profit versus target lessens payout but does not go to zero

Improvement or decline on one axis (sales or profit) alone impacts multiplier, but at a slower rate

EBIT: Earnings before interest and taxes

directly influence the company's long-term financial success partici-pate in a performance shares plan, with a payout based on EPS growth over a four-year period. We set up a new performance shares plan every three years to provide continuity and retention.

Finally, a small number of candidates for top management succes-sion are eligible for a restricted stock plan. The award is substantial and is intended to provide a premium over and above competitive opportu-nities. The program vests over ten years, so participants have signifi-cant incentives to remain with the company.

Several points about our approach to management compensation are worth highlighting. First, as noted, our program hasn't changed over the years, and it has been administered consistently by Jo Ann Harmon Arnold, senior vice president. Second, as also noted, a rela-tively high proportion of annual compensation is at risk. Good com-pensation is not an entitlement but instead must be earned every year. Above-market performance, however, means above-market pay.

Third, the annual bonus is based on performance measures, weight-ings, and targets that are common throughout the company and have been for decades. All rules apply to everyone, and everyone understands them. Fourth, during the year, Emerson's planning and control cycle ensures a constant stream of communication about progress against the targets, so there are no year-end surprises. Finally, targets reinforce the company's short-term financial goals, especially consistent increases in profits. We couldn't do that without an action-oriented organization, which is supported by this approach to compensation.

Summing Up: Action-Oriented Organization

The benefits of an action orientation are numerous. Policies and sys-tems ensure that decision makers make good choices and that their peers and reports in turn know what they must do to execute the deci-sions. People know what's going on and what's important, and they are motivated and rewarded for performing well. Organization reviews and planning put the right people in the right jobs. Accordingly, we experi-ence very low turnover for our type of business; relatively few of the high-potential employees leave the company, and fewer than 4 percent at the executive level depart. The average tenure of the top fifteen exec-utives with Emerson is twenty-six years. This continuity is invaluable.

It promotes a team-oriented, cohesive culture that is focused on winning and consistency.

We also work constantly to lower the barriers to effective action, applying the three tests and insisting on frequent, candid communications about the state of the business. This policy, too, has significant benefits: it prevents successful union organizing drives. Constant communication means that everyone knows what's expected. And our systems take the blame and the politics out of the organization. The result is an organization that acts quickly to meet expectations and stay on track over time.

The ultimate key to making our planning and control cycle work and to maintaining an action-oriented organization is effective leadership. In addition to identifying talented managers, grooming them through stretch assignments, and rewarding them for achieving results, we seek to instill in them the qualities of effective leaders.

LEADERSHIP: CREATING AN ENVIRONMENT
WHERE PEOPLE MAKE A DIFFERENCE

Emerson has a long tradition of inviting outside speakers to its annual corporate planning conference. One of our guests, in the autumn of 1979, asked me a question that I'd been pondering for a long time and still think about: "What makes an effective business leader?"

The guest was Marshall Loeb, a writer for *Time* magazine (and later managing editor of *Money* and *Fortune* and now at MarketWatch.com), and we had invited him to help us understand and anticipate the challenges of the 1980s. When would stagflation end? Would there be another energy shortage? What economic and diplomatic priorities would the United States have in the coming decade? I don't remember where we came out on these questions, but I do remember Marshall's question to me, which came at dinner after a long day of meetings and presentations.

Marshall did not catch me unprepared. At that point I was forty-three and had been at Emerson for six years. I'd been working with business leaders and thinking about business leadership for a long time. I framed my answer to him with a couple of general observations. First, I believe leaders are made and not born. Leaders are distinguished by what they do, and what they inspire other people to do, and not by their genes, their looks, their credentials, or their beliefs.

Second, there is no one right way to lead. I've seen many effective business leaders with many styles of leading. Some are take-charge people; others are good delegators. Some are energetic and outgoing; others are quieter. Some rely more on the carrot, others the stick. Some are exceptionally good in crisis situations; others seem better suited to the long haul. In my experience, however, all of these leaders share certain attributes, and these formed the basis of my answer to Loeb.

I like to make lists and especially lists of ten points. Many times I'll write a long list of points about a topic and stew over it for a while, then do some sorting and arranging, trying to understand the relationships. If possible, I'll boil the list down to ten points. Cutting the list shorter risks blurring distinctions and burying key points; making it longer is undisciplined. Ten is not a magic number, but getting the points right stretches the mind.

My answer to Loeb consisted of ten points, which he published in *Time* in February 1980 (see "Knight on Leadership"). The list struck a chord with readers, and it has stood the test of time. I received many favorable comments when it was published and still get mail about it from people who've seen reprints or been handed photocopies. Although we've changed the order and some of the language, we still use a similar list in training and development at Emerson.

Following are the ten attributes of effective business leaders, the ten keys to creating an environment in which people can and do make a difference (see the summary chart in chapter 1). As individual points, they may seem obvious. Collectively and cumulatively, however, they help create the environment for exceptional organizational performance.

1. Be Committed to Success. Leadership starts here, with a commitment to success. We all see people who we know will succeed, and most of them pour enormous energy into projects or assignments. They also have the perseverance to stay with an issue or a problem until it gets resolved. That combination of energy and perseverance is central to the commitment to success. And that commitment is contagious. It galvanizes an organization, big or small. And obviously, people like to be on a winning team. Similarly, people quickly spot a lack of commitment. That too is contagious, and it drags down performance.

John Berra is an example of relentless commitment. The head of our process control business, John is a chemical engineer who spent his early career at Monsanto. He joined Emerson's Rosemount division and quickly climbed the ladder. When we bought Monsanto's Fisher Controls division in 1992, a deal that provided a big boost to our process control business, John was already thinking bigger. He wanted to change the game, to lead Emerson beyond making and selling smart components to supplying those components embedded in an intelligent network—a flexible, open system to control virtually all operations at continuous-process plants. This vision was not shared by our competitors, which had (or still have) vested interests in proprietary systems.

John faced a daunting task in getting customers and competitors to change their thinking, but he did not let their vocal, and sometimes fierce, opposition deter him. He helped to form and then led the Field-bus Foundation, a global organization that includes all the major players in the industry. John then persuaded the members to endorse an open architecture for process control systems and to develop industry-wide technical standards. This involved years of hard work and managing through stiff resistance and countless frustrations. At one point, to avoid perceptions of conflict of interest, he donated several key patents held by Emerson to the foundation.

Under John's leadership, the open architecture and new standards prevailed, a game-changing outcome that was good for Emerson, its customers, and its competitors. That's commitment to success—adhering to a vision and bringing it to life through hard work and persistence.

2. Set Proper Priorities. No one disagrees with the critical importance of setting proper priorities, but time after time I've seen organizations struggle because their leaders didn't or couldn't do it.

They typically get into trouble for three reasons. First, it takes hard work and hard thinking to identify a limited number of actions and communicate them in a clear, logical sequence—to keep things simple. Second, leaders may pursue the wrong priorities, but they're just as likely—maybe more likely—to be unsure of what the right priorities should be, especially in a fast-changing world. They don't take the time and do the work to get their priorities right. Third, leaders often experience difficulty in managing the trade-offs among conflicting objectives, such as profit and growth. They don't know which to

KNIGHT ON LEADERSHIP

People who wonder what it takes to be a leader would do well to listen to Charles Knight. His father, Lester B. Knight, seventy-two, who is one of the premier management consultants, programmed young Chuck to be a leader ever since he grew up on Chicago's gilt-edged North Shore. At fifteen, Dad packed his only son off to a client's foundry in a small Canadian town for a summer's work to learn blue-collar life. After that there were summer jobs in Switzerland, Germany, and Argentina; engineering and business studies; and varsity football and tennis at Cornell. In his early twenties, Chuck Knight headed the European operations of Lester B. Knight & Associates; in his early thirties he took charge of the whole company. Then, startlingly, he revolted against Dad's grand plan.

At thirty-six, Knight skipped away from his family's company to join a valued St. Louis client, Emerson Electric, of which he soon became chief executive. Father was furious. The breach has healed in the seven years since then, in part because Chuck Knight has shown how well he learned his lessons. Emerson is on most short lists of the best-managed companies in the country, and with its sales having risen steadily to $2.6 billion last year, it is challenging bigger General Electric and Westinghouse in many product areas. Now 44, Knight is one of the youngest chairmen of a major U.S. corporation.

Knight believes that in business, in politics, indeed in any venture at all, leadership consists of ten basic ingredients. Some of them, he concedes, sound obvious, even corny, but together they make a compelling package. Here is Knight's list:

No. 1: You have to be able to set priorities. I always remember my father said, "Chuck, your health comes first; without that you have nothing. The family comes second. Your business comes third. You better recognize and organize those first two, so that you can take care of the third."

No. 2: You need an ability to grab hold of tough problems and not delegate them. It's not fair to let the guy below you take the brunt of making the hard decisions. The leader has to get deeply, personally involved in challenging issues and set the policy.

No. 3: Set and demand standards of excellence. Anybody who accepts mediocrity—in school, on the job, in life—is a guy who compromises. And when the leader compromises, the whole damn organization compromises.

No. 4: You need a sense of urgency. It is absolutely better to do something, recognizing that it may not be the right thing, than do nothing at all. If you don't have a sense of urgency, the bottom drops out of the organization.

No. 5: Pay attention to details. Getting the facts is the key to good decision making. Every mistake that I made—and we all make mistakes—came because I didn't take the time, I didn't drive hard enough. I wasn't smart enough to get the facts. You can't get them all, of course, but the last 5 percent or 10 percent of the facts may not really matter.

No. 6: You need commitment. You can always pick out the guy who has a commitment. He is the fellow who does not fly into town on the morning of the meeting but flies in the night before to make sure that he gets there.

No. 7: Don't waste your time worrying about things you cannot do anything about. Don't try to fix things that are impossible. Concentrate on the possibles.

No. 8: You need the ability to fail. I'm amazed at the number of organizations that set up an environment where they do not permit their people to be wrong. You cannot innovate unless you are willing to accept some mistakes.

No. 9: Be tough but fair with people. Being tough means setting standards and demanding performance. Probably the hardest part of leadership is to make sure that you will not compromise when choosing people. When we change a division president, 60 percent of the initial recommendations are compromises. But you cannot let emotions get in the way when making a choice.

No. 10: You can't accomplish anything unless you're having some fun. Of course, it is clear that I have fun on the job. I get to the office every morning between 6:30 and 7:30. The other executives know that, so they try to get in the office early, too. I hope they are having fun.

Marshall Loeb, "Executive View: A Guide to Taking Charge," *Time*, February 25, 1980, 82. Reprinted by permission of Marshall Loeb.

attack, in which order, and how moving in one direction affects progress in another.

The need to set the right priorities is one reason Emerson invests so much time in planning and replanning. Some people think we're nuts because we replan every business every year. As we've seen, however, our planning process and cycle gives us repeated opportunities to examine and question our assumptions and identify what's important. Planning also gives us the discipline to keep asking questions and to keep resetting priorities when circumstances change.

An important aspect of setting priorities is to communicate them to the people who must understand them and follow through. That explains why our top executives invest so much time in planning conferences. They aren't there just to manage their direct reports but also to manage all the people who in turn work for those direct reports. It's important to communicate our priorities to this wider audience. If only a few people understand what the priorities are, the organization will struggle. But getting hundreds of people lined up behind the priorities unlocks tremendous leverage. As noted, we like to say that no one at Emerson is wandering around wondering what is expected of them. People have to know.

A great example of setting and communicating priorities is Jim Berges, currently Emerson's president and a member of the Office of the Chief Executive. In the early 1990s, Jim was high on the fast track as head of our business in motors and drives when we asked him to take on a two-year corporate assignment as our first profit czar. Initially he was reluctant to move from a key position on the line to what could be perceived as a staff job. After he accepted the move, however, he did so enthusiastically and with clear priorities. At the corporate planning conference where we announced the appointment, Jim stood up and declared, "I'm not a technologist, and I don't care about growth. For the next two years I'm focusing on profit. Don't talk to me about anything else!" He did a fantastic job, setting up the systems and waterfall process that became central to our profit planning.

3. Set and Demand High Standards. A leader must have high standards for integrity, excellence, and performance. If a leader does not set high standards and observe them personally, the organization won't meet them. Compromises can be demotivating and debilitating.

Good leaders maintain a healthy level of productive tension. This does not mean that leaders impose a threatening atmosphere where people fear for their jobs. Instead, they promote the kind of tension resulting from people wanting to rise to extraordinary challenges and wanting to be held accountable. True leaders challenge their people, constantly, to do better. They ask basic questions and don't accept answers that haven't been thought through.

Emerson's Senior EVP and CFO, Walter Galvin, exemplifies these qualities and is a huge asset to the company. In meetings of the OCE, presidents' councils, financial reviews, and other gatherings, he has a knack for zeroing in on the numbers that open up the real issues we must confront. He asks tough, probing questions and is politely but firmly impatient with casual reasoning or evasive answers. The people whose work he will review know that they must be on their toes.

Walter is also widely recognized for his great integrity, continuing a long tradition in the CFO job. Decades ago, long before recent legislation mandated the practice, one of Walter's ablest predecessors, John Wilson, began requiring division managers to sign off on their financial results. The tradition of high integrity that John and Walter embody is evident in our financial reporting and our relationships with investors and other constituencies. It's no accident that our reporting is transparent and that we have credibility with analysts and investors.

Effective leaders like John, Walter, and many others at Emerson also visibly live up to their own standards. As a result, their people don't want to let them down.

4. Be Tough but Fair in Dealing with People. People want to be measured and they want to improve. Helping them requires the ability to be tough but fair.

The word *tough* is often misunderstood. In 1978, *Forbes* ran a cover story on Emerson, and in the accompanying editorial, then-editor James Michaels explored the meaning of *tough* in a business context (see "Not Brutal—Tough"). The dictionary's definition, he pointed out, is "having the quality of being strong or firm." "Being tough," Michaels noted, "does not imply being heartless or irresponsible." Rather, it's "what it takes to make a company run efficiently, to make capital productive, jobs steady and remunerative and to produce quality products at low cost for the benefit of society."

NOT BRUTAL—TOUGH

At dinner recently in the Ladue, Mo. home of Emerson Electric Chairman Charles Knight, *Forbes'* Phyllis Berman asked Knight's wife whether she had always known that Knight would be a great success. Joanne Knight, who had married Chuck when he was at Cornell, replied: "Yes." "Why?" Berman asked. "He's tough," Joanne replied. Her words sent us to our big Webster's dictionary, which defines *tough*: "Having the quality of being strong or firm . . ."

Toughness—strong, firm—is what it takes to make a company run efficiently, to make capital productive, jobs steady and remunerative and to produce quality products at low cost for the benefit of society. Sloppily run companies can produce neither profits nor steady jobs nor low-priced products. Being tough does not imply being heartless or irresponsible. It doesn't mean opposition to sensible social progress to alleviate suffering. But it does mean being supremely rational: If old Charley is no longer effective in his job, old Charley must go. If an old plant can no longer produce efficiently, it too must go. That's what capitalism is all about: shifting people and resources around to achieve the greatest possible efficiency for the greatest number of people even if some individuals must suffer.

Here, we expect, is one of the greatest grounds for misunderstanding between the business community and the rest of society. Outsiders, especially intellectuals, look at firings and say: How heartless!

Leaders must be tough—strong, firm—in demanding performance and accountability, just as boards of directors must be tough with CEOs and management teams. This is an area where people will quickly detect compromises and modify their behavior accordingly. This doesn't mean that leaders can be arbitrary or act too quickly in making changes. That's where being fair comes in. We don't trust managers who shoot from the hip, especially on personnel matters. You have to give people enough time to find out whether they can deliver. They must have room to fail and learn from failure. If problems persist, then it's time for a change.

They fail to see the whole picture. This was brought home to us recently when we received a copy of a speech made before the Modern Language Association by Edith Kern, professor of English at Hofstra University in Hempstead, N.Y. Professor Kern used a much-admired *Forbes* advertising campaign to launch a criticism of business morality. She asked rhetorically: "Is *Forbes* advocating a way of life in which the man who has 'arrived' is fated to be overcome and annihilated by one who has not yet succeeded . . . only to be defeated in turn, most likely by yet another . . . ? Is the poster to glorify or satirize a world of capitalism so brutal that victory depends upon another's defeat, and dog eats dog in unending repetition?"

The truth is, Professor Kern, we are advocating *nothing*. We are merely describing the world. People do grow older—to paraphrase the poet, hungry generations *do* tread them down. Combinations of people and resources do grow inefficient and must be rearranged with inevitable inconvenience and even suffering by individuals. Men like Chuck Knight, because they do lust for the boss' job, help keep business on its toes, with benefits to all.

Professor Kern speaks of the capitalistic world as "brutal." We think "tough" is a better word. And we think the tough qualities of men like Chuck Knight are a major reason why the American standard of living is as high as it is and why our society is as open as it is.

James W. Michaels, "Not Brutal—Tough," *Forbes*, March 20, 1978, 6. Reprinted by permission of *Forbes* Magazine © 2005 Forbes, Inc.

Managing this way is not always fun. But we firmly believe that people want to be measured, and when they come up short, they want help to improve their performance. The problem is that even though most managers can assess performance, few have the ability to help others improve themselves. Identifying and nurturing those who can help others is vital to an organization.

Bill Rutledge, Emerson's president and chief operating officer during the 1980s, possessed an extraordinary ability to help people improve. I once offered a $100 reward to anyone who could produce a memo that Rutledge had written. There were no takers. That's because his gift was to engage with people to a point where he could build and enhance their capabilities without having to write follow-up memos. He was tough, and he spoke bluntly when holding people accountable. This practice was balanced with a great sense of humor and charm that put people at ease. When Rutledge walked through a plant he was like the Pied Piper; people wanted to follow him because they knew they would learn something that would make them better at their jobs.

Among the most important decisions made by business leaders are promotions, and we don't always take the time to do that job well. We tend to take the path of least resistance: "Well, so-and-so has been loyal for many years and deserves a chance." That's human nature, but it's also a mistake. You've got to be tough enough to fight that tendency. It sounds harsh, but we hurt people more by putting them in jobs where they will fail than by passing them over. It's critical for leaders to choose the right people as their direct reports so that they maximize their time and capabilities. It's also critical to give these people room to do their jobs well. To paraphrase the axiom at the beginning of this chapter, a leader's success is the result of what other people do.

5. Concentrate on Positives and Possibilities. One of the best pieces of advice I received when I joined Emerson came from a veteran board member, Maurice R. "Dude" Chambers, chairman of Interco. He said, "In setting priorities, don't waste time and effort on issues that can't be influenced or problems that can't be fixed. Attack the issues where you can make a difference."

Leaders invest their time and energy in reaching ambitious but attainable goals. They don't squander their time and energy on trying to meet challenges that cannot be met or trying to undo outcomes that can't be undone. Nothing can be gained by tilting at windmills, but a great deal can be accomplished by focused efforts to achieve the possible, even if it takes a long time.

Earlier we told the story of John Berra's vision of changing the game in the process control industry, using it to illustrate the power of personal commitment. This story also illustrates the benefits of concentrating on possibilities and positives. John's vision was attainable, and it stirred thousands of our employees to help realize it. Emerson's history is full of such stories, and they are central to our consistent success. Another story that stands out is our perseverance and tenacity in completing the acquisition of Astec, a major move for Emerson that took nearly a decade to complete.

This saga began in the late 1980s, when we recognized the strategic imperative to build our business in electronics. We had five divisions that made electronic equipment, instruments, and components, but they were concentrated in North America and loosely coordinated. And even taken together, they did not give us the scale to succeed. So in 1989 we struck a deal with BSR International PLC, a British corporation, which included Astec, the world leader in high-volume switching supplies and other products. Headquartered in Hong Kong, Astec had an especially strong presence in Asia.

The deal had several moving parts. We swapped our five units in return for a 45 percent share of BSR. Then BSR sold its unrelated businesses and renamed itself Astec (BSR). This new entity, which now included our former units, immediately became one of the world's biggest power conversion companies. Emerson had management control along with an option to acquire the outstanding shares later.

So far, so good. The strategy proved right for the long term, although implementing it was not easy; integrating the constituent parts of Astec was especially difficult in the short term. The unit endured losses for several years while we took strong actions to restore its health under the outstanding leadership of George Tamke and David Farr, among others. These actions included plant closings, job moves, and suspension of dividend payments, all of which were controversial among some shareholders. In the mid-1990s, Astec turned the corner, becoming the strong performer that remains the foundation of today's Emerson Network Power.

But as difficult as the turnaround of Astec was, lawsuits from dissident shareholders and the glare of hostile press coverage of our actions in the United Kingdom made it a challenging experience to complete the acquisition. Emerson and its leaders endured numerous attacks, including some that were not only ill informed but also personal and vicious—that we were "bullies" bent on intimidating minority shareholders and were engaged in a "dogfight" to deprive them of their dividends.* Again, George, David, and their colleagues stayed the

---

*See, for example, "Thunder and Lightning in an Electric Storm," *Financial Times*, February 11, 1998.

course, preserving Emerson's legal rights while patiently explaining the reasons for our actions, the need to reinvest for growth, and the ultimate benefits to shareholders and the public. Eventually we prevailed in the courts of law as well as the court of public opinion. We finally acquired the last of the outstanding shares of Astec in 1999, ten years after it all started. By then, Astec had become the great business we had always known it would be. Despite the obstacles and the adversity, we made it by focusing on the possibilities and stressing the positives.

6. **Develop and Maintain a Strong Sense of Urgency.** We've never run across a real problem that went away because we ignored it. It will be there tomorrow, and it's going to get worse until it is resolved. It is particularly important to address operating and people problems quickly, because they will cause the most trouble in the short term.

Good leaders have a bias for action. They recognize that it's better to do something than nothing. If they don't get it quite right, they'll keep trying until they do.

Emerson's core beliefs and management process help instill urgency in everything we do. When we confront strategic problems, we search urgently for the facts to support the best decision. And after the decision is made, we act urgently to implement it. Two Emerson business breakthroughs of the past twenty years—smart sensors in process control and the scroll compressor in climate technologies—illustrate the point.

The genesis of our smart sensors business occurred not long after we acquired Rosemount in 1976. Rosemount was the leader in differential pressure sensors for process control applications, but by the early 1980s it was imminently vulnerable to next-generation electronic sensors and systems. We knew that unless we developed the next-generation technology ourselves, we would eventually fall behind competitors that got there first.

The stakes were huge for us. We had placed a major bet in acquiring Rosemount, and only a few years later we had to raise the bet again on a crash development program for smart sensors. We set up a program called Mount Everest that was led by Ed Monser. He and his colleagues created a skunk works that drew on our best people from all over the company. The team invented not only a wholly new product but also a wholly new and faster process for innovation, all in only fourteen months. Introduced in the mid-1980s, our 3051C digital pressure sensor proved a huge hit and gave us great credibility with customers.

That product also enabled us to get to the next step—from making components to making smart components—on the path to becoming a systems supplier in process control.

The story of the scroll compressor is similar. We bought Copeland in 1986 to get the technology, but it took years to make it reliable, figure out how to manufacture the compressors economically, and convince customers to make the switch. Bob Novello, Dick Peltier, and Earl Muir deserve huge credit for this, and for the decision and urgent implementation of the rollout after the technology was deemed ready.

Again, we placed a big bet: in our franchise strategy of the mid-1990s, ahead of demand, we built a dozen factories worldwide. We knew the risks but also knew that we would gain a huge advantage in being ready when the technology took off. The franchise strategy worked brilliantly. Not only did we preempt the competition, but we've also reaped huge benefits from being physically close to our customers with the capacity to meet their needs. Emerson today is by far the global leader in scroll compressors, a position we never could have achieved without acting urgently.

7. Pay Attention to Detail. We all make mistakes, and many—perhaps most—of them result from not having all the facts. Getting as much information as possible is critical to making good decisions. That takes hard work and there are no shortcuts.

Getting the facts right is vital to Emerson's success as an acquirer. Mistakes in this area can be costly. As a result, we developed what we believe to be a due diligence process second to none (see chapter 6).

The acquisition of Fisher Controls in 1992—Emerson's biggest transaction to date—demonstrates the benefits of doing a deal right and paying attention to the details. We had been interested in Fisher—a maker of control valves and process control systems owned by Monsanto—for some years as an excellent strategic fit with our process businesses. We did some preliminary valuations and other analyses and from time to time talked to Monsanto about a deal. Monsanto was happy with Fisher, however, and it wasn't until the early 1990s that the possibility became real.

Monsanto was reevaluating its strategy and looking for cash to fund investments in pharmaceuticals, and we learned that it might be interested in selling. Based on CEO-to-CEO contact, we agreed with Monsanto on a process whereby we could buy and preempt a potential auction of Fisher. We had to submit a bid that would be satisfactory to Monsanto and subsequently could not be negotiated, even after due diligence. Then for thirty days we had exclusive access for the due diligence to determine whether to complete the purchase at the bid price or walk away.

This process placed a premium on our ability to make a credible bid as well as to determine a short time later whether or not to live with the bid. A mistake would have disastrous consequences, so we had to get the facts right in both instances. Fortunately, our preliminary analyses and valuations provided an excellent foundation for making the bid. Monsanto accepted, and, during the next month, we mobilized for and conducted the biggest due diligence effort in Emerson's history. We formed two teams: one for strategy (led by Charlie Peters) and one for transaction planning and integration (led by Bob Cox). During that thirty-day period, we visited every Fisher location in the world to gather facts. We worked around the clock. In the end, we determined that the opening bid was fair, and we got the company. Two weeks later, we had negotiated the contract, separation agreements, and other details and became owners of Fisher Controls—not only the biggest but also one of the best purchases in our history.

There's no substitute for getting the facts. In addition to getting as much information as you can before making a key decision, it's important to recognize when you don't know what you don't know—a domain vastly greater than what you are ever likely to know. After a few mistakes and learning experiences, we've developed a keen sense about matters we should explore further. When we're not comfortable with an analysis or a decision, even if we can't explain why, we've learned to insist on doing more work.

8. Provide for the Possibility of Failure. Things rarely go exactly according to plan, and this is one reason we plan every year. We all want to limit and control losses, but an occasional failure is the inevitable price of innovation and learning. It took us a long time to commercialize the scroll compressor and to become the global leader in process control. In both cases, we tried things that didn't work, but we kept at it because we knew we were headed in the right direction.

An organization must find ways to motivate people to think boldly and creatively. To do this, we encourage programs and initiatives that are experimental and somewhat risky—if they are well thought out.

Emerson's Strategic Investment Program (SIP) provides many examples of our attitude toward opportunity and experimentation. Because we don't have a corporate R&D center and because each of the divisions operates on a tight budget, we created SIP to fund projects that division managers feel are too risky or cannot be accommodated within their budgets (see chapter 5). SIP gives them the flexibility to try new things, and it provides Emerson with some of its best growth opportunities. We've used SIP to fund big programs such as scroll compressors as well as many smaller innovations.

One of the most interesting projects involved variable-speed motors, an opportunity created by the integration of electronic controls with advanced motor designs. In the mid-1990s, we drew on SIP to fund a program on switched reluctance motors, a type of electronically controlled motor that is highly reliable and can be produced at lower cost than alternative types. Applications range from automotive steering systems and vehicle traction, to smart appliances, to microturbine generators, to industrial automation. Although we were interested in all these potential markets, the automobile industry garnered the most attention in anticipation of the eventual, inevitable switch from gasoline-powered to hybrid and electrically powered vehicles in the 2010s and 2020s.

Making variable-speed motors work at economical prices proved a tall order, however, and serious technical hurdles loomed in our path. We had numerous failures and at one point had invested more than $100 million. Yet finally we scored some key wins: a partnership with TRW in electric steering and braking, with the first cars on the road in France in the early 2000s; a starter-generator program with Caterpillar; and a smart washing machine with Maytag. Although the big payoff from variable-speed motors still lies in the future, we are well positioned to take advantage of the opportunities when they come. We couldn't have done this without SIP, which gives us room to experiment and learn from the results.

9. Be Personally Involved. Leaders have a much greater chance of doing well if they are engaged in the important issues. It's impossible to be aloof and inspirational at the same time. Yet personal involvement is a scarce resource: no one can give wholehearted attention to a great many issues.

At Emerson we use the concept of *loose-tight controls* to guide these decisions. We carefully identify what's important and align that with our skills. Leaders focus tightly on some issues while delegating responsibility and following loosely on others. This individual autonomy is another characteristic of high-performing organizations.

As CEO, I chose where to invest my energy by focusing on where I could have the greatest impact on performance. By spending more than half my time in planning, I challenged division leaders to think through their plans and choose their best options. I also met their reports and communicated my priorities to them. These sessions became occasions of high impact and leverage: I was able to work not only with the dozens of people who reported to me but also with the hundreds of people who reported to them.

I also personally attended to two other matters. First, I signed off on the pay and benefits packages at every plant, because our cost basis depended on it. For the same reason I looked closely at regular surveys of plant-level employees to be sure we were treating our people well. I'm proud that Emerson has not had a plant successfully organized by a union for decades, although some plants we've acquired are unionized. We've been able to operate efficiently without the restrictions and contentiousness that normally accompany collective bargaining in a unionized setting—a big advantage.

Second, I invested my time in organization planning and in making management appointments, because it is the high quality of the people at Emerson that ultimately accounts for our results.

Whatever the issues are that are most significant, it's important to stay with them. We've provided some examples of this personal involvement in the stories of John Berra in process control, Jim Berges as profit czar, and George Tamke and David Farr at Astec. Another leader who exemplifies personal commitment is Bob Staley, who directed our thrust into Asia in the 1990s. When Bob became chairman of Emerson Asia-Pacific he was a corporate vice chairman and a seasoned executive who had performed great service to the company. He was less than a decade from retirement, and he could have turned down another challenging assignment with no prejudice. But that's not Bob's style. He moved to Hong Kong and averaged more than two hundred days on the road every year, visiting our operations, talking with host country governments, recruiting and developing Asian managers, running planning conferences, and transferring the Emerson management process to the region. These efforts helped Emerson leap far ahead of other Western competitors in Asia, and we now have an especially strong foundation for continuing rapid growth in China. Our remarkable progress in the region is one of our greatest achievements of the past decade, and it owes a lot to Bob's leadership, energy, and involvement.

A final benefit of staying involved: it defeats politics in an organization. When the leader works hard and tenaciously on the most important issues, it sends a clear message to everyone. And that leaves no time for politics.

10. Have Fun. If you're not having fun, you're in the wrong business or the wrong career. If you don't enjoy it, it isn't likely that the people you lead and work with will enjoy it either.

Emerson experiences very low turnover in its management ranks, and a principal reason is that our people take pleasure in their work and are happy at the company. Sometimes the fun originates in traditions meant to help us relax and put aside the daily pressures. For thirty years we've run an annual golf tournament for our key customers called the Swat Fest. It's an elimination tournament played by some unusual rules that we make up as we go and differ from year to year. People get eliminated for crazy, arbitrary reasons. Every year, though, the event produces a lot of laughs and some great stories. It's a great way for our people to bond with each other and with our customers. Afterward everyone knows everyone else a little better and can call on these relationships when needed.

More fundamentally, though, the fun comes from collaborating with people who want to do well and from winning. Maintaining our record streak of annual increases in earnings, earnings per share, and dividends per share was fun. It provided motivation and pride. Now that the record is ended, starting another string of consistently strong performance is fun. So is the initiative to build the Emerson identity and brand, which is becoming a similar point of pride and fun for our people. There is a palpable feeling of excitement that arises when you work with smart and engaged people whose goals and commitment are the same as yours.

I've been asked how I was able to sit through twenty-seven years of planning conferences for some component division. "How can you stand it?" people have asked me, because this process required hundreds of intense hours for each division. But it was fun, because I was with people who were committed to making something better. Winning is what it's all about, and winning really makes it fun.

4

Operational Excellence

Profitability is a state of mind.

—Emerson axiom

Emerson is renowned for achieving consistently high profit margins. We strive for consistent high profitability because it is essential to creating shareholder value. At the same time, it lets us make acquisitions and invest in developing new products and markets while improving existing operations. High profits are our lifeblood and our promise to investors, and we organize ourselves to produce them, year after year.

During the past two decades, our average profitability, measured as earnings before interest and taxes as a percentage of sales, has run about 30 percent higher than that of a group of peer companies (see exhibit 4-1). We've done this through good times and bad, continually finding ways to maintain profit margins in spite of pricing pressures, competition, inflation, the dilutive impact of acquisitions (most of which had lower margins than Emerson), the costs of maintaining technology leadership, and other factors.

Our ability to deliver high profits consistently is a function of operational excellence, the fifth element of the management process. It consists of a fundamental belief: profitability is a state of mind. This

EXHIBIT 4-1

EBIT margin, Emerson versus peers: Consistent outperformance

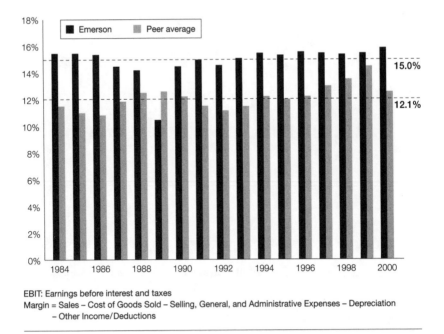

EBIT: Earnings before interest and taxes
Margin = Sales – Cost of Goods Sold – Selling, General, and Administrative Expenses – Depreciation
         – Other Income/Deductions

means that we take steps to ensure that we know in detail what our customers want and what our competitors are doing and that we anticipate and respond effectively. As competition has become more global, pressure on margins has increased markedly. As a result, the complexity and sophistication of our approach to operational excellence have steadily increased, as has the intensity with which we pursue it. In combination with our planning and control systems, our approach enables us to identify the challenges to our desired levels of profitability, take actions in response, and monitor our progress.

Some of our actions have deep roots in Emerson's history, whereas others are more recent additions. Achieving our profitability targets over the long term has never been easy, and it has constantly required us to think and act differently as we confronted new challenges and learned new lessons.

COST REDUCTION AS RELIGION:
EMERSON IN THE 1960s AND 1970s

Our interest in protecting margins began decades ago, when we were not technology leaders and thus had to compete primarily on price. To achieve low costs, we began using techniques such as value engineering to reduce material costs and improve the manufacturability of our products. We also relocated plants from our headquarters in St. Louis, Missouri, to lower-cost rural areas in Arkansas, Mississippi, and other southern states.

At the same time, we implemented an aggressive program of cost reductions. Through our annual planning process, we established profit margin targets by division and product line. We also identified the amount of cost reduction necessary to close the gap between available price increases and inflation in our cost factors (hourly and salaried compensation, materials and overhead costs). Before the year started we specified programs and steps to meet 70 percent of our annual cost-reduction target, with the remaining 30 percent identified and implemented during the year.

Each division president presented the identified cost-reduction programs at the financial review before the start of the fiscal year, and progress was reviewed with corporate management at division board meetings and the quarterly presidents' councils. Corporate manufacturing established the metrics by which actual versus planned cost reduction was measured, and each plant and division reported its actual results to headquarters monthly.

Cost-reduction teams of salaried and hourly employees in each plant and division headquarters bore responsibility for reaching the targets. The teams competed with other teams in the plant or division, and those with the best performance won recognition. In one of our plants in the western United States, the captain of the best-performing team got to ride the lead bull in the annual rodeo parade—and one particular captain made sure his team won every year! This was "employee involvement" long before the term became standard in textbooks on workplace productivity.

We achieved a large cumulative impact from multiple cost-reduction teams, in multiple plants, in multiple divisions throughout Emerson; it was sufficient to fill the annual gap between available price and cost inflation and to generate annual margin improvement. Many skeptics who questioned the magnitude of our annual cost-reduction target became convinced of its viability after visiting our plants and meeting with individual cost-reduction teams. These skeptics then understood what the managers of the company knew: that cost reduction had become a religion and a way of life at Emerson.

BECOMING A BEST COST PRODUCER
IN THE 1980s

Emerson's focus on cost reduction, in combination with other components of the management process, enabled us to deliver consistently high profit margins until the early 1980s. At that time we encountered selective instances of competitors located in low-cost countries offering comparable performance and quality but at much lower prices. Three incidents stand out.

In the first, in the early 1980s, we lost overnight a substantial, long-standing business in hermetic motors to a Brazilian competitor. We had been shipping millions of these motors every year from our modern, efficient plant in Oxford, Mississippi, to Whirlpool, which then incorporated them into home refrigerator compressors at its plant in Indiana. Whirlpool also bought assembled compressors from Tecumseh that likewise contained our hermetic motors.

This was a great business for us and had been for many years. One day, though, we got some bad news: Whirlpool notified us that it would no longer need our hermetic motors. Indeed, it planned to close its U.S. compressor plant and to cease buying compressors from Tecumseh. Whirlpool had found a Brazilian supplier that could meet all its needs, including new government-mandated higher efficiency levels, at prices far below those it was accustomed to paying in the United States.

There was no appealing the decision, but we wanted to understand what had happened. Al Suter, then head of our motor division, flew to Brazil to gather the facts. What he found was eye-opening. The Brazilian producer had licensed state-of-the-art technology from Europe, and its engineers and managers were well trained and highly competent. So were the factory workers. The facility itself was as modern and efficient as any of ours. Because of much lower labor costs and favorable steel and cast iron prices in Brazil, the producer could deliver assembled compressors to customers in the United States at prices 30 percent below the U.S.-manufactured price.

Whirlpool's decision hit hard. Not only did we lose a big, long-standing business, but also we were forced to close our hermetic motors operation in Oxford. We lost hundreds of hourly jobs, and a significant number of salaried jobs, at both the plant and in the division headquarters in St. Louis. We determined that such an experience would never happen again. We also learned two lessons: first, we could no longer take for granted that we were cost leaders in our markets; and second, we would have to keep a close eye on foreign competitors and realign our cost structure, as required, in time to prevent the complete loss of other product lines.

We soon had the opportunity to apply these lessons. This time it was an Asian supplier of temperature controls for small appliances like coffeemakers, which offered our OEM customers 20 percent lower prices on selected models. Therm-O-Disc (T-O-D), the Emerson division that made these controls, couldn't match the lower price, which was below its cost. At the same time, T-O-D managers realized that if their low-cost foreign competitor gained access to American customers in these limited lines, the competitors would quickly broaden their product offering to include all of T-O-D's models. This meant that we would lose another significant business along with as many as two thousand hourly and salaried jobs in the United States. T-O-D offered a smaller price reduction on all its models, which in total matched the Asian rival in limited lines; our customers stayed with us, albeit at a lower profit margin. T-O-D then developed a plan to realign its cost structure to restore the original profit level and prepare to meet further price competition.

T-O-D started a Mexican operation, which lowered costs to the point that it not only regained profit margin but also was able to increase exports to Europe. The net impact on U.S. employment was a loss of approximately three hundred jobs, whereas our actions saved seventeen hundred jobs.

As if we needed it, a third incident in the early 1980s drove these lessons home. Again, the trigger was a communication from one of our major motors customers, which showed us a letter from one of its suppliers. Ironically, the supplier was our Japanese partner, and it had written to apologize for a defect rate of 80 parts per million units in the motors it had shipped. That level was about ten times better than we had ever achieved in our best American plant. And here was another supplier—thankfully, not a competitor—with quality much better than ours apologizing to our customer and offering to make amends!

Together, these incidents showed us the error of our ways. Although we cut operating costs every year and customers rarely complained about quality, the competitive benchmarks were changing to reflect new standards: best-in-the-world, and not best-in-the-United States. In running our business, we were making the wrong comparison—namely, comparing ourselves to ourselves. What mattered to customers, however, was not how little our prices were increasing but rather what the alternatives were. With the global economy reaching a new state of maturity, our customers suddenly had attractive alternatives.

In the early 1980s, then, we realized that global competition had arrived in a limited number of product lines, and we projected that it would soon spread to the rest of our businesses. We would soon be under much greater price pressure than ever before. With falling prices, moreover, traditional cost reductions would not close the annual gap between available price increases and inflation. We could achieve productivity improvements faster through new management techniques and equipment, but not fast enough to meet our targets for profitability. We would have to do something different.

We responded to rising global competition in the 1980s by defining a new Best Cost Producer strategy. The idea was not to compete exclusively on price but rather on value—the optimum combination of products, services, and pricing—as perceived by our customers: best cost, not lowest cost.

The Best Cost Producer strategy originally consisted of six points (see "Emerson's Best Cost Producer Strategy: 1980s") that mingled old and new management policies and principles at Emerson. We maintained our traditional emphasis on formalized cost-reduction programs, effective communications, and ongoing capital expenditures. However, we stopped using ourselves as a benchmark and focused instead on the best-in-class competitors, wherever they happened to be.

For example, we set dramatically higher standards for quality, as defined by our customers, to reach the highest standard in the world.

EMERSON'S BEST COST PRODUCER STRATEGY: 1980s

- Commitment to total quality and customer satisfaction

- Knowledge of the competition and the basis on which it competes

- Focused manufacturing strategy competing on process as well as product design

- Effective employee communications and involvement

- Formalized cost-reduction programs in good times and bad

- Commitment to support the strategy through capital expenditures

Achieving this new standard required that we make significant changes in manufacturing management, factory organization, and other areas of our business. We adopted statistical quality control methods and just-in-time inventory management, which required that we provide additional training for factory personnel and renegotiate terms and modify relationships with some suppliers and customers. As we improved quality to meet customer requirements in terms of reject rates, we realized that our increased costs—our investment in quality improvement—were more than offset by reductions in internal scrap and rework as well as fewer returns from customers. Higher quality not only met competitive requirements but also became another way to reduce costs.

To implement the enhanced quality improvement programs throughout the company, we appointed a corporate officer to lead the change. D. Seals, formerly president of our In-Sink-Erator division, agreed to take on this assignment. He operated with minimal staff and worked with division management on setting targets, providing training, and monitoring results.

The hardest part of implementing the quality improvement program was convincing people that investing in quality actually reduced costs over time. Most managers believed that building in quality created an added cost. This was a communications challenge that we eventually overcame through demonstration and persistence. Another big issue was getting our managers to stop comparing their current and projected performance to their historical performance. We needed them to compare themselves to their toughest competitors, and that also took a change in mind-set.

FROM COST REDUCTION TO CONTAINMENT

A key premise of the Best Cost Producer strategy was that productivity and quality improvement programs, no matter how ambitious and successful, could not by themselves make us globally competitive as long as our manufacturing and procurement bases were still situated in high-cost countries. We needed to complement our cost-reduction programs, which primarily reduced labor and materials content per part or product, with containment of the annual increase in the unit cost of labor and materials; in other words, we needed to reduce the annual rates of inflation of these unit costs and, if possible, make them negative. Developing cost-containment programs in turn required us to change the way we managed because it required different analysis, actions, and monitoring than traditional cost-reduction and productivity improvement programs.

We focused first on hourly labor costs. We had experience in a number of our divisions with plant relocations and job moves from high-cost to low-cost areas of the United States. We set a metric of measuring annual inflation in hourly compensation at the division level, with a target of keeping wages flat. By blending into each division's payroll mix new jobs in lower-cost countries, we could stop and perhaps even reverse the long-standing inflation in these costs.

Managers in many divisions initially resisted moving jobs. They were concerned about the cost and risk of establishing new, offshore facilities as well as the impact on the welfare of U.S. employees. However, as increasing global competition forced our prices down in a broad range of products, the economic case for relocation became overwhelming. Divisions under the greatest pricing pressure, such as T-O-D, were the first to move. T-O-D's success in establishing a facility in Mexico allevi-ated the concerns about cost and risk. At the same time, we could demonstrate that the net loss of jobs in the United States was much less than if we delayed job moves and became increasingly uncompetitive. Even as U.S. employment declined, our American employees main-tained high levels of productivity.

As other divisions invested in Mexico, we found that after an initial start-up period our new Mexican plants achieved quality and produc-tivity levels equal to or better than those of our U.S. plants. This perfor-mance reflected the wage and salary differential between Mexico and the United States. This meant that we could employ people with a higher level of education in staff, supervisory, and technical positions and still save significant sums. A degreed engineer in Mexico cost only 25 percent of the annual compensation of a high school graduate in the United States, whereas a Mexican vocational high school graduate with a thorough knowledge of math and blueprint reading cost only 15 percent of a counterpart north of the border.

As more of our divisions encountered stiff competition in a broader range of their product lines, we needed to accelerate job moves from high-cost to low-cost countries. Meanwhile, it also became clear that American consumers made purchases on the basis of price, given equivalent performance and quality. "Buy American" campaigns were not going to save U.S. manufacturing jobs. We even found instances of our own employees buying imported goods that were competitive with the products made in our plants. Eventually, sometimes reluctantly, our management teams in divisions facing global competition realized that establishing jobs overseas meant survival of their businesses and saving of U.S. jobs that otherwise would be lost.

This message received and understood, we acted swiftly. Between 1983 and 1988, we closed fifty plants in the United States and estab-lished roughly five thousand jobs in low-cost countries. We mounted a particularly strong push into Mexico, taking advantage of the *ma-quiladora* program to locate plants along the border, a free trade zone from which we could ship back to the United States while paying tar-iffs on only the value added. Many of the divisions also set up addi-tional operations in Mexico—in Monterrey, Guadalajara, Mexico City, and other locations.

PROFIT PLANNING IN THE 1990s

A fundamental tenet of Emerson's process called for continuous expansion of operating margins to offset the dilution of acquisitions that added product breadth and global reach. In the early 1990s, however, we began to struggle and actually incurred down margin in some years. Looking back during our corporate planning conference preparation in the fall of 1992, we were concerned to see that the base company—the company without the impact of acquisitions and divestitures figured in—had experienced minimal improvement in margin over the five-year period. We needed a new approach.

We reassigned Jim Berges from a significant operating role and charged him to revitalize and enhance our profit improvement process—to fix the problem and fix it fast. As profit czar, he presided over the small corporate staffs of procurement, industrial relations, information technology, manufacturing, and international development.

Berges and his team spent their first weeks together trying to analyze what had gone wrong. They went back to 1987 division planning conference books to understand the makeup of plans that had forecast a 3.5-point margin improvement by 1992, with the aim of figuring out why we had fallen short. The work yielded a number of significant findings:

- *A shortfall in growth:* We had forecast growth at 7 percent, but the recession of the early 1990s had resulted in an actual five-year growth rate of only 2 percent. We had expected to gain leverage through fixed costs, but that did not occur.

- *Pricing pressure:* We had projected price increases at 1.5 percent annually, below the average of the early 1980s. But because of the recession and increased global competition for available volume, actual price realization was only half of plan.

- *Inflation in materials cost:* Cost reductions from redesigns, procurement actions, and price adjustments had not been enough to overcome inflation in our direct materials costs.

- *Inflation in salaried payroll costs:* Salaried costs had increased relative to sales because of a lack of volume leverage and an annual inflation of employee benefits in excess of 4 percent.

Although we had reduced the headcount of salaried employees during the recession, this action did not offset the lack of growth and price increases.

- *Insufficient benefit from containment of hourly payroll costs:* Hourly labor costs relative to sales improved slightly but not nearly as much as we had forecast. We had counted on sales growth to fill the new plants in low-cost areas. Without growth, the proportion of our factory workers remaining in high-cost locations was much higher than we had planned.

- *Higher medical benefits costs:* We experienced significant increases in medical costs that had not been anticipated.

- *Margin pressure in Western Europe:* Our margins in Europe were less than those in the United States and had been declining for some time because the divisions had not yet mounted a push to establish jobs in low-cost areas.

In the weak price and volume environment in which we found ourselves in the early 1990s, we needed to redouble our efforts to contain the annual increases built into our costs. We attacked this challenge on several fronts.

The Profit Waterfall

The first step was to develop better ways to measure and understand our profit problem. Jim Berges, with the help of Senior EVP and CFO Walter Galvin and the rest of the team, developed an Excel-based data package that provided a rigorous basis for developing a five-year forecast. This software tied together volume, price, and the components of cost (materials, hourly labor, salaries, and overhead) and evaluated the forecast in the context of the previous five years' actual results. This analytical tool became known as the *profit waterfall*, and it was quickly adopted as the basis of the one-year financial review as well as the five-year plan.

The total package consisted of forty-five exhibits that captured in a uniform way the effects of volume, price, gross and net inflation, cost reductions, leverage, job moves, product line mix, currency, and make-buy decisions on individual line items for review and discussion. We differentiated actions to contain inflation from those that reduced costs through improved productivity. We separated the hourly compensation savings of true job relocations from those that depended on the products made in one facility growing faster than others. Each cost-reduction program could be tied directly to its impact on materials, labor, salary, and overhead costs in the fifth year of the plan. The profit waterfall package was developed in November 1992, tested at the first division conference in January 1993, and rolled out to the rest of the company by the end of August.

We established guidelines for the use of this new tool, starting with conservative assumptions about volume growth and pricing. We had found that our traditional planning approach placed too much emphasis on growth. Typically, we expected to hit our target margins based on optimistic forecasts of sales growth combined with traditional cost-reduction measures. We found that our sales forecasts were invariably too bright in terms of both volume and price increases, and we fell short of achieving the target margin in many of the divisions and in total for the corporation.

To stop such unrealistic forecasting and force management to think through the strong actions necessary to improve margins in a tough environment, we insisted that divisions make conservative assumptions in planning profits. They were not allowed to predict that they would grow faster than the market or that future pricing would be better than or even level with that of the prior five years. They also had to allow for the unforeseen cost contingencies that always occurred in the prior years' actual results but were never anticipated. We provided inflation assumptions on wages, salaries, and benefits by world geography, and

THE VALUE OF DILIGENCE

The extraordinary emphasis on detail in the waterfall process enabled us to focus early on challenges and necessary cost options in each of our businesses. "There is no place to hide in the waterfall analysis," says EVP Jean-Paul Montupet. "But if you trust the process and do the analysis correctly, it will show you what needs to be done."

materials by major commodity. Hourly wage and benefit rates were to be flat or down during the period. We then set tough targets for five-year margin improvement for each division.

Consider the challenge in context: no leverage from growth, little or no price improvement, continued inflation in costs, and the task of growing margin, sometimes significantly, in that environment. We knew that this was a tough assignment, but it was essential that we take it on, given the economic and competitive conditions we saw ahead. Our conservative assumptions and the rigors of the waterfall would trigger, we believed, widespread awareness of the need for more, and sometimes tougher, cost actions.

THE PROFIT REVIEW

The division planning conference had always included a discussion of profit margins. This dialogue was generally led by the VP of operations but was limited by the scope of the agenda to one or two hours at the end of the day. Because we had lacked an integrated development tool like the waterfall, in many instances the margin improvement plan did not hang together with other presentations.

It quickly became apparent that we needed more time to present, challenge, and critique the deep analysis required by the waterfall. As noted in chapter 2, we decided to split the traditional planning conference into two sessions. One was focused on profit planning based on conservative growth assumptions, and a second conference was focused on volume growth planning.

We also decided that we wanted more involvement and commitment to the profit plan from the people who would implement it. Berges and his team traveled to each division headquarters for profit reviews and asked for participation from a broader range of managers than would normally attend a planning conference in St. Louis. The operations executives were charged with developing the plan and completing the waterfall exhibits.

At the review, the VP of operations presented an overview of the plan, including a facilities strategy that featured shifts to lower-cost areas. Plant managers presented productivity programs, engineering managers presented product redesign and materials substitution projects, human resource managers presented five-year wage and benefit plans for each plant, and procurement managers detailed plans to offset expected inflation in materials costs. We were also interested in programs to hold down payroll and headcount (including salaried workers) and to improve capital efficiency, particularly inventory. Financial managers attended the meeting but generally did not present; this show belonged to the operating experts.

In addition to gaining a deep understanding and commitment to the profit plan from a broader base of division management, these sessions gave people in each of the functions an opportunity to understand their area's direct impact on the success of the division. It was fun, for example, to see human resource managers tie wage and benefit plans to margin impact; they all became significantly more aware of their role in containing inflationary pressures and the need to communicate to factory employees the reality of the market we faced. These meetings also gave us an opportunity for a thorough assessment of the operating managers in the divisions.

At the end of every profit planning meeting, we accepted the plan as presented or gained the agreement of management on changes (lower growth or price assumptions, more jobs in low-cost areas, better material productivity) to be incorporated in a resubmission. When the final plan was in hand, Berges documented it in a memo to the CEO, the COO, and the business leader, and the division president presented a brief summary at his growth conference a month or two later.

Walking Through the Waterfall

The following example (see exhibit 4-2) illustrates how the profit review process works using the waterfall for a typical division. The chart demonstrates the way that the impacts of negative cost and offsetting actions flow through the waterfall model.

The profit waterfall begins with the historic actual values and future assumptions of price, volume, inflation, cost reduction, and other cost factors and converts them into their impact on operating profit margin over the past and future five-year periods. Mapping past performance into the waterfall provides a benchmark for future expectations. When a division projects, for example, a positive change in margin that is inconsistent with past results, it identifies a risk to its plan that needs to be discussed.

EXHIBIT 4-2

2000–2005 Emerson Division X profit waterfall analysis

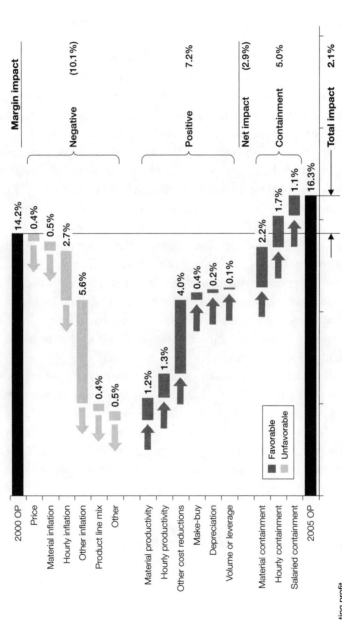

OP: Operating profit

In this example, the division plans to improve operating margin from 14.2 percent to 16.3 percent over five years—the black bars at the top and bottom of the chart. To achieve this performance, the division will have to overcome some headwinds—the negative cost factors from "Price" to "Other." If the division takes no action to improve profitability, these pressures will severely erode its profitability.

Price changes flow straight to the bottom line. As noted, our profit review guidelines were developed at a time when economic and competitive pressures pushed prices down. To prevent unrealistic margin forecasts, we insisted that pricing forecasts be no more favorable than in the previous five years, and this sample is forecasting a reduction in price, with 0.4 percentage points of margin impact. Of course, the division is not bound to this restriction when executing its plan; if it succeeds in increasing prices, the impact on margin will be positive.

Gross inflation is the amount that costs grow in the open market. The waterfall model subdivides gross inflation into its constituent parts: materials inflation, hourly compensation inflation, and other inflation. Gross materials inflation corresponds to historical or projected increases in commodity prices. Hourly compensation inflation includes increases in both wages and fringe benefits. Other inflation includes the growth of compensation for salaried workers as well as that of overhead costs such as rent or freight.

Product line mix captures how the growth rates of various product lines affect profitability. If more profitable product lines grow faster than less profitable ones, then the division will see positive product line mix. In this case, the division expects its less profitable product lines to grow more quickly than its more profitable ones. As with price trends, Emerson profit review guidelines stipulate that product line mix not be any more favorable than in the past.

The other negative is a catchall category that allows the division to plan for unforeseen costs. For planning purposes, this category again can be no more favorable than in the past.

The sum of all the negative impacts is 10.1 percentage points. If the division takes no actions to improve profitability, the combination of negative factors will shrink profit margin from 14.2 percent to 4.1 percent.

Below the negative cost pressures, the chart specifies actions that the division will take to improve profitability—the bars between "Material productivity" and "Salaried containment." The first several bars illustrate cost reductions to lower the cost of the materials or labor that goes into manufacturing a product. Materials cost reductions generally involve a product redesign that lowers the amount of materials used in manufacturing or allows cheaper, lower-cost components to replace more expensive ones. Hourly productivity permits a single worker to build more units or allows fewer workers to build one unit. Hourly productivity can also be improved by the use of more efficient machines. Other cost reductions apply to salaried headcount and other overhead.

In this case, the division expects to generate 0.4 percentage points of cost savings through make-buy actions such as outsourcing a job to a more efficient supplier. If a division can build a component for less than a supplier does, it will save by conducting this step in-house.

Depreciation can impact operating margin in either direction. The depreciation effect is a measure of how depreciation cost changes over the period. Often a division's cost-reduction programs will require the addition of capital equipment that will increase depreciation cost. A division that uses lean manufacturing techniques or outsourcing to reduce capital would get an operating margin boost from the lower depreciation.

The profit review guidelines mandate that the impact of leverage be no more favorable than in the past. The division achieves leverage when it is able to spread its fixed costs across greater sales. It is important to understand the tight relationship between cost reductions and leverage. For example, when a division develops a program that allows an engineer to design products more efficiently, it reduces its cost of engineering. If a division simply sells more products based on the same design, the fixed costs of that engineer will be spread across greater sales and thus will generate leverage.

The sum of the positive cost actions is 7.2 percentage points. The net of negative cost headwinds and positive cost actions presents the challenge that faced many of our divisions in the 1980s and 1990s. Significant pricing pressures from global competitors resulted in flat or declining margins when our response was limited to traditional cost-reduction activities. Even with enhanced management techniques such as Six Sigma, cost-reduction efforts alone were not sufficient to achieve our margin targets. Therefore, containment actions become necessary.

Containment actions are closely related to gross inflation. They consist of the division's efforts to offset those rising costs. To contain materials costs, for example, the division would find lower-cost suppliers for the same material. Emerson procurement offices have put in place a number of initiatives to drive materials cost containment. We draw on this capability to find the lowest prices for inputs, and we leverage materials purchases across multiple divisions to gain volume discounts. Emerson also has procurement offices throughout the world to find and develop suppliers in low-cost countries.

To contain the costs of hourly compensation, divisions find lower-cost labor that can do the same job. This metric includes the savings both from moving a job from a high-cost to a low-cost facility and from increasing the output of a low-cost plant relative to that of a high-cost alternative. Both actions lower average hourly compensation and generate cost savings. In this example, the division is able to contain only 1.7 percentage points of the 2.7 percentage points of hourly inflation; so the average hourly compensation would increase during the five-year period. To offset hourly inflation completely, the division would need to move more jobs to low-cost countries.

Salaried compensation containment is similar to hourly compensation containment. When a division replaces a high-cost Western European steel buyer with a lower-cost one in Central Europe, it contains its salaried cost.

Together, these containment actions contribute 5.0 percentage points of margin, allowing the division to hit its target: an improvement of 2.1 percentage points in operating profit margin. Note that containment efforts require a different allocation of resources compared with cost-reduction programs. Experience shows that containment efforts generally offer a better return and require fewer resources than cost-reduction programs. By shifting engineers from redesign projects to procurement qualification efforts, a division can realize the most efficient allocation of its salaried headcount. With low-cost engineering (achieved through salaried job moves), a resource-constrained division may be able to implement both cost-reduction and containment actions.

All five-year profit plans have upside potential and downside risk. Starting with conservative assumptions requires undertaking more aggressive containment actions, which in turn increases the probability of meeting or exceeding target margins.

INTENSIFYING CONTAINMENT

In addition to instituting a new profit planning process, we redoubled our efforts to rebuild margins. Our analysis revealed that we had lost momentum in containing payroll cost, in part because of low growth but also because divisions under the most pressure during the 1980s had already moved a significant portion of their operations to low-cost areas. Many divisions, however, had not yet followed. Their management typically argued that the technical nature of their product or processes was unsuited for Mexican manufacture. But three years of tough sledding at the start of the 1990s and the rigors of the waterfall analysis began to convince even these managers that they had to move some production to remain competitive. By that time, our motor plant in Monterrey was operational, using all of our best processes, operated by indigenous Mexican management, and exceeding the performance of the domestic counterpart plants in every performance measure. One by one the doubting division managers visited Monterrey and came away impressed and convinced that they, too, could succeed there. The pace of Mexican activity picked up dramatically.

Europe was another matter. The same low-growth, low-price environment that had afflicted our divisions in the United States had eroded margins in many European divisions, and rigid labor laws made it impossible to deal with the relentless wage increases that national unions were demanding and winning. During the 1980s several divisions had set up operations in Ireland, but the renaissance of that country as a high-tech location had begun to drive wages up significantly, and some difficult union encounters dampened our enthusiasm for this solution.

With the collapse of the Soviet bloc in the late 1980s and early 1990s, Central Europe held some appeal. Steve Cortinovis and his small international team traveled through Hungary, Slovakia, the Czech Republic, and Poland looking for existing facilities or sites where we could build factories. They visited a number of industrial parks under development by Western contractors, quickly learning that the cost of new facilities would be high, and time to production too long, to meet our pressing needs. Instead, we identified a Slovakian company, Vuma, as a target for acquisition.

Based in Nove Mesto, Vuma had several large manufacturing

buildings—a little worn but structurally sound—as well as an office complex. It had been a supplier of automation equipment to Soviet military plants and had talented designers, machinists, and machine builders, but no orders. Wages and salaries were one-tenth those in Germany. The company had been privatized, and we were able to buy the shares at a reasonable price. We had found our European equivalent of Mexico.

We set about upgrading Vuma's facilities to accept divisions from Western Europe, and six quickly moved in. Emerson corporate provided finance, human resources, building maintenance, and logistics services, but each division took responsibility for its own operations. Later other divisions joined, and today we have more than two thousand employees in Nove Mesto, including design engineers and, for the most part, indigenous Slovakian management. We found additional, smaller sites in Hungary, Poland, and the Czech Republic that are equally successful today (see exhibit 4-3).

EXHIBIT 4-3

Emerson is established in Eastern Europe and Russia to serve local markets

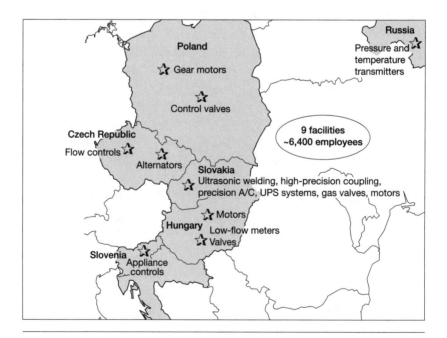

Meanwhile, the divisions became creative in controlling wage and benefit inflation in our older plants in high-cost areas. Armed with facts regarding the realities of global competition and the education gained from profit reviews, plant managers and HR professionals communicated the need for change and moderation to our traditional workforce. The average rate of annual general wage increases in the United States, for example, fell from more than 4 percent to less than 3 percent. We made lump sum payments in lieu of general wage increases in alternate years. Two-tier wage structures were introduced, and the use of temporary employees was expanded. Medical plans were redesigned, and employee copays were increased. Ideas spread from division to division as management teams scrambled to meet the targets of the profit review process. Despite these tough actions, our opinion survey scores actually went up, a testament to the tremendous strength of our communication policies and our people's understanding of the challenges we faced.

In the first five years of the profit review process, we contained the annual increases in average wage and benefits cost to 1 percent per year or less, a record that continued under succeeding profit czars: Al Suter, Craig Ashmore, and Ed Monser. Meanwhile, we added more operations in low-cost areas of Asia, especially in China. We acquired a significant, successful manufacturing operation in southern China and leveraged its facilities and capabilities to support the divisions' moves into the region. (See chapter 7 for a detailed account of Emerson in China.) As elsewhere, after we had some successes in China, other divisions followed, setting up operations there and in other Asian countries through joint ventures or acquisitions or by building new, wholly owned facilities.

In the early 1980s we had basically no meaningful hourly jobs in low-cost countries, but after twenty years of continually investing in such locations, nearly 40 percent of our hourly employment was in low-cost areas helping, as noted, to contain total annual hourly compensation inflation to approximately 1 percent. This compares with an annual inflation rate of 3–4 percent in our remaining U.S. plants. Reducing the inflation in total compensation cost by 2–3 percentage points represents savings of $50 million annually at 2000 volume levels. At the same time, basing nearly 40 percent of our total hourly employment in low-cost countries yields annual savings of more than $900 million—about 6 points of margin.

A NEW FOCUS ON MATERIALS

Our analysis of the 1987 plan also opened our eyes to a glaring weakness in controlling materials inflation. We had accepted price increases from our suppliers that exceeded our ability to pass on to customers—a cardinal sin! Further, it was becoming obvious from some of our more aggressive divisions that relocating jobs could not sustain us forever. By the early 1990s, some divisions already had 70–80 percent of their jobs offshore.

More than 40 percent of our total cost was tied up in direct materials. However, in our autonomous management approach, procurement had traditionally been left under the control of division management. We had a small corporate group that negotiated contracts for a few commodities such as motor lamination steel and magnet wire, but it was becoming clear that we could achieve large potential savings by leveraging purchases across multiple divisions.

We were fortunate in 1992 to have Larry Kremer join us from Whirlpool as VP of corporate procurement. As a supplier, we had watched while Kremer changed the game at Whirlpool, centralizing commodity management, leveraging buying power, consolidating the supply base and looking globally for best-cost sources. In fact, it was Kremer who brought the Brazilian compressor supplier into the United States, opening our eyes in the early 1980s.

Kremer's new challenge proved daunting. He came from a relatively homogenous company with common systems and part numbering schemes, fewer vendors, and relatively few commodities made up the majority of the buy. In his new job, he found approximately sixty divisions buying from more than two hundred locations, with no common part numbers or vendors. The diversity of commodities was enormous—from nuclear-grade stainless steel and explosionproof castings to power semiconductors and microprocessors. On the day he started, we could not tell him what we bought, how much we bought, what we paid for it, or where we bought it.

Kremer and Jim Berges put their heads together to figure out how to attack the problem. The profit waterfall included a simple exhibit that sought to quantify materials inflation incurred in the past five years, with a forecast for the next five years. We identified seventy broad commodity categories, and we retained an economic forecasting firm to provide historic and forecast inflation rates for each category.

The divisions were to assign their annual purchases of relevant commodities and tabulate the inflation they had actually incurred for each category in the past as well as a forecast for the next five years.

The numbers from the outside forecast were called *gross inflation*, the incurred and expected inflation was called *net inflation*, and the difference was called containment, or sometimes the *spread*. These were crude calculations, but within nine months we were able to roll up the entire corporation and get a sense of how we were doing compared to the government data provided by the outside firm. We could now identify the commodities we were buying in the largest volume and begin attacking them in a more coordinated way. It was clear, however, that we needed to do much more work in this area.

At the same time, Kremer and Berges decided that it would be nice to know how other global multiple-industry companies were managing procurement. We retained a consulting firm that had recently published a benchmarking study on best-in-class procurement practices. It was assigned to survey our divisions and grade them against those metrics. We helped design the survey and trained some of our people to conduct it so that we could complete the work in a cost-effective and timely manner.

The results were revealing, and they led us to adopt the following course of action, presented at the 1993 corporate planning conference:

1. Procurement Organization

    – Increase the number of degreed personnel in procurement.

    – Centralize procurement within divisions.

    – Raise the visibility of the division procurement leaders.

    – Centralize procurement of major commodities at the corporate level.

2. Supplier Relations

    – Consolidate purchases with fewer suppliers.

    – Develop long-term agreements with rigorous metrics.

3. Strategic Plan

    – Develop a multiyear strategy for each commodity.

    – Devote more resources to strategic versus tactical procurement.

  4. Information Technology

    – Greatly increase IT resources devoted to procurement.

Because of our tradition of division autonomy, the actions were taken at the division level. Division managers used the waterfall exhibits and other analyses to set measurements and targets during the profit review and financial review process. Initially, we centralized major commodities at the corporate level by assigning a few people to lead teams made up of the representatives of the largest-using divisions of each category. These teams took on an enormous exercise in data gathering. We knew from the crude waterfall data how much we spent annually on, for example, aluminum die castings. But to consolidate suppliers effectively and to leverage our volume for better cost, the teams needed to know alloys, wall thicknesses, die condition, die ownership, current volumes, incumbent suppliers, piece prices, freight terms, and more.

Despite the hurdles, the teams made progress. And the divisions responded to the challenge, upgrading procurement staff, elevating procurement leadership to officer level (generally reporting to the president), including procurement as a major topic at every division board meeting, and taking most buying responsibility out of the plants and giving it to a high-performance team at division headquarters. And we began to see the results. Our data told us we had beaten gross inflation in the late 1980s by only 0.3 percentage points, but by the middle 1990s we were beating the outside forecast by a full percentage point annually, a $40 million improvement.

Meanwhile, we worked to improve on our first, crude efforts to collect data. The commodity list was expanded to 475 codes, creating finer granularity to help the commodity teams identify the best opportunities for leverage. We developed an inflation model that allowed the divisions to forecast expected price changes by month for every part number in a commodity class. When this data was aggregated at the division and corporate levels, it provided an early warning system and a direction for focusing our attention and resources. When annual financial plans were set in August, Kremer and his team set stretch inflation containment targets for every division. They were charged with taking actions to beat back the increases (or improve the decreases) in materials costs forecast in the inflation model.

TAKING PROCUREMENT TO THE NEXT LEVEL

Our early success was encouraging, but we had begun to see year-to-year pricing of our goods and services go from modest increases to outright decreases. Containing inflation was no longer acceptable; we needed to drive absolute reductions in our materials costs. We challenged Kremer to take our game to the next level. As we prepared for the 1998 corporate planning conference, he presented his plan:

1. *Invest in full-time corporate commodity teams for major purchases.* The ad hoc teams—made up of a corporate leader and division personnel assigned on a part-time basis—had experienced some success, but more attention was needed. The division employees already had full-time responsibilities and weren't always available for team meetings. Personnel assignments kept changing, and the lack of continuity slowed things down. Kremer wanted full-time professionals to drive the programs to help him meet his challenge.

2. *Staff an Asian procurement office (APO).* Divisions that were early movers to Asia, such as Therm-O-Disc and Astec, had found highly capable, low-cost suppliers of components like plastic moldings, metal stampings, and screw machine parts. The addition of a corporate resource center that could develop sources for all divisions would be a tremendous tool.

3. *Develop a corporationwide material information network (MIN).* Data gathering for negotiations was still laborious, and that limited the number of commodities that could be attacked in any one year. Many classes of materials were too small for our limited resources but nonetheless were, in total, significant, creating fruitful opportunities. We needed a way to look painlessly and accurately into all of our materials requirements systems and mine the data for price reduction opportunities.

Kremer's proposal generated heated debate in the OCE. Centralizing the commodity teams at the corporate level attacked the sacred notion of division autonomy. Who would bear responsibility if a supplier selected by a corporate office failed to deliver on time or had a quality problem? A central decision could affect the profitability of a division. We could see ownership of the financial results slipping away from the people we had always believed were best equipped to deliver our superior results. Adding significant staff at the corporate level flew in the face of a lean, nonmeddling central staff and the long-standing minimal corporate charge to the divisions of 0.67 percent of sales. We had always been skeptical of large IT investments, which never seemed to provide a payback. Kremer's project was going to be big and expensive.

But our customers were expanding their supply base to global sources, and the reality of the resulting price pressure dictated that we take aggressive action. The business leaders agreed to support Kremer's proposal, and it was presented to a wider audience of division leaders at the corporate planning conference. It was also agreed that the corporate charge would be increased to 0.70 percent to pay for this initiative. We kicked off the meeting by telling the group that we could no longer afford to allow autonomy in procurement, and we expected full and complete cooperation with the new initiative. We were on our way to the next level.

With full-time, professional personnel engaged, the intensity of our major commodity effort picked up notably. Although the teams still needed division buy-in and cooperation, they no longer had to beg for resources. These teams became global in scope, scouring the world for best-cost suppliers. When necessary, they helped suppliers develop processes to meet our specific needs. Our teams worked with a Mexican steel producer to make electrical-grade motor lamination steel, and with a foundry to make gray iron lost foam castings.

We staffed the Asian procurement office with experienced local professionals and began the missionary work to develop a new supply base and introduce it to our divisions in the United States and Europe. The APO team realized early that a supplier development effort would be required to bring local sources up to expected quality and delivery standards. With the aid of universities in the region, we developed training programs that, along with capability assessment tools, provided avenues for new suppliers to meet our requirements. In many cases, however, we found suppliers that were already meeting the rigorous standards of other multinationals. Large divisions added their own people to the corporate office to accelerate the development effort.

We were still struggling with gathering direct materials data in a timely and reliable manner. We conceived the material information network as a data warehouse that could provide easy and reliable access to key information about our global purchases. The approach involved a system that could extract relevant data from division systems in 247 locations in 27 countries, involving 1.1 million unique part numbers and 33,000 suppliers. Each part number was to be linked to a specific corporate commodity code, and each supplier to a specific identifier. Standardizing units of measure, converting currencies, translating languages, and developing validation software all presented significant challenges.

We approached MIN in two steps. First, we focused on the dynamic data, such as price and volume, that changed regularly; this was the easy part. In phase two, we attacked descriptions. Where possible we used manufacturers' part numbers, but in most cases we had to develop parametric data—such as the alloy, size, weight, and wall thickness of a casting—to enable eventual aggregation of like parts. To help with this effort we established a Global Material Data Center in the Philippines, where talented, locally educated engineers scoured division databases and drawings to extract the information required to complete the descriptive fields.

In 1999 we piloted the use of an Internet-based technology called a *reverse auction*. Qualified global suppliers of certain commodities bid for orders on electronic exchanges, with prices falling throughout the bidding process. The dynamics of these reverse auctions are fascinating as suppliers from India, Southeast Asia, Latin America, Eastern Europe, and other locations vie for the business. The initial results of this pilot showed savings in excess of 20 percent. We established a corporate team to manage the process and train division personnel. We've now adopted the reverse-auction process as a comparative tool throughout the corporation. Its use has grown markedly each year, aided by our corporate commodity teams, our MIN data warehouse, and the Asian procurement organization. Today we use MIN to automatically gather part number data for reverse-auction projects and to track implementation of completed reverse-auction processes by part number.

The reverse-auction process also provided a newer, lower benchmark cost for the outsourcing of noncore technologies and manufacturing processes, such as metal stamping and turning, aluminum die casting, plastic molding, and others. In many instances, by outsourcing we not only lowered part costs but also reduced capital requirements—a double plus in terms of return on capital.

Such steps as building MIN and purchasing via reverse auctions proved an excellent way to save money because we could more easily match our needs with sources of low-cost materials. Meanwhile, we also followed the recommendation to increase the educational level of procurement personnel at both the division and the corporate level. We established relationships with universities that had developed MBA programs with concentrations in procurement or logistics, and their graduates became prime sources for new hires.

The overall materials inflation containment program gained momentum quickly. By the early 2000s, the corporate commodity managers increased their control to up to 60 percent of the total buy, 10 percent of the annual buy was put through reverse auction, and 15 percent was sourced from Asia. As the program grew in impact, the annual spread (the difference between gross and net materials inflation) increased to more than 2 percentage points, an annual materials cost reduction (or avoidance) of more than $100 million.

LEAN MANUFACTURING

We also rethought our approach to quality. The initiatives of the 1980s and 1990s brought our product quality up to world standards, but we were chasing a moving target. Customers now routinely expected high product quality and began to push for additional benefits. From routine customer satisfaction surveys, we discovered that demands for reliable delivery and shorter lead times headed the list, and we had to address these expectations as aggressively as we had addressed product quality.

Organizing ourselves to meet these needs required another round of fundamental changes in how we organized and operated our factories. Speed—speed of materials flow, of information, and of changeovers—became the new imperative. Ray Keefe, an executive who joined us from Eaton Corporation, led us in adopting principles and techniques of lean manufacturing. He set the objective to cut lead times in half and to significantly improve our delivery reliability. To get there, we had to deal with a number of internal performance issues, including accelerating productivity improvement and improving asset management. These issues, too, became objectives of our lean manufacturing program.

Lean manufacturing is a structured approach to decreasing the throughput time of materials flowing through the plants, eliminating waste and non–value-adding activities, and ensuring quality at the source of production. Implementing the program at Emerson involved several steps:

1. We trained more than four thousand executives and managers on the principles of lean manufacturing and exposed them to the fundamental changes that they would be expected to lead.

2. We established a lean champions development program to create a critical mass of leaders and implementers and minimize use of external consultants. To date, more than five hundred people have graduated from the program.

3. We use consistent methodology that identifies the key manufacturing strategic goals, maps the relevant processes in detail, and identifies and sets priorities among projects to be implemented.

4. We developed a metric to measure a division's involvement in lean manufacturing from initial planning through full implementation, and we report this metric to corporate headquarters throughout the year.

5. At all planning conferences and profit reviews, we hold mandatory discussions of plans and progress on lean manufacturing initiatives.

Results since this effort began in 1999 indicate that it has had a significant impact on our operations and has yielded valuable benefits to our customers. Many divisions report that they are successfully meeting lead-time requirements that are as small as one-third of their level when we started. The number of late deliveries has been cut in half. Productivity has improved approximately 25 percent. We're using our assets much more efficiently, maintaining high production volume from 20 percent less space. Inventory turnover has been another success story, increasing 32 percent and helping to generate more than $500 million in equivalent cash flow.

Currently, the lean manufacturing program is evolving and expanding. We're using Six Sigma tools to help eliminate process variation. We set up a lean enterprise program to spread lean principles beyond the factory floor to business process improvements (ranging from order entry to design), supply chain management, and demand management. The latter program focuses on knowing and understanding customers' real demand patterns rather than reacting to orders.

E-BUSINESS

During the late 1990s, through profit planning and a mix of traditional productivity and newer containment actions, we were able to maintain our operating margins. By 2000, more than one-third of the employment base was in low-cost countries, and our materials containment program was well along. Still, in an environment of continuing price declines, we needed more elements to bolster our operational excellence programs.

We turned to the new technology of e-business, which we had successfully employed in a number of selected cost-reduction and -containment projects. Charlie Peters moved from a key operating role to become our e-business champion. He developed a companywide analysis of the benefits available in a range of specific applications, including the following:

- Basing a percentage of our salaried engineering jobs (for product design and project implementation of process control systems) in low-cost countries.

- Consolidating warehousing and shipping of raw materials, parts, and finished products throughout one global logistics operation.

- Establishing customer service call centers and functions (such as accounts payable) in low-cost countries.

- Increasing the productivity of administrative personnel by automating information flow and eliminating manual interfaces with customers and suppliers as well as internally.

- Centralizing procurement of travel and maintenance, repair, and operating (MRO) services.

In total, Peters's analysis initially identified 2 percentage points of margin improvement. Not only would e-business techniques save us money, but they also would deliver other benefits. *Swarm engineering*—assigning numerous engineers to tackle a project in concurrent (as opposed to sequential) steps—could reduce product development cycles dramatically (see chapter 5). Similarly, well-staffed customer call centers could improve customer service significantly.

As Peters worked on his recommendations, it quickly became clear that a division-by-division approach to e-business would be not only impractical but also costly and time-consuming. There were tremendous economics of scale in implementation, and the complexity of implementation and ongoing system operation challenged many divisions. Meanwhile, common customers of multiple divisions were insisting on single points of order entry.

We developed an approach that included standardization of software, hardware, and telecommunications systems to support e-business applications; the consolidation of suppliers; and the use of software engineers in low-cost areas to assist with development and implementation. The economics of this approach were overwhelming, and the ongoing success of the centralized approach to procurement also helped gain support for a centralized, shared-services approach from division management.

We developed two metrics of the progress of the overall e-business initiative: the percentage of salaried administrative jobs to be located in low-cost countries, and the total cost reduction or containment to be realized by application by divisions. The metrics became part of the division presentations at presidents' councils, financial reviews, and profit reviews. The 2002 profit review included plans to increase the percentage of salaried administrative headcount in low-cost countries to more than 30 percent within five years, with the total cost reduction or containment equal to 2 points of margin by then.

Our work to determine the best approach to the application of e-business throughout the corporation also established the advantage of outsourcing. Many companies in India, the Philippines, and other locations can provide customer call centers and engineering services at much lower cost than we can internally. Global logistics companies provide services that leverage not only global warehouse and container utilization throughout compatible Emerson division shipments, but also the needs of their other customers. The result is a greatly reduced cost of warehouse space used and materials shipped. Outside firms also operate larger data centers, leveraging their overhead costs over their total customer base and providing us with lower unit storage and transaction costs than we can achieve in our own facilities.

Although recent profit reviews indicate that the original estimate of a 2 percent margin benefit from e-business would be achieved by 2007, it is clear that we can achieve additional benefits in the future.

SUMMING UP OPERATIONAL EXCELLENCE

During the past several decades, Emerson has steadily worked at improving operational excellence, focusing on new and better ways to understand customers and competitors, to compete aggressively around the world, and to use its assets more efficiently. Despite adverse circumstances, we managed to grow and remain profitable, but it has been a long, hard slog, and it isn't getting any easier. We've succeeded by making difficult choices, by taking strong actions, and by changing when we had to change before it was too late.

Exhibit 4-4 summarizes some of the techniques, tools, and programs we've instituted over time in striving for operational excellence, starting from our strong foundation in cost reduction and manufacturing management. With globalization and intensified competitive pressures in the 1980s, we added new programs and initiatives, such as a focus on designing in—as opposed to inspecting in—quality and opening new factories in low-cost countries. Later, as competitive pressure continued to escalate, we stepped up our efforts, focusing on matters such as improved purchasing and supply chain management, lean manufacturing, containing salaried payroll costs, utilizing e-business, and outsourcing noncore activities and processes. In many of these initiatives, we appointed corporate officers to lead the charge. Operating with minimal staff, these champions worked directly with division management on setting targets, providing training, and monitoring results.

So far, our approach has worked. Not only did we outperform our peers in operating margins during the 1990s (recall exhibit 4-1), but we also found that basing facilities and jobs in low-cost locations had no adverse impact on quality. On the contrary, quality improved dramatically. As a number of management experts have noted, achieving better quality goes hand in hand with lowering costs.

Emerson would not have been able to achieve this performance without our commitment to operational excellence as a key component

EXHIBIT 4-4

Best Cost Producer and operational excellence activities over the past thirty years

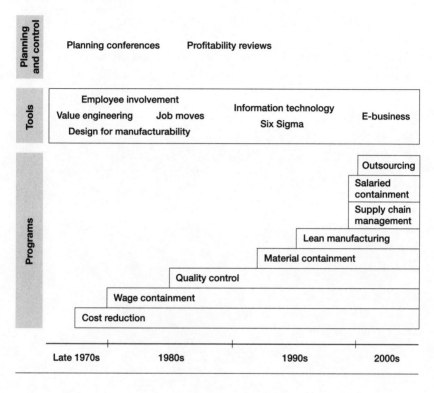

of the management process. We've also learned that we can never relax this commitment, because the business environment will continue to pose major challenges. The particular actions we emphasize and support in achieving operational excellence will undoubtedly change as customer requirements and expectations evolve, as competitors develop new strategies and offerings, and as new technologies become available. As long as we observe the major principles of operational excellence—satisfy our customers, know the competition, develop a competitive global plan, and manage our assets well—we will remain a profitable and healthy company.

5

From Technology Follower to Technology Leader

*Technology leadership creates a
sustainable competitive advantage.*

—Emerson axiom

I n the early 1970s, our planning throughout Emerson showed that we were facing two serious technology-related challenges. First, we were market followers—fast followers, but not leaders. We believed that this position was not sustainable over the long term: we couldn't continue to deliver consistently strong financial performance unless we attained technology leadership in our businesses.

Second, we needed to upgrade our technology base. Most of our products featured mechanical, electrical, or electromechanical technologies, and the world was quickly moving toward electronics. Somehow, we had to boost the level of technology in the company or risk mediocre performance.

Meeting those two challenges—which were related—is one of Emerson's biggest achievements of the past thirty years and one of which I am proudest. We are now number one in all our major markets, and we spend more than $500 million every year on engineering and development (E&D). New products account for about 40 percent of sales, up from less than 3 percent in the early 1970s.

This chapter describes how we achieved this record. Our success is the result of a deep commitment to technology-based competition and an effective process for managing it.

TECHNOLOGY LEADERSHIP AND
COMPETITIVE ADVANTAGE

Achieving technology leadership in products as well as processes is costly and requires steady, ongoing investment at a high level. But the benefits of leadership far outweigh the costs. These benefits include the following:

- Opportunities to add significant value for customers by improving the performance of their offerings and their fundamental economics

- Differentiated products that resist commoditization, have staying power, and command price premiums

- Opportunities to augment advanced products with state-of-the-art design and support services

- Opportunities to bundle products and services into higher–value-added solutions that are the foundation of enduring relationships with customers

- More efficient processes that realize significant savings in operating costs

- Early access to new technologies, with the potential to define the state of the art and change the competitive game

- Proprietary intellectual property that can be exploited for competitive advantage

In short, the benefits of technology leadership are overwhelming. In the early 1970s we weren't yet aware of all these benefits, but we knew that the best way to control our destiny, become industry leaders, and achieve truly superior performance was to become a technology leader. The issue was how to get there from where we were.

FUNDAMENTALS OF TECHNOLOGY MANAGEMENT AT EMERSON

Emerson transformed itself into a technology leader through our management process. We start with shared beliefs about the importance of the objective, including a high-level commitment from the board of directors and the top executive team. Then we set stretch goals, plan how we will meet them, track and control our progress, and pay for results. We are selective and disciplined in limiting spending to programs and projects that are likely to yield new products and to help us in the relatively near future. Thus we focus on applied technology, as opposed to pure research, and in doing so, we talk about "D, not R," and "E&D, not R&D."

At the same time, we've developed distinctive practices and techniques during the past three decades that enable us to apply technology effectively. For example, we've invariably increased our investment in E&D spending every year. We plan for and track new product sales. We provide special funding for programs and projects that are beyond the means of a single division. We open new channels to outside sources of critical technologies. We integrate stand-alone products across divisions into higher-value customer solutions. We champion new technology projects and programs and support them with corporate resources. Finally, we honor achievement.

Commitment to Leadership

We knew that the costs of attaining leadership would be high but more sustainable than the costs of continuing to follow. Therefore, achieving technology leadership and upgrading our technology base became top priorities. In this we had the staunch support of Emerson's board of directors, with several longtime directors leading the charge. Gen. Bernard ("Bennie") Schriever, USAF (Ret.) served as our leading technology advocate on the board for twenty-six years, until his retirement in 1994. A career Air Force officer, Schriever had directed

America's intercontinental ballistic missile programs in the 1950s. The ICBM was one of the most complex technology deployments in history, akin to World War II's Manhattan Project to develop atomic weapons, and Schriever was one of the country's most outstanding technology experts. He was joined on the Emerson board in 1973 by Gerry Lodge, a venture capitalist who had great insights into electronics-related industries, and later by Vern Loucks (from Baxter) and Dick Loynd, who had many years of experience guiding technology development in industrial businesses.

Our first step was to win the commitment of the board and the organization to invest in technology throughout the company for the long term. We translated this top-level commitment into dollars by beginning a cycle of building our investment in E&D. Beginning around

EXHIBIT 5-1

Increased engineering and development spending every year

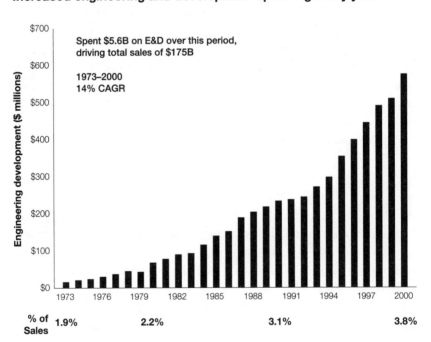

Spent $5.6B on E&D over this period, driving total sales of $175B

1973–2000
14% CAGR

CAGR: Compounded annual growth rate

1975, we made it a point to increase our spending every year, and for the next quarter-century, engineering and development climbed annually as a percent of sales (see exhibit 5-1). Regardless of the economic situation, we added to our capacity to deliver superior technology to customers.

Accelerating New Product Programs

In addition to our firm commitment to annual spending increases on E&D, we made new product development another top corporate priority. An internal review convinced us that we had a serious problem in this area, and we knew we had to manage it differently. From Trane we recruited Bob Staley, a Cornell-trained engineer whom I'd known for years, to champion new product development.

Staley started by developing a new metric: we defined new product sales as those stemming from a product that offered new functionality and had been introduced within the past five years. We then calculated the percentage of revenues originating in new product sales and developed targets for improvement. The initial findings were discouraging. In 1973, only 2.1 percent of Emerson's revenues came from new products. At this rate, we realized that we were regenerating Emerson's product line only on roughly a fifty-year cycle and that, at any time, the average age of our products exceeded twenty-five years. With the rate of change in technology accelerating, and given that electronics-related activities were leading the way, we knew that we had to make profound changes.

Staley began working closely with the divisions to accelerate the pace of new product introductions. As a comparative measure throughout Emerson, the new products sales metric allowed us to bring the technology emphasis to virtually all of our operations. This metric became a required agenda item at division planning conferences, where we dived into the details. Even with our metric established, however, there was confusion in the early years, and for clarity, we tracked adjacent categories such as line extensions and buyouts. These categories were important to our division managers, who were frustrated by the dearth of development activity. Tracking these other categories at least allowed managers to say they were making progress, but these benchmarks also highlighted the need for change.

EXHIBIT 5-2

New product sales

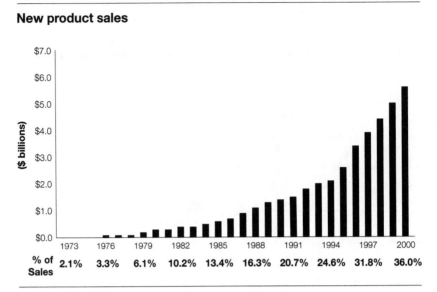

	1973	1976	1979	1982	1985	1988	1991	1994	1997	2000
% of Sales	2.1%	3.3%	6.1%	10.2%	13.4%	16.3%	20.7%	24.6%	31.8%	36.0%

Meanwhile, we required division management teams to increase investments in product development activities as a step to accelerating growth. We used these new product activities to fill the gap between our base sales programs and the growth objectives of the overall company. By detailed investigation and tracking of each new product program, we developed a map for increasing new product activity and for shortening product life cycles, division by division. And we generated significant numbers of new products every year (see exhibit 5-2).

The Strategic Investment Program

Our progress to technology leadership was challenged by our tradition of division autonomy, including the expectation that each division would fund its own technology development. Our strong profit ethic was in constant tension with the need to make long-term investments. Our best division managers balance these contrary pressures and create the necessary investment capacity to sustain their technology commitment. However, at times, the best opportunities and strategies are simply too large and have too much potential for a given division to fund. We designed the Strategic Investment Program (SIP) to deal with such instances and have sustained it over three decades.

As noted in chapter 3, SIP helped fund game-changing programs such as Rosemount's Mount Everest (a first-generation smart sensor), Copeland's scroll compressor, Emerson's variable-speed motors and drives, and scores of other initiatives with lesser but still significant impact. Each year we review proposals that would soak up two or three times the available SIP funding. We work through our priorities—supporting some, supplementing divisional money in other cases, and rejecting or delaying still others.

SIP has worked well, as an objective review of the most important technology foundations at Emerson attests. The program allows corporate management to take risks at times when division management cannot.

Reassigning Roles and Responsibilities for Technology Development

With Emerson traditions and our management process in mind, we established the objective to get the divisions to take the initiative in upgrading our technology capability. We appointed a corporate technology champion—later the chief technology officer (CTO)—whose mandate was to help the divisions in their efforts.

We have had several key technologists as CTO, but no one played a more important role in creating a first-class corporate technology function than Hal Faught, who led this function from 1979 to 1992. Formerly a senior research manager at Westinghouse and the U.S. Postal Service, Faught raised awareness of technology issues, developed training programs, put people in touch with other Emerson colleagues who could help them on technology issues, and opened channels to best practice on the outside.

Randall Ledford, a PhD physicist who followed Faught as CTO, also made significant contributions, equipping us with much more sophisticated approaches and tools for planning and managing technology. A technique called *technology road mapping*, for example, helped the divisions plot the sequencing of their product and technology development efforts and coordinate them with suppliers, customers, and other Emerson divisions.

EXHIBIT 5-3

New Emerson patents

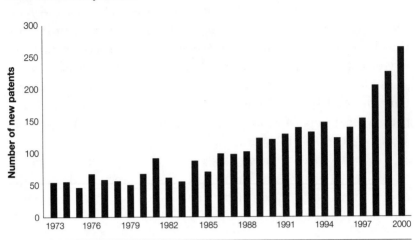

We bolstered our technology program by appointing outstanding technology business leaders to serve as counterparts of the CTO in the divisions. These people led the charge at the operating level, and, at the level of the businesses, some joined together in the Emerson Technology Council, which was chaired by the CTO. The technology council meets periodically to share information and insights and to identify trends and potential discontinuities having significant potential impact on our businesses. The group also champions major technology initiatives in areas such as software, electronics, and materials that may affect multiple divisions and businesses. Similarly, Emerson holds occasional special conferences of its technical people and outside experts to deal with particular technologies or emerging technology issues.

The corporate technology function is also responsible for managing Emerson's intellectual property, especially its ever-increasing number of patents (see exhibit 5-3). In technology-based competition, it is vital to preserve technological advantages. Thus we've protected our key developments such as variable-speed motors, the scroll compressor, smart sensors, and process control systems and networks in a number of patents that we enforce vigorously. This intellectual property is a major corporate asset, and we do everything we can to ensure that we realize its full value.

Opening New Channels to Technology Sources

Yet another key step in our transformation was our effort to access the world's leading technologies. We relied in part on our acquisition program, seeking companies that were clear global leaders in technologies that could form a foundation on which to add. This thinking led us to some of the most important acquisitions of recent decades, including Rosemount, Micro Motion, and Fisher (in process management), Copeland (in climate solutions), Astec and Avansys (in network power), and Leroy-Somer and Switched Reluctance Drives Ltd. in our motors and automation businesses. These deals extended our technology capability in important ways.

Emerson's approach to creating technology internally also underwent significant changes. In the 1970s we depended largely on a centralized model built upon a series of corporate development laboratories. The idea was that a separate group would be responsible for creating new technologies that would be driven to market by independent divisions. But we found that this approach simply didn't work. These efforts lacked focus, were underfunded, and generally proved ineffective. We developed a different approach, one that was designed to support divisions in the efforts they managed, as opposed to the corporate center independently developing specific products. The new approach also recognized the broader applicability of technology, extending work beyond product development to encompass manufacturing needs, electronics and communications capabilities, and, specifically, the materials-related sciences.

At the heart of the new approach was an effort to create centers of technological expertise, in some cases focused on businesses and in other instances focused on technologies. Starting in the late 1980s, we invested in centers of excellence to exploit important technology trends that were impacting a range of divisions or where operations required direct support. These centers evolved into five principal groups:

- Motor Technology Center

- Solid State Center for Process Control Applications

- Advanced Design Center

- Software Center of Excellence

- Emerson Design Engineering Center

These centers serve multiple purposes. The Motor Technology Center, for example, conducts focused E&D studies of motors, drives, and controls having potential impact on multiple divisions. It works on enhanced product performance as well as more efficient ways to build motors. The center looks at both near- and long-term possibilities, including conceiving next-generation approaches to advanced motors.

An example of Emerson's commitment to keeping our organization on the leading edge involved expanding the Motor Technology Center via the mid-1990s acquisition of Switched Reluctance Drives Ltd., a U.K.-based consulting group. SRDL was focused on applying a broad range of revolutionary motor technologies. As the declining costs of electronic components continually make known motor applications economically feasible, this consulting firm's application experience is a valuable capability. Its teams lead motor development programs in next-generation products in appliances, HVAC, and automation as well as in applications new to Emerson, such as electric-powered steering and electric vehicles. Leroy-Somer, meanwhile, participated in the design team for Peugeot's electric automobile.

Emerson's approach to technology development also broadened with the recognition that manufacturing processes can be a source of competitive advantage. In the 1980s, as we competed for leadership in process control, sensor developments were the key determinant of product performance. In response, Emerson created the Solid State Center, a wafer fabrication facility that allowed our process control divisions to push back the frontier on sensor performance while internally protecting our intellectual property. This manufacturing process turned out to be a critical element that established Rosemount and its counterpart process control divisions as the technology leaders in instrumentation. This expertise ultimately became a critically important building block in the PlantWeb initiative (discussed later in this chapter).

Through the years, other advances in electronics presented tough challenges for most of our businesses. Our technical people found themselves confronting new demands for software, applications for communications protocols, and the use of advanced hardware components such as application-specific integrated circuits (ASICs). Initially, we formed small groups of experts and made them available throughout the company, dedicating them to either specific technologies or specific applications, such as HVAC or appliance controls.

At the same time, the corporation's technology leadership established important relationships with entities such as Battelle Research Institute, a renowned center for research in materials technology; Edison Welding Institute; and various universities that have deep research capabilities in areas central to our businesses. Each of these relationships provides an excellent source of knowledge and serves as a center in its own right, an effective clearinghouse for state-of-the-art thought and information on particular technologies and best practices in technology management. Our efforts initially were focused on the United States, but as our business globalized we added more centers overseas and ultimately linked them into a global technology network. With centers all over the world—including in India and China—this network gives us a formidable competitive advantage.

In the 1990s, we formalized our network of expertise into the Advanced Design Center, which provides consulting and assistance to all divisions in their design processes. Located in Columbus, Ohio, where it is tightly coupled to the Battelle organization, the Advanced Design Center leverages our internal and external resources to help Emerson divisions with product development, manufacturing, and materials-related problems. The network now links more than one hundred independent organizations, forming a virtual network of the premier technological minds in the world, which are applied to Emerson's most urgent challenges.

We've used a similar model in software. Housed at Carnegie Mellon University, a world leader in computer science, the Software Center of Excellence supports Emerson's needs in this key technology.

Virtual networking has also helped us establish strong technical links outside the United States, as illustrated by the story of our Material Characterization Center in China. In the mid-1990s we recognized the vast potential of China as a low-cost area for manufacturing and sourcing (see chapters 4 and 7). It was clear, however, that we could not rely on technical resources based in Western countries to support expansion in China. So we launched an initiative to identify and develop local resources to meet our needs.

We started by forming a relationship with Wang Qilong, a prominent professor at Harbin Institute of Technology, who facilitated introductions to leading universities. Next, we began sponsoring PhD programs. This initiative was kicked off with fanfare at a signing ceremony in

1996 in the Great Hall of the People in Beijing. Emerson divisions identified topic areas for research, and we set up projects at Harbin Institute of Technology, Tianjin University, Tsinghua University, Shanghai Jiao Tong University, Jilin University, and the Research Institute of the Welding and Machinery Industries. These projects and others that soon followed have proved very successful. They have generated more than fifteen patents for Emerson, helped identify future employees, and strengthened our relationships with the institutions. Emerson businesses and divisions in China now routinely and extensively draw on this technology network in meeting everyday needs.

In 1998, we took the next step, establishing the Material Characterization Center at Shanghai Jiao Tong University. We contract for two full-time university staff, who, in turn, act as a gateway to the university's outstanding materials department as well as other research institutes near Shanghai. The contract staff is responsible for identifying the best people to work on our projects, overseeing the work, and preparing the final reports. We started with about twenty projects in the first year. Their success prompted a surge in demand, and within a few years the center had more than two hundred projects under way. We've since established a similar research center at South China University of Technology (SCUT) in Guangzhou.

Consolidating our resources and aligning with best-in-class institutions in China and elsewhere put Emerson designers in contact with world experts. The Advanced Design Center organizes divisional support in several modes, including consultations, projects in technology, and creativity exercises for specific applications. Today there are more than a hundred resources—universities, national laboratories, and technical institutes—in our virtual technology network around the world.

However, the most effective use of this virtual resource network is through a business process formalized in the 1990s that we call the *design review*. This approach is applied to major new product programs throughout the company. A design review draws on the resources of people from the virtual network and Battelle, as well as other academic or industry specialists, to add value before a new product approach is finalized. The team is formed and makes a two-day visit to a division's new product design team. On the first day, the outsiders listen to the division's presentations on the design and the technology decisions and challenges. This is a one-way communication, and no challenges or discussions occur. At the end of the day, the outside review team caucuses and then offers its perspective on design issues and challenges. This then serves as the basis of the second day's discussions.

The design review process has made a significant contribution to new product efforts from many viewpoints. It provides excellent direct input into our designs before final approaches are frozen. Division engineers and designers get significant exposure to the world's top technology minds in specific disciplines. Finally, this process cements the relationship between Emerson and outstanding industrial technologists, who subsequently contribute to us in many ways.

A final example of a center of excellence created by Emerson's technology leadership is the Emerson Design Engineering Center situated in Pune, India. This effort represents the first time in our history that a corporationwide engineering center has been developed to serve multiple divisions and businesses in a common facility. Its purpose is to provide our divisions easy access to resource capabilities in India in a cost-effective environment. The center operates with first-class design processes and can design product platforms that span multiple geographies using robust processes for building knowledge and for protecting intellectual property. Today, nearly thirty divisions operate in this center in support of Emerson's growing development resource needs and technology sophistication.

Employee Recognition

Given the overall importance of technology, we give great emphasis to employee recognition in this area. Starting in the mid-1980s, we instituted a technology awards program that includes two levels of recognition. The first, the Emerson Technology Award, honors project- or program-based achievements. We present two or three of these awards each year. The second level is the Emerson Technology Leadership Award. We've given out about a dozen since the program began.

The technology award recognizes teams that create outstanding new products based on advanced technologies that prove themselves in the marketplace. Each year twenty or more divisions nominate programs, and only about 10 percent are chosen. The winning teams are invited to St. Louis, and their awards are celebrated in front of the entire Emerson management team at a dinner at our corporate planning conference. This has become a company tradition, and the awards are coveted.

WINNERS OF THE EMERSON TECHNOLOGY LEADERSHIP AWARD, 1987–2002

1987	Maurice James (Emerson Industrial Controls); Steve Quist (Rosemount Inc.)
1988	Hal Faught (Emerson Corporate)
1989	Vern Heath (Rosemount Inc.)
1990	Joe Adorjan (Emerson Corporate)
1991	Bernard Schriever (director of Emerson)
1992	Neal Royer (Emerson Motors)
1994	Bernard Brown (White-Rodgers)
1995	Earl Muir and Richard Peltier (both with Copeland Corporation)
1996	Neal Stewart (Astec)
2000	John Berra (Emerson Process Management)
2002	Charles Knight (Emerson Corporate)

The technology leadership award is a lifetime achievement award for individuals whose dedication has made a significant contribution to creating our technology advantages. These are special people, ranging from experts in specific technologies to champions of highly successful but risky new product programs. Corporate executives and board members are eligible, as are our operating and technology managers.

BECOMING A TECHNOLOGY LEADER

By the mid-1980s, our steady investment in E&D, our commitment to technology leadership, and the many programs and techniques we adopted in our management process were paying off. Virtually every division was making significant progress, and some, such as motors—our oldest business—made huge gains. We made investments to add electronic controls and other high-technology content to motors and to manufacture them more efficiently, and these actions transformed us from an also-ran into a leader; we overtook Westinghouse and GE in the United States as the number one producer. Based on a steady stream of innovations and improvements emanating from the Motor Technology Center and from our Leroy-Somer division in Europe, we were well on the path to global leadership in motors.

Among many success stories, the benefits of technology leadership proved most evident in the rise of Emerson Climate Technology, Emerson Process Management, and Emerson Network Power, our three largest and fastest-growing businesses. New technology and shrewd technology management enabled us to reinvent entire industries, gaining an advantage over bigger traditional rivals and attaining global scale. Although strong organizations, great leaders, excellent plans, and effective execution all played important roles in the respective technology developments, the root of success was our ability to bring to market technologies that customers valued. Finally, these businesses led the way through an important internal transition in which the traditional autonomous division structure of the 1980s gave way by the late 1990s to an effective integrated business organization.

The Scroll Compressor

The first powerful technology advances in what is now Emerson Climate Technologies took place in the late 1980s and early 1990s at our Copeland division. At the time, Copeland was one of several successful producers of reciprocating compressors used in high volume for residential central air-conditioning units. Pending legislation for energy efficiency foretold increasing demands on compressor performance to satisfy system requirements.

In the 1980s, Copeland committed to the research and development of a new compression technology called "scroll" (named for the scroll-like shape of the compressing elements in the unit, which offered significant efficiency advantages over the reciprocating approach). Through aggressive development of the scroll mechanism, as well as aggressive, preemptive investments in capacity, Copeland led the industry transformation to the scroll in the United States and around the world. The magnitude of these investments was staggering, both to perfect the scroll and to tool up for global growth. SIP funding and strong support of Emerson and Copeland management during the long, difficult development of the technology proved critical to its success.

Bob Novello, an engineer and MBA who had joined us in the 1970s with the acquisition of an instruments business, led commercialization of the scroll. For this he relied on well-crafted strategies for new product platforms, global manufacturing investments, and industry partnerships. To gain meaningful market positions in both the Asian residential and the European commercial markets, Copeland created platforms that were deployed globally. With increasing energy efficiency requirements and increasingly stringent limitations on refrigerants, scroll technology continues to outperform all other approaches and underlies Copeland's consistently strong results (see exhibit 5-4). Furthermore, Copeland is the centerpiece of Emerson Climate Technologies, a business that involves more than a dozen divisions and is the leading hardware supplier to the global air-conditioning and refrigeration businesses.

EXHIBIT 5-4

HVAC sales driven by scroll

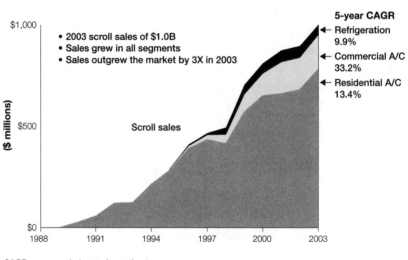

- 2003 scroll sales of $1.0B
- Sales grew in all segments
- Sales outgrew the market by 3X in 2003

5-year CAGR
Refrigeration 9.9%
Commercial A/C 33.2%
Residential A/C 13.4%

CAGR: compounded annual growth rate

PlantWeb

New technology and superior technology management also changed the game at Emerson Process Management. Our involvement in the process industry began in the 1960s but dramatically increased following the 1976 acquisition of Rosemount, the world leader in differential pressure sensors (see chapter 6). During the 1980s, the instrument business prospered, but Emerson was an also-ran in other segments of the industry such as control systems, and we had no position at all in control valves.

The acquisition of Fisher in 1992 remedied these deficiencies in a single stroke, providing a global leadership position in control valves and a competitive control system called Provox. The Fisher deal gave Emerson all the dimensions of a possible breakthrough in process control. Because we were organized as little more than a collection of independent companies, however, integrating these dimensions would prove a major challenge.

We were fortunate that our management challenge coincided with a key turning point in technology. The process control industry was just managing the transition from an analog to a digital approach to control. As we examined the prospects for digital control, it was apparent that the new technology offered Emerson significant advantages, given our strong positions in both instrumentation and control valves. Because the transition seemed to favor our field devices (where Emerson was the world leader) at the expense of centralized "big box" control (the strong area of our traditional competitors), no one was moving forward to develop the new technologies. With the realization that digital approaches were the key to Emerson's future and that they required development of multiple technology platforms, we put in motion a number of development programs under the leadership of David Farr and John Berra.

To build a digital process control architecture, the industry required a combination of these elements:

- *Digital communication protocols that were open to all industry suppliers.* Emerson responded by becoming a charter member of an industry initiative to define protocols tailored to the process control applications. This effort formed around a group of industry leaders cooperating under a consortium titled Fieldbus Foundation, and John Berra served as the architect and founding chairman.

- *PC-based control systems designed to manage information flows, and smart instrumentation as opposed to the historical central processing of all control decisions.* Emerson's Process System division began a major initiative to develop the industry's first PC-based control system, branded as DeltaV.

- *Smart field devices, including instruments and control valves with the capability to provide control decisions in the field as well as provide predictive diagnostics.* Emerson's instrumentation and control valve divisions aggressively invested in microprocessor technologies based on Fieldbus Foundation protocols that took advantage of the new capabilities made possible by advances in electronics.

In the late 1990s, we combined these elements into an integrated architecture called PlantWeb. At the same time, this initiative spawned a fourth new business called Asset Optimization Services. This new division's objective was to integrate and use all the new information available from the devices to optimize plant performance. In addition, our approach enabled substantial improvements in maintenance and capacity through effective use of this information.

The Emerson PlantWeb story is an excellent example of industry transformation based on technology change. The new technology was designed, piloted, and perfected within a five-year span. It yielded dramatic opportunities for process customers to reduce capital costs while simultaneously increasing efficiency, capacity, and productivity. Customers gained an ability to compete at new levels. All this was made possible by the foresight of the Emerson organization and its execution in delivering sound, reliable technologies to its customer bases.

Beyond offering great value to customers, the new architecture required our divisions to work together in an integrated and comprehensive fashion, providing solutions that pulled together a multitude of our technologies and products. This was the basis of the transformation that changed Emerson Process Management from operating as roughly fifteen independent divisions to providing a common approach to global customers supported by powerful solutions to their problems and challenges.

Our customers value our approach, as evidenced by high rankings in *Control* magazine's annual survey of top performers. In 2005, Emerson swept twenty-eight product categories and placed in the top three in forty-one of forty-two of the most relevant—by far the best result among global competitors. For the fourth consecutive year, PlantWeb won the top ranking for control systems. The rewards of such performance have been significant: during the past five years, our market share in process control has jumped from slightly more than 10 percent to 15 percent of the global market.

Reliable Power

An enhanced technology capability is also central to our strategy in the area of network power. The original divisions constituting the business were technical leaders in their domains: Liebert, in both precision environmental control and uninterruptible power supply product lines; ASCO Valve, in high-powered switching equipment; and Astec, in large unit-volume power supply applications. Each business operated independently until the 1990s, when the information technology revolution dramatically expanded demand for these applications. As the world became more dependent on information, there was strong interest globally in better system reliability. This created a substantial growth opportunity for Emerson, but one that was feasible only if we could remain at the forefront of these dynamic technologies.

We began to build a business platform around the network reliability theme. Several acquisitions in the late 1990s brought global scale to our relationships with telecommunications customers. We bought several previously captive power supply operations from major telecom equipment suppliers, including Nortel, Ericsson, and ultimately, Huawei in China. This network of companies gave us strong participation in the installation of telecommunications networks on every continent. It resulted in two significant opportunities: allying the components business with Astec's high-volume power supply design and manufacturing operations, and merging each entity's systems businesses with the existing broad product lines of Liebert and ASCO.

Emerson's technology strategy for these initiatives differed from those in climate technologies and process management. The keys in network power were the high rate of introduction of new and lower-cost power electronic approaches along with the need to manufacture components in low-cost areas. These capabilities had to be linked to the capacity to provide customized solutions locally in each of the world's regions. We built manufacturing operations in low-cost areas, aggressively consolidated designs into global platforms, and created a large technical and development engineering resource base of unparalleled global scale, also in low-cost locations.

The key to pulling together this approach was the acquisition of Avansys, Huawei's captive power electronics components business in

MORE BANG FOR THE E&D BUCK

Emerson's expanding reach into low-cost regions of the world opens new ways to use engineering dollars more efficiently. In China, India, the Philippines, and other countries, the cost of engineering talent is a fraction of that in the West, and it is talent of a high order. Engineers in these locations are the products of excellent technical educations. Their availability, coupled with instantaneous communications and collaborative software, greatly increases our "engineering bandwidth."

Not only can we employ more high-quality engineers at a constant level of spending, but also we can deploy these additional engineers in new ways. Swarm engineering, for example, is a technique that assigns large teams of engineers to swarm to a project and break it into steps that can be accomplished in parallel rather than sequentially.

Exhibit 5-5 illustrates the point. The traditional approach to developing a new direct current system might take more than four years as fifty engineers sequentially develop components of different amperages. Under swarm engineering, ninety lower-cost engineers working on some components in parallel can complete the system in about two-thirds the time. The practice not only saves money through faster development cycles but also enables us to incorporate newer, more powerful, less expensive electronic components. In short, it reinforces our cost leadership.

EXHIBIT 5-5

Swarm capability example: DC Systems

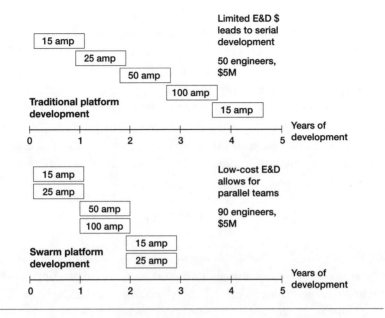

China. This deal brought us a well-deployed selling network in China and the rest of Asia. More important, it provided an established base of engineering personnel in China who were already engaged in applying state-of-the-art power electronic approaches. In conjunction with marketing efforts to define the specifications of next-generation global platforms, management rapidly expanded the size of the engineering force and the scope of its work.

After this transformation, Emerson has substantially more developers working on each product area than do our competitors. We further extended our leverage by simplifying the global product platforms. This means that our resources are applied across product lines on a global scale—and therefore in greater volumes—than are those of individual competitors, which operate in only one region of the world.

This development leverage is a critical ingredient in our network power strategy. It makes Emerson more effective than the competition in applying technological advances. By employing the concept of swarm engineering, Emerson brings new power electronic applications to market more rapidly than the competition, giving us the advantage of speed. Most important, this high rate of introduction creates shorter product life cycles and greater advantages for our customers.

Today, Emerson Network Power has strong advantages in the global reach and breadth of products and services on which to build and support network infrastructure needs throughout the world. Our capabilities related to power reliability range from power components to climate and power systems. Applications range from broad telecom and computing grids down to reliability issues even at the chip level. Above all, our technology leverage and scale enable us to meet new challenges for reliability in these applications and make our strategy distinctive.

SUMMING UP TECHNOLOGY LEADERSHIP

By the 1990s, Emerson's transformation from technology follower to leader was complete. Throughout our businesses, we had upgraded our technology base from electrical and electromechanical technologies to electronic technologies, in the process changing how our customers and other observers viewed the company. Our business platforms featured state-of-the-art technology, and we were realizing important benefits.

Our ability to manage our evolution from a supplier of components to a supplier of services and solutions has been particularly important. Everywhere at Emerson, in all businesses and divisions and in all geographies, we are positioned to meet our customers' highest value-added needs. And this capability benefits not only our customers but also our shareholders because meeting such needs translates directly into faster growth.

Technology management is now well established as a high corporate priority, and it will continue to be a critical element of Emerson's strategies in the future.

6

Acquisitions and the Management Process

*Effective due diligence is fundamental
to making good acquisitions.*

—Emerson axiom

A cquisitions have been central to Emerson's growth and success for decades. They are a vital component of our financial model (see exhibit 2-1 in chapter 2): we cannot consistently reach our target of double-digit annual earnings growth without doing deals. The organic growth of our existing businesses, even with our ability to improve operating margins, won't get us there.

Beyond their contribution to our financial performance, acquisitions generate additional valuable benefits: they help us diversify and reposition our portfolio and gain access to new technology, markets, capabilities, and people. For all these reasons, then, it is essential that we do acquisitions well.

Over time, we've learned how to do deals. Between 1973 and 2000, we completed more than two hundred acquisitions for a cumulative investment of more than $10 billion. For companies owned more than five years, Emerson achieved an average internal rate of return of approximately 15 percent, with more than 80 percent of the dollars

EXHIBIT 6-1

Acquisitions have been an important part of our process

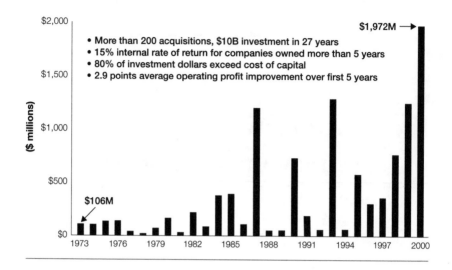

• More than 200 acquisitions, $10B investment in 27 years
• 15% internal rate of return for companies owned more than 5 years
• 80% of investment dollars exceed cost of capital
• 2.9 points average operating profit improvement over first 5 years

invested exceeding our cost of capital (see exhibit 6-1). This success rate is unusually high. Numerous academic studies have found that acquisitions are a risky way to generate growth and on average generate returns significantly below the cost of capital.

The Emerson management process has been the key to our success in this area, just as it was pivotal in our becoming a technology leader. The process helps us select good candidates and manage post-merger integration effectively. At the same time, it helps us achieve strong results quickly in the companies we acquire.

BECOMING AN EFFECTIVE ACQUIRER

Emerson became an active acquirer in the mid-1950s. Between 1957 and 1970, we bought more than twenty companies. Several of these companies—White-Rodgers, U.S. Electrical Motors, Ridge Tool, Therm-O-Disc, Browning, In-Sink-Erator, E. L. Wiegand, and Alco Controls—added significantly to total revenues and made strong contributions to corporate profits. These deals brought new businesses, new customers, and new people to Emerson. The decision to retain management and operate these units as autonomous divisions had profound implications for the company and for the genesis of the annual planning and control cycle.

During these years we also bought some nonperformers, such as a small producer of undifferentiated electrical lighting products. Another was a maker of consumer electronic equipment that had a good brand but lacked the technology and scale to compete with the Japanese. These deals indicated that we had much to learn about the kinds of businesses in which Emerson could succeed, as well as about the kinds of companies that could thrive under our direction. We lacked discipline and a rigorous process for evaluating potential deals and for integrating them into the company.

In 1970, we essentially stopped doing deals of strategic significance. Our longtime outside counsel advised the board that major deals faced increasing scrutiny from federal antitrust officials. Emerson shifted its focus to small deals to extend its product lines and gain access to new technologies.

Soon after I became CEO in October 1973, it became apparent through the planning process that Emerson would not be able to maintain healthy earnings growth without restarting the flow of large deals. In addition, I wanted us to capture the other benefits that such deals bring (discussed in the next section). I appointed Joe Adorjan as the new head of corporate planning. Adorjan had joined Emerson several years earlier as a financial analyst, and he had the high level of energy, intelligence, and commitment to tackle the assignment. Assisted by a small staff, Adorjan began to identify acquisition candidates and shape a more systematic approach to the process.

We became more active in mergers and acquisitions almost immediately and since then have undertaken several, sometimes many, significant deals every year. We differ, however, from many active acquirers. We buy exclusively for the long term. We don't do deals to reap a quick financial return. We are not a holding company that makes money through financial engineering but rather an operating company that owns certain types of businesses in which our participation can add significant value. We are especially interested in the quality of management and organization in the companies we acquire because they are critical to the success of our post-deal integration strategy.

GUIDING PRINCIPLES

Every year since the mid-1970s, we've looked at hundreds of acquisition candidates, each with its own management challenges and risk profile. To deal with so many opportunities, we've developed an acquisition program that reflects decades of experience and learning both from successes and failures.

The program includes a process to identify and evaluate strategic alternatives by a small staff of full-time, experienced professionals. We describe the program in greater detail later in this chapter. Following are the guiding principles that inform it and are essential to its effectiveness.

1. All Acquisitions Require Top Management Involvement. Given the significance of acquisitions to our strategy and financial performance, all transactions, no matter how small, require the active involvement and final approval of the CEO. This is not a formality. Rather, it entails the CEO's day-to-day involvement in the acquisition process, including all significant decisions regarding the target's business plan, its valuation, and the quality of its management. No prices or price ranges can be discussed without the CEO's prior approval. The CEO is also involved in due diligence findings, as well as in price and other significant contract negotiation issues. We also rely on the experience and knowledge of the Emerson board, which reviews and approves all transactions greater than $10 million. This is a far lower threshold for board involvement than is typical of companies of Emerson's size.

2. Every Transaction Must Have a Sponsor. We've learned to demand that every deal have a sponsor, a senior operating executive who has a sense of ownership and will take responsibility for the transaction. Depending on the nature of the deal, the sponsor may be a division president or a business leader. The sponsor must be willing to sign off on and commit to delivering on the acquisition business plan that supports the price we are willing to pay for a target. The sponsor also takes responsibility for being the spokesperson and selling the acquisition to the CEO, the board, and the rest of the Emerson management team. In the Emerson culture of vigorous, sometimes heated, debate, this challenge can be a difficult one. Hence the Emerson axiom "There are no deals without pain."

Equally important is the role played by the sponsor after a deal is closed. It becomes the sponsor's responsibility to ensure that the acquisition plan is executed and that the expected synergies are realized, while at the same time guiding and assisting the new management in its integration into Emerson. The sponsor chairs a board that sets the agenda for integration and oversees progress.

We rarely violate this requirement for deal sponsorship, because the consequences are generally unpleasant. An example is our 1998 acquisition of a Japanese company named Okura Intex Ltd. It was a very fast-paced transaction. One of our top executives in Asia identified and promoted the prospect, but his other responsibilities prevented him from sponsoring the deal.

Although no one else stepped into the role, we went ahead for several reasons. We'd been looking for a long time to find businesses to acquire in Japan, and, although the Okura deal was small, we believed that it could pave the way for more to come. One of the most significant obstacles to penetrating the Japanese market in many of our businesses is an inability to establish a significant presence in local distribution channels, which tend to resist outside entrants. Okura was primarily a distribution company, and it appeared it could provide a channel for many of our process control products.

We bought Okura, but it struggled for many years after the acquisition and has never met expectations. Looking back, I believe that one of the primary reasons is that Okura had no true sponsor, no operating executive to take ownership. It's not that anyone resisted or didn't want to make the deal work. Rather, no one was committed to follow through and make it a success.

3. No Transaction Proceeds Without a Plan. Emerson's commitment to planning is evident throughout our acquisition program. The disciplines we employ every day in planning for our existing businesses are directly applicable to evaluating potential acquisitions. In running their businesses, our managers develop the strategic, financial, and operational planning skills that are precisely those required to analyze, understand, and prepare a business plan for an acquisition target. Thus we have a wealth of talent and experience to draw on in carrying out due diligence on a target.

More important, applying our basic planning methodology to acquisitions means that before we close a transaction we have a detailed plan in place that lays out the necessary actions, step by step and quarter by quarter, to realize the synergies and financial performance on which the price of the deal is based. I believe that this detailed planning approach is a principal reason our success rate with acquisitions is so high. Elsewhere, in many cases, it seems that deals are done based on general, high-level assumptions about strategic value and potential synergies. Only after the closing does anyone develop a detailed plan to attain the target synergies and return. In my view, this is a formula for disaster. At Emerson we have a simple rule: "If you can't plan it, you can't value it."

4. The Emerson Management Process Creates Value. Our management process, in and of itself, creates significant value in our new partners. At first glance, especially at the highly structured planning and control cycle, many of our new partners are apprehensive and wonder whether all the effort is really necessary. These feelings are particularly strong in small private companies, but they are also present in the public companies and divisions of large public companies we've bought. Almost without exception, however, after a year or two, we hear managers in these new partners rave about the process. They like that it enables them to understand their business in new and meaningful ways and that the planning and control cycle provides the tools and structure they need to close the gap between planning and execution.

We have learned to install Emerson's tight financial controls in new partners as a first order of business. Not only does this quickly reveal any issues that may need to be addressed, but it also creates the basis for tracking and monitoring progress against the acquisition plan. In the environment following the Sarbanes-Oxley Act, it is even more urgent to establish financial control. To keep management from being overwhelmed, we can implement other aspects of our management process more deliberately.

The Emerson management process has been effective everywhere we've instituted it, in companies as diverse as Leroy-Somer in France and Avansys in China. Time after time, the management process has led to significant improvement in the profitability of new partners. This is an element of value that can be important in pricing strategic transactions, especially in competitive bidding situations.

5. Ego Has No Place in Deal Making. Emerson is disciplined in its approach to pricing acquisitions, and we try to avoid getting caught in the heat of the moment and overpaying for a deal. This common temptation is strong in auctions or when investment bankers are pushing a deal. The leading investment bankers are adept at creating a highly competitive, high-pressure environment in which acquirers are tempted to pay whatever it takes to win. This could be a challenge at Emerson because of our competitive nature and our strong desire to win, but our disciplined approach prevents it.

The management process keeps us focused on the main objective: not to win every negotiation but rather to create value for our shareholders. As long as the price we offer is supported by a detailed acquisition plan, we won't go very far wrong. Perhaps the most important measure of the value of our disciplined acquisition approach is not the deals we have done but rather the deals we have walked away from. We have seldom regretted these decisions. In fact we often say that the best decisions we've made are the deals we didn't make.

In 1985, we dropped out of the bidding for Allen-Bradley, a leader in industrial automation that we had been looking to acquire for years. We believed that the acquisition would complement several large Emerson divisions and in a single stroke make us one of the market leaders in the industry. An investment bank arranged the sale of Allen-Bradley through an auction. Our due diligence reinforced our sense of the value of the property to us, and we were confident that it would be a great deal for us. It also seemed that Allen-Bradley's board and management would welcome Emerson's bid.

The issue for us was to get the company at the right price. We prepared an aggressive bid at the highest price we could justify. As the auction proceeded, however, North American Rockwell (now Rockwell International) bid a sum well above our limit. We were invited to raise our bid to match but decided against it. We could have afforded the higher price, but we would have lost a significant part of the expected benefit. So we walked away.

6. Acquisitions Are About People. One of the most important tasks in our acquisition process is the assessment of the target's management team. In general, we believe anyone can buy assets, but only people can create value. This is not to devalue assets such as patents or manufacturing process and know-how that may not otherwise be easily available; but these types of intellectual property are the direct creation

of their inventors and developers, and their value is short-lived without the people behind them.

This principle is particularly important as we've made many small acquisitions to strengthen our capabilities in services and solutions. These deals rarely involve hard assets but instead center on people, including entrepreneurs and those who enjoy working in small organizations. It's vital in such deals to ensure that the key talent not only remains but also remains motivated. We learned this lesson the hard way in several small deals that proved less than successful after certain critical people left, and we ended up dismantling or disposing of the units. So we've learned to listen closely to these individuals to understand their needs and see whether we can structure a deal that satisfies both parties.

As a rule, we will not pursue an acquisition unless we are comfortable that the target management team is solid and will fit well at Emerson. The managers don't have to be superstars. One of the great benefits of our management process is that it tends to transform good managers into very good managers. Of course, we prefer to start with very good managers who will continue to thrive at Emerson and for whom we can offer new opportunities for growth and advancement. As noted in chapter 3, several of our top managers came to us through acquisitions.

7. Never Stint on Due Diligence. Acquisitions are inherently risky propositions, and mistakes can be costly to shareholder value. The seller has a clear advantage in knowing everything about the property, whereas potential buyers initially know only what is available publicly, and this information can be meager in the case of a privately held company or a division of a public company. When a deal reaches an appropriate stage of seriousness, then potential buyers undertake due diligence—that is, they get access to nonpublic information for the purpose of deciding whether to proceed and, if so, how much to bid.

An effective due diligence process is the key to Emerson's ability to minimize and manage the risks of acquisition. Proper due diligence involves all aspects of a target's operations and activities and requires that in a very short time we gain a full understanding of the target; determine the validity of the financial data we have been provided; assess all of the target's known and potential liabilities; assess its business plan for reasonableness and determine its risks and hopefully its unrecognized opportunities; assess its core technologies; determine the synergies that we can plan on enjoying after a deal; and assess the target managers and their likely fit with Emerson. In short, we must learn very quickly everything there is to know about the target. Clearly this is a difficult challenge, but the effort to meet it must never be compromised.

Although sellers often try to limit the degree of due diligence, we must not allow ourselves to be talked out of doing what is necessary to assess the risks inherent in a deal. Determining and quantifying significant risks require judgment born of experience. As always at Emerson, clear lines of responsibility are established with respect to managing the due diligence process.

Our corporate development department includes people who have a long history of doing deals. The department has responsibility for assessing the risks in a potential transaction, determining how the due diligence will be staffed and will proceed, and organizing and coordinating the process. Given the high cost of discovering a problem after the closing of a deal that should have been discovered in due diligence, corporate development takes its responsibility seriously. In turn, Emerson personnel called upon by the department to support a due diligence effort are highly responsive.

The corporate due diligence team works closely with experienced people from our operating units to do the operational due diligence. Given our long history of deal making, the combined team is accustomed to mobilizing on short notice and working under intense pressure and tight deadlines. This is an outstanding capability, something that is often validated by investment bankers and by management in many of our targets. It is not unusual for us to hear, after a couple of weeks, that we know their business better than they do. Without question, the high quality of our due diligence has been critical to our successful acquisition record.

Our basic due diligence process resembles that of other companies active in acquisitions. What makes us particularly effective, I believe, is the involvement of top corporate management, as well as our experience—which allows us to identify and focus on the significant issues—and our attention to detail in execution.

Any first-class law firm or public accounting firm has a standard due diligence checklist for acquisitions that probably does not differ significantly from the one we use. Again, the real difference at Emerson lies in how the output of the process is organized and the importance placed on the findings by top management. All the teams involved produce written reports of their work and major findings, which are organized and summarized in a due diligence book for each transaction. The book includes an executive summary that outlines all significant issues discovered and their resolution, whether through contract protection, price negotiation, or corrective actions to be taken after the closing. Our top executives review the books thoroughly before we proceed with a deal.

EMERSON'S ACQUISITION PROGRAM

The principles just described guide the process by which Emerson identifies, considers, and screens target companies. To reach closure of a deal, an acquisition candidate must satisfy four criteria: strategic fit, strong management and organization, compatibility with our management process, and acceptability of the valuation.

Interestingly, acquisition programs at most other active acquirers depend heavily on the first and last tests as well as on other quantitative measures. In our experience, however, these are no more important than the qualitative assessments about the strength of the organization and management and its compatibility with our management process. We believe that our successful record as an acquirer reflects how seriously we take all four tests together.

Strategic Fit

In screening a candidate's fit with our strategy, the process operates at three levels. Our corporate-level strategy is continuously to seek new business platforms that generate growth and opportunities to create value. We attempt to find new businesses that can be built on a cornerstone acquisition or an existing, but possibly less prominent, division—as you've seen in the stories of Climate Technologies, Process Management, and Network Power.

At a lower level, our late-1980s reorganization around businesses was driven by the need to keep abreast of industry strategies and to identify opportunities to add to or reposition our portfolio. We discuss these opportunities, including acquisition priorities, in our annual strategy reviews for the businesses. It was in these sessions that we conceived such game-changing deals as Copeland, Astec, Fisher Controls, and Avansys.

In addition to the internal mechanisms that generate prospective deals, we use advice from investment bankers. Cultivating this source is important. Through the years, Emerson management has maintained effective relationships with a broad range of firms covering all parts of the world.

Strong Management and Organization

All Emerson deals, regardless of the reasons we pursue them, bring new human assets to the company. This is so important that the first questions we ask as we narrow our focus on an acquisition candidate are not where and how the money is made but how the company is organized and who is on the management team.

There are several reasons for the focus on people and organization. The most important is that no company has excess management talent sufficient to meet the demands of a large acquisition program without affecting its core businesses. From another perspective, we understand that industry experience and insight into the culture and organization of the acquired business are key determinants of success. The management team of the acquired company is the best source of this experience. Thus in planning an acquisition we go to great lengths to ensure continuity of the management team while minimizing losses of people and the need to inject Emerson resources.

Compatibility with the Emerson Process

The third test is the organizational fit—the ability to transfer the Emerson management process and use it to boost the value of the target company. Over the years, this consideration has remained an explicit component of our deal analysis, and we periodically review our acquisition successes and failures with it in mind. These reviews are replete with lessons.

In 1990, for example, we analyzed fifty Emerson transactions completed between 1970 and 1985. Each was assessed in terms of the price we paid, the actual cash generated during the interim years, and the current value of the business to our portfolio. We calculated financial returns for each investment, thereby obtaining a performance ranking for all the deals. Using return as a proxy for success, we then examined these deals for characteristics correlating with success and failure.

The results matched our intuition: when we bought businesses that were compatible with our management process, we fared well; when we didn't, the results weren't as good. The "Emerson-type" businesses—those in which we succeeded—displayed common characteristics. When we bought market leaders in industries with some inherent growth, high returns became likely. Also successful were companies we were able to help expand into new geographical areas or adjacent technologies.

Not surprisingly, the analysis showed that we favored companies that were profitable but operated at margins below Emerson's. Through our focus on profitability and our operational excellence and Best Cost Producer disciplines, we knew how to help these companies. Finally, a more subjective finding involved the speed at which a company assimilated into Emerson: the faster a company's adjustment, and hence the more receptive it was to our management process, the greater the likelihood of a high return.

Emerson generally does not buy companies in need of a turnaround. (Skil was an exception because we believed it would complement our tools group and open up additional opportunities, something it did eventually through our joint venture with Bosch.) Profits are a barometer: if they're present, then we know that the management team is able; if they're below our levels—almost always the case—then we can improve profitability through our management process. Companies that adapt easily to joining a bigger corporation find themselves on a fast track to improvement.

In short, we think about how the management process and deal criteria are linked. If we don't see such a fit, we don't do the deal.

Valuation

The final hurdle for any acquisition target is its value. In traversing the lengthy acquisition process from contact to closure, the acquiring organization must continually revamp its view of valuation.

During the 1980s and 1990s, Emerson built a financial model that allowed us to generate many alternative valuation scenarios for a particular deal. The entire organization understood the drivers of this valuation approach: sales growth, profitability, capital intensity, risk, and required investment. This model created a common language that enabled us to discuss value and the impact of our plans for a new division. In addition to the model, we calculate the valuation based on a detailed analysis of the proposed acquisition's business plan, which we subject to the same scrutiny we give to our own division, business, and corporate plans. The plan must be well reasoned and based on a thorough analysis of reliable information.

As we learned from our valuation work, understanding a deal from multiple perspectives often allows us room to be creative about its structure. In determining whether to proceed with a transaction, we often consider a range of structures beyond a simple purchase that may better suit a situation, as you've seen in the stories of Astec and F. G. Wilson (see chapter 2). These purchase arrangements can range from partial equity investments, to swaps of assets, to joint venture structures with defined end points. In some cases we may even include third parties as partners, often as intermediate structures that lead to a further objective.

The key point is that a thorough quantitative deal analysis, including the seller's and other bidders' perspectives, yields insights and allows creativity to find its way into the deal structure. This flexibility increases the probability of our completing a successful transaction.

DOING DEALS

Emerson's ability to move swiftly without compromising thorough due diligence creates an advantage over less skilled buyers and makes more transactions available. Treating the target company's organization with respect during the process pays important dividends during post-deal integration.

We segment the deal-making process into three stages (see exhibit 6-2). In the early evaluation stage, we push the candidate through several screens and carry out preliminary legal, financial, and pricing analyses. There are several go–no-go decision points in this stage.

EXHIBIT 6-2

Stages of the acquisition process

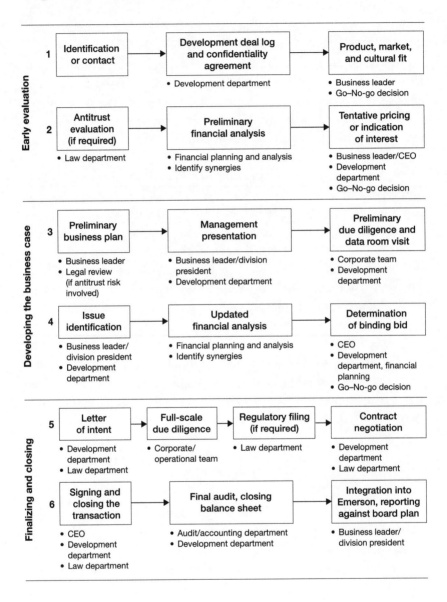

If the lights remain green after the first stage, the next stage entails building the business case for the deal. This means preparing a detailed analysis of the deal for discussion with top management and ultimately with the board of directors. At the end of this stage, which involves preliminary due diligence and typically engages management at both business and corporate levels, we identify issues that may be sticking points or subject to negotiation, and we prepare the initial bid. The final stage consists of the formal letter of intent, full-scale due diligence, contract negotiation, and, if successful, the closing.

Several points in this approach deserve special comment. As noted, Emerson pays close attention to developing the business plan for a new acquisition. We judge value based on two perspectives: the value of the base company and the synergy plan. In general, we calculate the value of the base company on the assumption that the target will continue to operate as an independent company. We focus on this analysis to understand alternative bidders' thoughts on value and to communicate to the seller our view of the stand-alone value of the property. This analysis is a key step in our approach to negotiating price.

Synergy value is built from the base value as well as opportunities that may be realized after the target becomes a part of Emerson—opportunities for sharing and leveraging capabilities, reducing costs, stimulating sales, and so on. We depend on the operating managers who sponsor the deal to specify these opportunities thoroughly. Their commitments are reviewed and documented so that assumptions beneath the forecast are well articulated and understood. From the synergy forecast, we create what we call the *board plan*, and it is against this plan that we evaluate the performance of the acquisition during its first five years as a part of Emerson.

Due diligence divides generally into two categories: strategic and technical investigations. *Strategic* analysis focuses on customers and distribution channels and may use third parties for market studies. We also verify the competitiveness of the target, a process that entails design cost analyses, technology reviews, and manufacturing process comparisons. *Technical* due diligence, on the other hand, requires a cadre of experts in areas such as auditing, legal matters, human resources, and specialized topics such as environmental impact assessments. To carry out this work we rely on trusted third parties such as accounting firms, law firms, and consulting firms. We blend these resources with internal resources and hold them all accountable.

Post-Deal Integration

The final critical aspect of our acquisition program is our approach to post-deal integration, which is designed to make this transition as smooth as possible. Any change in ownership opens opportunities for improvement, and many well-meaning participants at the corporate level and in the businesses are eager to pursue them. The combination of many things to do and many people to do them can create problems for any new acquisition, and its management may become overwhelmed with "help."

The sponsor of a deal plays a critical continuing role in integrating our new partner. Typically this individual must approve any corporate contacts, bearing in mind the priorities for value creation and organizational retention. This approach enables us to focus on the three or four most significant opportunities for value creation. Other opportunities can wait, possibly for a year or more, before they are pursued.

The rhythms and disciplines of Emerson's management process itself aid integration. As our new partners become exposed to our planning and control cycle, financial policies and systems, and distinctive practices such as organization reviews and our operational excellence and Best Cost Producer approach, they gain access to our senior executives and insight into what makes Emerson tick. The norm is for the new Emerson unit to record significant performance improvements during the first few years. After two or three passes through the cycle, most acquired units are thoroughly integrated into the company. This pattern holds true regardless of the industry, the type of business, or the geographical location of the acquired company.

THE ROLE OF DIVESTITURES

Emerson acquires for strategic reasons and therefore intends to keep the companies it buys. However, market imperatives and strategies change. Some deals, moreover, do not work out. In these instances, or when we determine that a particular business no longer makes strategic sense for us, divestitures may follow. This happened in our consumer products and government and defense businesses in the 1980s and early 1990s (see chapter 2).

Managing divestitures requires great discipline. Often they call for leadership to understand and acknowledge mistakes so that corrections can free up resources for better opportunities to create value. Financial reasoning does not always lead directly to the right divestiture decisions. Often our valuation analyses show that we lose value on divestitures, especially if taxes on gains are involved. The key point to remember, however, is that a company like Emerson has finite management resources, and they must be deployed to exploit the best opportunities. Bad deals and strategies can consume great managers, and the resulting opportunity cost can be heavy.

Given our culture, it is often difficult to make the case for divestitures. Emerson managers typically are confident and believe that we can fix most difficult situations. But it is also an important management duty to extricate the company from draining situations.

In sum, acquisitions are the biggest and riskiest decisions a company like Emerson can make. A success can have a huge positive impact on growth and profitability, but a mistake can destroy significant shareholder value. For these reasons, we focus intently on doing acquisitions well.

7

The Globalization of Markets and Competition

The management process is adaptable on a global basis—
it is effective everywhere.

—Emerson axiom

In the early 1970s, Emerson's international sales totaled about $110 million. Most sales originated in Canada and Latin America along with small joint ventures in Japan (for motors and appliance components) and a motor licensing agreement in India. Only one division—Ridge Tool—had operations in Europe.

Now Emerson is a global leader in most of its businesses. Slightly more than half of our employment, 40 percent of our revenues, and 30 percent of our investments in property, plant, and equipment are outside the United States (see exhibit 7-1). These statistics reflect Emerson's anticipation of and response to the evolution of the global economy, and we expect all these percentages to grow in the future.

Emerson's international growth came in two periods (see exhibit 7-2). In the first phase—the 1970s and early 1980s—we pushed overseas through exports and followed our traditional customers, which themselves were expanding abroad.

EXHIBIT 7-1

Emerson has made substantial commitments outside the United States (2002)

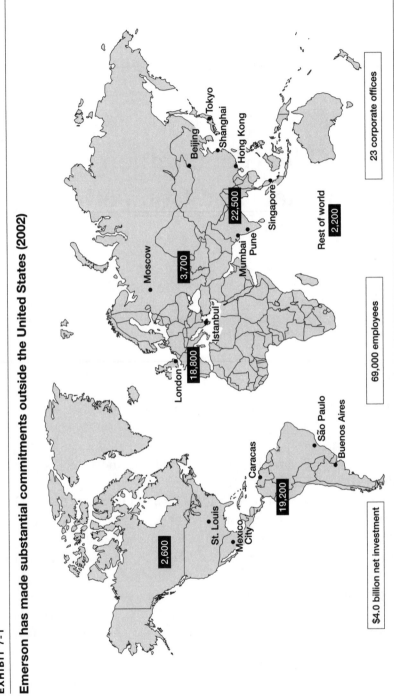

23 corporate offices

69,000 employees

$4.0 billion net investment

EXHIBIT 7-2

International sales have grown at 16% compounded annual growth rate

Europe drove growth in the 1980s and early 1990s. Developing markets will lead growth in the new millennium.

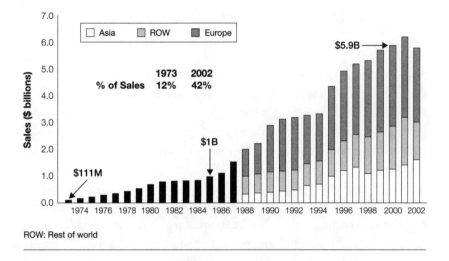

ROW: Rest of world

By the mid-1980s we reached approximately $1 billion in international sales. With the globalization of our markets and competition entering a new stage, we accelerated the pace. We ramped up investment in operations outside the United States, including acquisitions, and stepped up efforts to penetrate non-U.S. customers.

And we succeeded: our international sales climbed to almost $6 billion by 2000. We built a leading position in Europe primarily through acquisitions and bolstered our position in Asia and Latin America through direct investment and organic core growth. The establishment of the businesses in the late 1980s and early 1990s provided a strong boost, and several of today's business platforms—Process Management, Network Power, and Climate Technologies—are global leaders in their respective industries.

Emerson transformed itself into a global corporation in much the same way that we became a technology leader and an effective acquirer: we relied on the management process. We identified the need, defined new measurements, and installed a corporate officer to lead our growth. Then we planned, executed, and followed up. We started modestly, learned and applied our learning, and continued to make progress. As we've attained global leadership in our businesses, we are focused on maintaining our lead.

GETTING STARTED, 1973–1985

In 1973, only 12 percent of our revenues originated outside the United States, with by far the biggest portion in Canada. To become a significant factor in international markets, we had a long way to go, and getting there would be a huge challenge. I believed we could meet it by paying attention to management fundamentals: set ambitious goals, plan how to reach them, develop metrics to track progress, and get going, making sure to follow up.

Our initial push overseas had been haphazard and poorly coordinated. We tended to move into the easy, English-speaking countries. We also moved passively, often at the request of our major customers. For example, Tecumseh, a big purchaser of Emerson motors, urged us to license our technology abroad to support its foreign operations, and in the 1960s we set up our first licensing deals in the United Kingdom, Italy, France, Australia, and Japan. Subsequently, we set up minority joint ventures in Europe and Japan to manufacture motors, and we signed a motor licensing agreement in India.

We followed an export-led strategy and were reluctant to make investments overseas in advance of revenues. We were a conservative Midwestern company, and we didn't want to make any mistakes. We were still growing rapidly in the United States. We were torn, moreover, between managing our international expansion at the corporate versus the division level. Our small corporate office in Europe was attempting to get the divisions to pay attention, but we weren't making much headway.

A few divisions were pushing ahead on their own. Ridge Tool was fairly advanced, with a well-considered approach to Europe. As one of its officers put it, "You don't go out and sell one hundred countries at once. You take two or three countries a year, and you put all your investment in those. You get a critical mass, and you get an organization in place before you move to the next country." Few other divisions, however, followed suit.

When I became CEO in 1973, I recognized that international markets represented a huge opportunity and made international growth a priority. Our international sales were about $100 million in 1973, and I set a goal of $200 million by 1975. To get there, we followed an approach similar to the one we followed in technology and new product development (see chapter 5). We deemphasized the small corporate office in Europe and began pushing the divisions, as appropriate, to expand overseas on their own.

We appointed a corporate officer, Charlie Dill, as corporate vice president, international, and we assigned him to work with the divisions to develop international plans. A bright young MBA from Harvard, Dill had come to Emerson as an assistant to my predecessor and had carried out a number of corporate staff assignments. As head of our international effort, Dill was influenced by Ridge Tool's example. To track our progress he developed a measure called a *footing*, defined as having at least one full-time employee of a division in another country. One person or a hundred people, it was still one footing.

We began reporting and tracking footings in divisional and corporate planning conferences. At the start, we had 20 footings, but we soon began to make faster progress. We reached the 1975 goal of $200 million in international sales and set a new goal of $500 million by 1980. We continued to prod the divisions and had 106 footings by 1978. Our success reflected not only Dill's efforts and more aggressive management at the division level, but also the impact of several U.S. acquisitions.

The most important was Rosemount (1976). The world leader in differential pressure sensors, Rosemount had a growing business serving the European process industries. Rosemount's success abroad was an early signal of the vast global potential of the process control industry and a foundation on which we would continue to expand internationally. Like Ridge Tool, Rosemount provided a high-profile example to inspire other divisions to keep pushing.

In 1980 we surpassed the $500 million goal for international sales. By then, twenty-nine Emerson divisions accounted for 155 footings in thirty-six countries. But not all the news was good. The relatively low profitability of much of our international business constituted a limiting factor on our growth. This became a more significant concern in the early 1980s with the slowdown of the world economy, including a double-dip recession that hurt especially in Europe. Although we continued to encourage growth overseas, our international sales remained flat through the middle of the decade as we concentrated on improving margins.

Meanwhile, the nature of our challenge shifted in fundamental ways with the globalization of markets and competition. We began encountering stiff foreign competition in our home market. Previously, we had believed that achieving leadership in the U.S. market would give us significant scale and cost advantages that we could exploit both at home and, via export, abroad. In the early 1980s, however, we learned a different lesson. The coincidence of a strong dollar, tough economic times, and rising imports in the United States showed us that world scale was critical and that we had to become more competitive globally.

As explained in chapter 4, meeting the new competitive benchmarks entailed following the Best Cost Producer strategy. We undertook a major restructuring. We located more plants and people overseas, spent for higher quality and productivity, and redesigned products and processes for a more competitive world. Beyond that, we realized that we had to accelerate the shift from an export-led to an investment-led strategy so that we could compete in world markets. Investing to manufacture more overseas not only improved our cost position but also put us in position to gain market share, especially as we ingrained the Emerson management process in our international operations.

As we set up operations in Mexico and along the Pacific Rim, we confirmed that our management process would transfer readily to other cultures. In manufacturing, the Best Cost Producer approach worked as well in Mexico and Singapore as it did in Arkansas and Minnesota.

Our management process also worked effectively in our international operations as they built scale. Retired Emerson Vice Chairman Bob Staley explains:

> *The process gives us two important advantages that apply everywhere. First, it requires us to look at the details of the business to determine whether it is progressing and further, to explain that result. The process gives us a way to look at the business that allows us to understand what's driving it and how best to run it. Second is the cumulative impact of our discipline. The calendar of events that occur year after year means that we're constantly on top of the*

business. At the same time, top management is directly and intimately involved in these events. Our top people are constantly asking questions and pushing for better answers. Again, it doesn't matter where in the world we are because we focus on fundamentals that apply everywhere.

ACCELERATING ABROAD AFTER 1985

By the mid-1980s, we had come a long way toward becoming a more internationally minded company. We were no longer novices: the divisions were more comfortable with international markets, and we had developed some seasoned international managers. We had significant operations on the ground in every major region. With the Best Cost Producer strategy in place, we were poised to take advantage of the recovery of world markets. And our international sales picked up, reaching $1 billion in 1985.

The next step was to transform Emerson from an internationally minded company to a truly global one, in which the divisions would pursue global customers and manage on a global scale. To encourage them to take a more global view of their markets, in planning conferences we stopped talking about footings and instead emphasized global market share. We asked the divisions to tell us in detail what they were doing to boost it.

It didn't take long for the message to sink in. During the next fifteen years we made significant progress in all regions, with especially rapid headway first in Europe and then in Asia.

Europe

During the late 1980s and early 1990s, Europe represented one of our fastest growth markets. Between 1986 and 1995, revenues in the region skyrocketed from $570 million to $2.7 billion (see exhibit 7-3).

Several factors accounted for this performance. The region was reaching a new stage in the long process of economic and political integration that had begun after the Treaty of Rome in 1957. In 1990, Lester Thurow spoke at our corporate planning conference and proclaimed that the 1990s would be "the decade of Europe," during which

EXHIBIT 7-3

Emerson's European sales, with major acquisitions noted

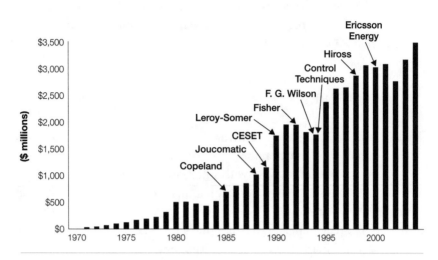

he predicted the European Union would outgrow and outperform the United States. That didn't happen, of course, but it was indicative of our bullish outlook toward Europe at the time. The collapse of the communist bloc in the late 1980s and early 1990s reinforced this optimism by opening new areas for low-cost manufacturing and creating opportunities for aggressive investors to seize a competitive advantage.

The growing maturity and sophistication of our divisions and businesses also contributed to our results through good fundamental management. As before, we benefited from acquisitions of U.S. companies having significant European operations. We also began making significant acquisitions in Europe, an approach we accelerated as we gathered the divisions into businesses. Process Control, Industrial Motors and Drives, Industrial Components and Equipment, and Motors and Appliance Controls became particularly active acquirers.

The acquisition of Copeland in 1986 provided a strong boost in Europe. The division had large facilities in Germany and Belgium as well as a growing base of customers in the region. We soon followed with several acquisitions of European companies, including Joucomatic (a French valve company that complemented our ASCO Division) and CESET, an Italian motor manufacturer with a strong position among European appliance OEMs.

In 1990, we acquired Leroy-Somer, a French maker of motors and drives, through a friendly tender offer prenegotiated with Leroy-Somer's management. Several of our U.S. and European rivals coveted the company, and our ability to close the deal proved quite a coup. In our planning process we had identified Leroy-Somer as a target, and Leroy-Somer's management, almost at the same time, decided to approach Emerson rather than other potential buyers, based on our reputation in the industry. The deal not only brought us a strong company but also led to several others in related fields in Europe: in 1994 we added to our portfolio both Control Techniques, a U.K. manufacturer of electronic drives, and F. G. Wilson, a family-owned manufacturer of diesel generator sets based in Northern Ireland.

These acquisitions were the most prominent of more than two dozen European companies we bought between 1985 and 2000. The creation of the businesses proved helpful in identifying new opportunities. The acquisition of PLASET (1998), added to CESET in Italy, increased the scope of our appliance components business in Europe. In electronics, Hiross (1998) and Ericsson Energy Systems (2000) increased our local presence. In process control, the 1992 Fisher deal included strong European operations, and we added a series of European deals to improve our ability to serve the sizable European chemical and energy industries. We called these various deals throughout our businesses *bolt-on* acquisitions because they strengthened existing foundations.

Fueled by acquisitions, Emerson's sales in Europe climbed, accounting for almost 30 percent of total sales in 1990. This number has since come down as a result of extraordinary revenue growth in Asia and acquisitions made in other parts of the world, but it seems likely to remain in the 25 percent range.

Meanwhile, the high hopes that the 1990s would be the decade of Europe slowly dissipated, as proponents of the single currency underestimated the pain involved in achieving it. Across the region, economic growth was sacrificed as countries pursued austerity programs. Despite this more difficult environment, Emerson continued to fare well in Europe during the decade, gaining market share at the expense of European competitors in almost every business. We understood, earlier than most European competitors did, the new opportunities afforded in Eastern Europe, and we developed and implemented strategies to benefit from these ahead of our competition.

Our rapid penetration into Europe in this period hastened the true globalization of the Emerson management process: instead of a one-day European review, we started holding full divisional planning conferences, profit reviews, and organization reviews in Europe, spending several days a year focusing strictly on our European businesses. Instead of inviting a few European managers to the corporate planning conference in St. Louis, we started holding corporate planning conferences in Europe, attended by 150 to 200 European managers.

The Emerson management process was well received and well implemented by our European management, although some aspects of the process, especially the Best Cost Producer strategy, had to be implemented a little differently. Implementing job moves to low-cost countries is more difficult in Europe than in the United States. Shutting down an American plant to set up operations in Mexico is relatively straightforward. In Europe, in contrast, such moves are more controversial and difficult, necessitating a more gradual approach. The opening up of Central and Eastern Europe in the early 1990s illustrates the point.

One of the first manufacturers to understand the magnitude of the opportunity in Central and Eastern Europe, Emerson was also one of the first to benefit from it. We identified four countries where we believed we could establish a manufacturing presence: Slovakia, the Czech Republic, Hungary, and Poland. We started to look at potential acquisitions in these countries that could serve as a base for transferring part of our Western European manufacturing activities. In most cases, we preferred to enter via acquisitions because this approach allows a more gradual transfer of activities, consistent with the constraints under which we operated in Western Europe.

We asked all of our European divisions to establish a manufacturing presence in Central and Eastern Europe. For those divisions that did not have the critical scale to justify investing on their own, we developed the concept of a multidivisional manufacturing facility managed by Emerson Corporate Europe, which acted as a landlord to the divisions and provided all the services required to operate efficiently. Eight divisions employing more than two thousand people are colocated in a facility in Nove Mesto, Slovakia. Today, one-third of Emerson's European manufacturing headcount is located in Eastern Europe, a ratio higher than that of any of our European competitors.

We succeeded because we initiated the process early and were able to rely on strong European managers who were persuaded of the merits of the strategy, able to explain it convincingly to employees, and able to implement it effectively.

In the early phases of development in Europe, strong corporate support was required for the divisions, with a main corporate office located in Brussels (and later in London) along with several corporate offices across Europe, particularly Eastern Europe. As the divisions reached critical size in Europe by the end of the 1990s, such support was no longer required. We disbanded the offices, thereby freeing resources that could be redeployed in other parts of the world, particularly Asia, where Emerson was still at an earlier stage of development.

Although local corporate support was no longer required, Europe was so important strategically to Emerson that high-level guidance remained necessary. At the end of 1998 we created a European Advisory Council headed by John Major, former prime minister of the United Kingdom. Also on the council are Theo Waigel, former finance minister of Germany and "the father of the Euro"; Henning Christophersen, former member of the government of Denmark and of the European Commission; and Sir Robert Horton, former chairman of BP and Railtrack and a longtime Emerson board member. The council meets several times a year with Emerson's senior management. Members of the committee are also available on an ad hoc basis and have often provided significant support in making contacts with local, national, and supranational governments and assisting in acquisition negotiations.

Although Emerson's rapid expansion in Europe was significant in and of itself, it also facilitated the company's globalization. Many companies acquired in Europe had established strong positions in Asia and other parts of the world outside the United States. Joucomatic, Leroy-Somer, and Control Techniques, for example, had a greater presence in Asia than did their North American counterpart divisions. Several of these operations helped us as we pushed into Asia in the 1990s.

European acquisitions also played a key role in shaping or reshaping some of our global businesses such as distributed power generation. When Leroy-Somer was acquired in 1990 it had a $70 million division making alternators for diesel generator sets ("gen sets"). We initially considered this business a candidate for divestiture, because it did not seem to fit with anything else at Emerson. However, as noted in

chapter 2, Leroy-Somer led us in 1994 to an opportunity to acquire
F. G. Wilson, located in Northern Ireland, one of the leading European
manufacturers of diesel gen sets.

We viewed this deal originally as a way to expand Leroy-Somer's alternator sales and to participate in a fast-growing business. F. G. Wilson had developed a relationship with Caterpillar, the world leader in
gen sets, and Emerson's arrival led to the creation of a joint venture between Caterpillar and Emerson in which we were the sole-source supplier of alternators. Again, as noted, we ultimately sold our interest in
the JV to Caterpillar but remain Caterpillar's exclusive supplier of alternators. Meanwhile, we acquired Kato Engineering and the alternator division of MagneTek in the United States. As a result of these
deals, Emerson is the world leader in the manufacture of alternators for
diesel and gas generator sets, with sales in excess of $500 million, and
manufacturing facilities in the United States, France, the Czech Republic, China, and India. Caterpillar has become one of Emerson's top
five customers.

Into Asia

Emerson had limited success in Asia during our first period of international growth. In the 1960s we set up joint ventures and licensing
agreements in several Asian countries and had wholly owned operations in Japan and Southeast Asia. Rosemount established a facility in
Singapore in 1979 and was doing well serving the process industries of
the region.

Otherwise, our progress was slow. Protectionist policies in some
countries kept us out, whereas in Japan, we, like other American manufacturers, faced a combination of capable local rivals and nontariff
barriers. We recognized, however, that Asia constituted an extremely
attractive growth market, and we were determined to accelerate our
growth there as we had in Europe after the mid-1980s.

Between the mid-1980s and the early 1990s, Steve Cortinovis, our
VP international, led an initiative to establish corporate offices across
Asia from Bombay to Tokyo, with Singapore, Bangkok, Kuala Lumpur,
Jakarta, Hong Kong, Taipei, and Seoul in between. Initially, some of
these were one-person operations, but all of them represented re-
sources on which the divisions could draw.

Some divisions followed the trail blazed by Rosemount and invested in new facilities, and others pooled their resources and colocated in the region. The process control divisions led the way, and the business in the region essentially doubled following the Fisher acquisition in 1992. During these years we also formed several joint ventures in India. Rosemount again set the pattern, although Copeland, Liebert, Fisher, and ASCO Valve also established JVs there.

As we had done in Europe in the 1970s and early 1980s, we were essentially planting footings throughout Asia as the best way to gain experience and build critical mass. By 1991, we had achieved $421 million in sales in the region. Many of our customers remained American or European companies, however, and we had a limited position in Asia, and the developing world generally, except through these customers. Booming economic growth throughout Asia and the emergence of liberal economic policies in China offered much brighter opportunities—if we could seize them quickly.

In 1993, we intensified our focus on Asia and particularly on China as by far the biggest opportunity in the region. Not only was the Chinese economy itself enormous, but also it was growing much faster than the U.S., Japanese, and European economies. It was clear that China was fully committed to a capitalist economy (see "Expanding in China").

Liberalization had begun earlier, of course, and Rosemount had licensed its DP 1151 transmitter technology in 1979. In the 1980s, many Western companies opened facilities in the special economic (free enterprise) zones near Hong Kong (Ba'oan, Shenzhen) and near Shanghai (Suzhou); from there, they exported throughout Asia and elsewhere.

Emerson's first real introduction to China occurred in 1989, as we restructured our electronic power components business via the sequenced acquisition of Astec (see chapters 3 and 6). Based in Hong Kong and with operations elsewhere in Asia, Astec provided a wealth of knowledge and experience about how to compete in the region. At the same time, the need to restructure Astec's operations and integrate them with ours afforded an opportunity to make our initial direct investment in China with an electronic components facility in Ba'oan. That served as a magnet for attracting other Emerson divisions, and by 1993, six divisions were operating on their own or in joint ventures in

EXPANDING IN CHINA

As we anticipated increasing our investment in China, I had an opportunity to meet with Premier Zhu Ronghi in Beijing. At the meeting, I asked the Chinese leader three questions:

1. Considering China's financial regulations, would Emerson have the financial flexibility to earn adequate profits, reinvest in China, and pay dividends?

2. Could we protect our intellectual property?

3. Would we be able to find enough employees with the right backgrounds and education?

The premier's response was encouraging. He said that making a profit was up to us, but he felt that the economic climate would provide us with the normal financial flexibility we had encountered in other world markets. He also said that the best way to protect intellectual property was to always use written contracts in all business dealings.

On the subject of identifying excellent employees, he said that without a doubt there were extremely bright Chinese executives interested in working for American-based companies and that we could help ourselves by supporting good business curricula in the top universities. Subsequently, Anheuser-Busch and Emerson, along with Washington University in St. Louis and Fudan University in Shanghai, established one of the top executive education programs in China.

Ba'oan, Tianjin, and Shanghai. As the legal umbrella over these activities, we created Emerson Electric China Holdings, a wholly owned subsidiary of Emerson.

At the 1993 corporate planning conference our theme was a renewed emphasis on growth, with Asia-Pacific clearly identified as a key geographic opportunity. We decided to push the accelerator. Within a month, two of our most promising executives—Jean-Paul Montupet and David Farr—were on their way to Hong Kong to establish the

Emerson Asia-Pacific corporate office. A few years earlier we had opened an office there, but the thrust now was to increase our focus on the region to achieve a growth rate of at least 15 percent per year, thereby doubling the business every five years.

We followed an approach similar to the one initially developed in the 1970s: multiply the footings for every business, increase corporate support through an array of corporate offices, attract divisional management to the region, and motivate them to make growth in Asia a key part of their total growth plans.

As we had done before in Europe, we intensified local implementation of the Emerson management process. Instead of a one-day annual Asian review, we started local divisional planning conferences for every division, including those with still a very limited presence in the area. In the Hong Kong office we set up an organization room modeled on the one in St. Louis (see chapter 3), and we started a series of Asia-Pacific organization reviews. Again, as in Europe, we started to hold an annual corporate planning conference attended by all our key Asian managers.

These steps were a prelude to a major thrust in 1994, when we established Emerson Asia-Pacific under vice chairman Bob Staley, who assumed the additional title of chairman of the new entity. We set a new goal to achieve sales in the region that would boost our corporate growth rate by at least 1 percent within five years—meaning that we would have to generate an additional $500 million in sales in Asia by 1998. Staley brought strong leadership and high visibility to this effort. His duties included accelerating the pace of transactions, bringing the Emerson management process to Asia, and cultivating local management talent and human resources.

In some respects, Emerson Asia-Pacific resembled earlier corporate initiatives to support new product development and international expansion. This time, however, with a corporate vice chairman in charge and backed up by some of our best executive talent, the profile was higher, reflecting a higher corporate priority.

We challenged the divisions to make the investments to win in Asia, recognizing that it would require a different strategy than had worked in Europe or in Latin America. We couldn't buy our way in through acquisitions, for example, as we had done and were doing in Europe. Nor could we necessarily expect to find our American or European customers already there to pull us along. Rather, we had to build business from the ground up, finding local customers and generating enough demand to justify additional investments. We called this process "getting over the Asian hump."

Exhibit 7-4 depicts the Asian hump in 1994 and shows the relative progress of our divisions. Many were just beginning to penetrate the region and faced a steep learning curve as they invested to establish a local presence and recruit local talent. About ten divisions were beginning to build scale in this process, although they still had plenty of work to do. Finally, a half dozen divisions were over the hump and rapidly gaining momentum. We used the concept of the Asian hump to indicate to the divisions where they stood in the process and what to expect as they moved ahead.

Getting over the hump required not only strong corporate leadership and support but also significant business- and division-level investments of management time and financial resources. We insisted, for example, that each of the businesses appoint at least one high-profile executive to lead the charge in Asia. These executives, who reported directly to the business leader, were based in the region and had the authority to make things happen.

We also required the businesses to develop a strategic road map for the region that we reviewed in planning conferences and incorporated into our forecasts. Each business was asked to produce an Asia staff development plan to be discussed at our organization reviews. We made a special effort to recruit talented Asian managers, and we tapped our management development and human resources budgets to train and help them succeed. Finally, we developed a program to identify and rank our best opportunities for new product development in Asia. We tracked the progress of and discussed these initiatives at planning conferences and technology conferences.

During the next few years, we made huge strides in China, organizing more than thirty companies and joint ventures throughout our businesses. We had opportunities everywhere, but the biggest were in electronics, process control, and heating, ventilating, and air conditioning (HVAC), where we could serve an expanding local market as well as export from our extremely efficient Chinese facilities.

In electronics, our strength at Astec and other divisions enabled us to gain share rapidly in serving local industry and telecommunications companies. Our success in penetrating Huawei, the leading Chinese

EXHIBIT 7-4

Getting over the Asian hump (1994)

- *Cannot acquire your way to top of hump, as in Europe*
- *Will not always find U.S. and European customers; must seek out and serve the customer in Asia*

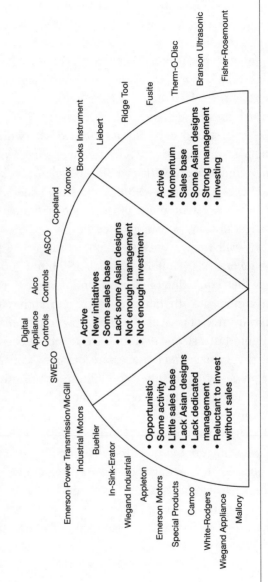

Digital Appliance Controls
Alco Controls
ASCO
Copeland
Xomox
Brooks Instrument
Liebert
Ridge Tool
Fusite
Therm-O-Disc
Branson Ultrasonic
Fisher-Rosemount

SWECO
Industrial Motors
Emerson Power Transmission/McGill
Buehler
In-Sink-Erator
Wiegand Industrial
Appleton
Emerson Motors
Special Products
Camco
White-Rodgers
Wiegand Appliance
Mallory

- **Opportunistic**
- Some activity
- Little sales base
- Lack Asian designs
- Lack dedicated management
- **Reluctant to invest without sales**

- **Active**
- New initiatives
- Some sales base
- Lack some Asian designs
- Not enough management
- Not enough investment

- **Active**
- **Momentum**
- Sales base
- Some Asian designs
- **Strong management**
- **Investing**

supplier of telecommunications equipment, led directly to the opportunity in 2001 to purchase Avansys (see chapter 6). This acquisition
gave us not only production capacity but also a nationwide distribution
network in China through which to pump other Emerson products.
Similarly, in process control, a series of direct investments and JVs enabled us to surge quickly to the number one position in Asia, and this
complements our leadership in North America and Europe.

In HVAC, our world-class production facility for Copeland scroll
compressors in Thailand and later in Suzhou, China, gave us entrée
into the burgeoning market for air conditioning and refrigeration in one
of the hottest and most humid areas of the world, and it gave us a
strong base for exporting. We've also made headway in motors and appliance components, with a wholly owned motors plant in Qingdao and
a significant purchasing commitment from Haier, the leading (and fast-
growing) Chinese producer of white goods (household appliances such
as refrigerators and washing machines).

With all this activity, destination sales in China began to soar,
climbing past $100 million in 1993–1994, to $700 million in 2002 following the acquisition of Avansys, and to more than $1 billion in 2004.
With annual growth rates in the region surpassing 20 percent, we
quickly overtook our goal of adding 1 percent to corporate growth rates.

Behind this strong performance lay our successful efforts to trans-
plant the management process to our new colleagues and partners.
"Our process is well suited to Chinese organizations, which are both
very entrepreneurial and very disciplined," Staley points out. "What we
had to offer made sense to the Chinese and was adopted quickly."

In 1994, we began the formal transfer of the process by starting
Asia planning conferences for all units in the region. Top corporate
and business leaders attended. I well remember the first conference
in Shanghai, where I gave an overview of the Emerson management
process, including the six points listed in chapter 1. My talk generated a lot of questions and discussion. The next morning, I visited a
nearby factory operated by one of our divisions. When I got there,
management had already translated the key points of the management process and had posted them on a huge scroll on the plant wall.
I viewed this as a clear example of how our Chinese employees understood the process and were eager to put it to work.

We realized early that the management process works because it
deals with strategic business issues, which don't change with geography.

EXHIBIT 7-5

Emerson's Asia-Pacific expansion

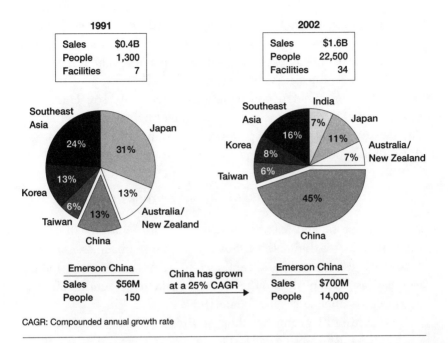

1991	
Sales	$0.4B
People	1,300
Facilities	7

2002	
Sales	$1.6B
People	22,500
Facilities	34

Emerson China	
Sales	$56M
People	150

China has grown at a 25% CAGR →

Emerson China	
Sales	$700M
People	14,000

CAGR: Compounded annual growth rate

Tactics, however, may differ by geography, particularly in employment practices. For this reason, we elevated the role of human resources management and set a policy in Asia of having the general manager of a specific operation on board first, followed immediately by the human resources manager.

The following year, under the aegis of Emerson Asia-Pacific, we launched a management training program for our key Asian executives. We even began holding special organization reviews in Asia, again with business leaders and senior corporate officers present. We also instituted other key elements of the Emerson management process, ranging from our mantra that profitability is a state of mind, to the six points of the Best Cost Producer strategy, to creating a flexible, action-oriented organization.

We hasten to add that our performance in China, which makes Emerson one of the top U.S. investors—far ahead of our direct competitors—reflects more than the advantages stemming from low-cost production and our management process. We also aggressively localized our operations in China, using few expatriates as managers and relying on local suppliers of raw materials and components. Thus we built the infrastructure to support rapid growth, and we have reaped the benefits. Our fast start in China enabled us to weather, with little ill effect, the financial crises that afflicted Japan throughout the 1990s and much of Southeast Asia late in the decade.

We also continued to grow rapidly elsewhere in Asia, reaching $1.6 billion in 2002 sales across the region—quadrupling our volume in a decade (see exhibit 7-5). Our performance in China is by far the biggest driver of our success in the region.

International Growth Beyond Europe and Asia

Although Europe and Asia accounted for most of our growth outside the United States during the 1980s and 1990s, our businesses and divisions also established significant operations in Latin America and the Middle East. Our push into these regions gained momentum after we organized the businesses in the late 1980s.

As these entities came together, our Process Management and Network Power businesses moved fast to serve customers around the globe. The vast energy industries of the Middle East became a big market for process control, as did the energy and process industries of Latin America. Network Power grew rapidly in the 1990s in Latin America, serving the region's expanding telecommunications infrastructure. Between 1995 and 2000, Emerson's revenues in Latin America more than doubled, from $254 million to $546 million.

By 2000, Emerson had substantial sales volume in all parts of the world—about $3 billion in Europe, about $1.25 billion in Asia, and almost $1 billion combined in Latin America, the Middle East, and Canada. It seems clear, however, that Asia will dominate our international growth in the next few decades.

Globalization and E-Business Opportunities

Our experience in international markets reaches back for decades, and our managers are accustomed to operating abroad. We have many thousands of employees on the ground in Europe, Latin America, and

Asia, and we are confident that our management process will help us identify and take advantage of new opportunities in these regions. The revolution in communications that accompanied the Internet and the World Wide Web is helping us in many ways, especially in our on-going efforts to operate more efficiently. The new technology enables dramatic changes in purchasing, engineering, and back office functions, which we can now situate in low-cost areas of Asia and Latin America (see chapter 4).

The new technology also opens up new possibilities for global growth through e-business (see chapter 8). Emerson engineers in China and India, for example, can provide cost-effective design and support services to North American and European customers looking for solutions. The abundance of high-quality intellectual resources at low cost in these countries and in the Philippines enables us to offer a range of services that would be prohibitively expensive to provide using comparable resources in the developed world. An example of these services is swarm engineering (see chapter 5)

Emerson's growing presence in Asia is a foundation for growth not only in the region but also around the world.

NEW CHALLENGES AND NEXT FRONTIERS

Since the 1970s, Emerson has traveled far from its roots as a Midwestern U.S. manufacturer serving primarily the U.S. market. International business can be risky and our record hasn't been perfect, but we've learned that we can succeed most of the time by following the management process. We now operate from strong bases in most regions of the world and have attained global leadership throughout our businesses. We have also internalized many valuable lessons about operating abroad. We're experienced in working with host country governments. We can manage the risks. We can build local organizations and recruit resident talent on our own or with local partners in joint ventures. And we know that our management process will work to make us stronger.

With all this progress and experience, there is yet no limit in sight to our evolution as a truly global company. Looking ahead, we see many challenges and opportunities. Robust operations in Asia complement our traditional strongholds in North America and Europe, but our revenues are far from geographically balanced. Some of our businesses have yet to get over the hump, not only in Asia but even in Europe and Latin America. And in those businesses in which we are currently global leaders, we must take advantage of the opportunities that will come our way during the ongoing evolution of—and inevitable consolidation in—these global industries.

Another challenge is to find ways to grow successfully in the developing world. To date, underdeveloped countries have not been good markets for most of our goods. Eventually that will change, as gross domestic products rise and economic resources become more evenly distributed. We must be ready to win in countries where we already have export operations, as well as in regions of the world where we are underinvested—for example, southeastern Europe, the Middle East, and parts of Africa. In the coming decades, emerging economies will offer huge new opportunities, with the biggest perhaps in Russia and India, where we have already established significant footings in the higher-technology businesses.

Our record in managing to achieve global leadership offers ample reason to be optimistic about Emerson's future as an increasingly global organization. We could not have traveled so far nor fared so well without our management process and the rigorous analysis and disciplined implementation it requires. We expect that our management process will also guide us successfully through the next challenges of globalization.

8

Growth

The Ultimate Challenge

Match the passion for profits with a passion for growth.

—Emerson axiom

By the early 1990s, Emerson possessed a secure reputation as a leading global industrial company. Helped by our Best Cost Producer strategy, we had increased our earnings every year for more than three decades, through good times and bad. We had also stepped up the rate of top-line growth through our initiatives in new products, acquisitions, and international expansion.

Our success, however, masked a serious weakness that became increasingly exposed as the Western economy emerged from a sharp recession. Investors' expectations were tied to rapid growth, and we weren't delivering quickly enough to satisfy them. For the first time in years, the performance of our stock fell behind that of some peer companies and below the S&P 500 Index. To return our share price to the premium level we believed it deserved, we took on the ultimate challenge: faster top-line growth.

Meeting the growth challenge proved more difficult than any other initiative we had undertaken. As we discovered, the challenge was multifaceted. Meeting it involved some things we could control directly, such as setting new targets, making new investments, and beefing up our capabilities in marketing and other areas. It also involved some things we could not control, such as relatively slow underlying growth rates of several of our major businesses.

Along the way, we learned that our management process and mind-set, which were finely tuned to delivering better profits year after year, would require major changes to enable us to grow faster. We were forced to reexamine some of our long-standing orthodoxies, such as the intense, almost exclusive focus on profitability and the importance of divisional autonomy. As we grappled with growth, we found ourselves evolving into a different kind of organization, albeit one still driven to achieve consistent results through rigorous management.

These unexpected dimensions of the growth challenge made it the ultimate challenge. We could not meet it by simply grafting new initiatives onto our existing foundation; instead, we had to modify part of the foundation itself. This process continues. Although we've made significant progress—and suffered some setbacks—growth still represents the ultimate business challenge for our current management team and our management process. It is likely to remain so for the foreseeable future.

UNDERSTANDING THE PROBLEM

Over the years, Emerson had instituted a number of policies and actions to stimulate growth. The most significant were our initiatives in new products, acquisitions, and global expansion. In our planning conferences we had also relied on a tool called the *sales gap chart*. It displayed current sales and made projections for the next five years based on an analysis of the sources of growth: the market's natural growth rate, the division's change in market penetration, price changes, new products, product line extensions, and international growth. The idea was that if projected growth did not meet or exceed our target, the division would face a gap. Then it became division management's job to tell us the specific steps it would take to close the gap.

The sales gap chart proved a useful tool, but in the early 1990s it became apparent that we needed to do more to generate faster growth. Several factors concerned us. First, although we considered ourselves a premium company, we found that investors were beginning to disagree, based on our plans to grow 10 percent per year. Analysts pointed out that some of our peer companies would deliver 12–15 percent earnings growth, and although Emerson had been recognized for decades as among the best-managed companies in America, we needed to achieve and sustain faster growth. Meanwhile, the rapid expansion of the world economy—brought on by the advances in information technology and the corollary enhancements in productivity—raised investors' expectations for growth rates in market leaders like Emerson.

Our internal analysis uncovered the second cause for concern. When we examined the underlying growth rates of what we call "the base company"—our continuing operations without the impact of acquisitions factored in—we saw that growth was slowing. At the same time, it was apparent to some of us that our management process, which worked well to produce consistent margins, was not generating sufficient growth in the base company. Our challenge was magnified by intense downward pressure on prices, which restricted our ability to grow by raising prices (see chapter 4).

In 1992 we received still more confirmation of the problem from another internal initiative. We had recently reorganized the company to create the business platforms, and we sought to give the business leaders new ways to look at their opportunities. We created a management task force consisting of the eight business leaders, three corporate officers, two division managers, and two external consultants. We asked the group to address a simple question: "What are the issues facing our company, and where are the opportunities to improve our process?"

The group came back with three major recommendations: (1) the company must develop a passion for growth comparable to its passion for profitability; (2) the roles and responsibilities of the business leaders must be clarified with respect to the roles and responsibilities of the corporate executives; and (3) the company must improve its organization development process to better cultivate future leaders. In listing the growth challenge as a top priority, the group urged us to address it immediately.

Finally, Emerson was not alone as we confronted the growth challenge. To help us address it, we engaged consultant Gary Hamel, who was writing, speaking, and advising on the topic. Like other companies, we were unsure of how big a problem we faced. The restructuring of the preceding decade had given many corporations a means to reduce overhead and grow profits. But as Hamel pointed out, "You can't shrink yourself to greatness." He argued that companies with great legacies like Emerson would have to reconsider their futures and reinvent themselves and their industries. He pointed out to us in particular the need to create a growth process that would run parallel with our profit process. We accepted Hamel's advice and began to address the growth challenge head-on.

THE FIRST PHASE: 1992–1997

Our initial efforts to modify our management process centered on two main actions: dividing our divisional planning conferences into separate sessions devoted to growth planning and profit review, and identifying and investing in a host of growth programs.

Growth Conferences

In 1992, as noted in chapters 2 and 4, we restructured the divisional planning conferences, our most important meetings of the year. We moved all discussions of profit actions to the separate profit review under our profit czar, Jim Berges. We renamed the traditional planning conference the growth conference and focused it exclusively on growth. The CEO attended each growth conference, an important symbol of the company's priorities.

This structural change was overdue. The planning conferences had devoted most of their time to profitability, especially if there was a problem. Thus we tended to focus on cost reduction, productivity increases, job moves, asset management, and similar topics while giving short shrift to growth. It seldom received the sustained, intense attention that it needed. Even our discussions of the sales gap chart failed to stimulate the performance we now needed—not merely to hit a reasonable growth target but to find and pursue breakout growth opportunities.

We also shifted the time horizon of the growth conferences. The divisional planning conferences traditionally had covered sales and marketing initiatives as well as "gap fillers." The agenda now became growth strategy, moving well beyond near-term tactical measures to discuss programs that would accelerate growth. We established growth priorities and reviewed the resources required to implement and track them. We also dwelled on ways to achieve quantum improvements in reducing the time and expense required for new product development and introduction.

The growth conferences provided a forum for emphasizing the importance of growth as a corporate imperative and for stimulating business and division leaders to think differently about their growth opportunities.

Growth Programs

To generate faster growth, we needed the businesses and divisions to identify and pursue their most promising growth programs. We were prepared to support these ideas with corporate funding, but we also wanted to be sure that the businesses and divisions were maximizing their use of available resources.

We developed a broad definition of growth programs to include acquisitions and joint ventures as well as internal developments. We stipulated that programs have a measurable sales impact and require measurable investment above and beyond normal sales and marketing activity.

Throughout the company, management teams began working to identify and submit programs for review at the corporate level. We classified the programs in three groups: core programs that were vital to ensure continuing leadership in our businesses; funded *adders*, or additional programs to boost growth; and unfunded adders, which would proceed only if the businesses or divisions could find means to pursue them. At corporate headquarters, we aggregated and tracked these categories, and we needed contributions from all of them to reach our growth target.

During the next few years, we generated nearly one thousand growth programs and reviewed them in depth. Clearly, we had plenty of promising initiatives, but it created a new challenge to evaluate so many programs and decide which to fund.

Reflections on the First Phase

In the mid-1990s, Emerson's underlying growth rates began to pick up. We were pleased with the progress we were making, but we also became aware of the limitations of our approach. On reflection, we realized we had taken a classic Emerson analytical approach to a problem that was less amenable to the exacting analysis that works so well in controlling profits.

First, we created too many programs and were not realistic about the management resources necessary to bring them to closure. With nearly one thousand programs in place, we had too many cars on the road. We found that an 80/20 rule applied—approximately—with 85 percent of sales growth produced by 30 percent of the programs. So we began to narrow our focus to those with the greatest potential impact, finally settling on thirty-nine programs. We grouped them into eight areas and treated them as major corporate priorities.

A less obvious problem, we believed, was that our timing often differed from that of our customers. To our surprise, we had a great many ideas for which our markets were simply not ready. We competed in many businesses in which market inertia would not permit us to grow at the rate we needed. In other cases, we had some great ideas, but our business fundamentals or positions in the relevant industry weren't strong enough to leverage them.

We also were constrained in our use of resources. Normal economic cycles inevitably require cutbacks at least every three or four years, even in the most prosperous times. Our long-standing focus on containing headcount was a great strength, but it also came with a cost: we were reluctant to invest in new people and overhead to support growth. Thus we lacked capacity to support our new programs. We also lacked sufficient skills in three areas: software, marketing, and technical support. Nothing in our thinking enabled us to see how to add these resources and still sustain our record of earnings growth.

Looking outward and ahead, we had too little infrastructure in Asia, certainly compared with the investments we had in Europe. Many of the best opportunities, moreover, were in service-related businesses, and, because we were a manufacturing company, our strategic thinking and management process on the subject were limited. Finally, customers were changing their expectations of suppliers, beginning to

purchase solutions rather than simply buying components. Our ability
to provide solutions, however, was hindered by our traditions of divisional autonomy and management independence. Because we grouped
our products and sold them across divisional lines, our organization
structure and management approach made it difficult to pursue opportunities to grow.

THE SECOND PHASE:
CHANGING THE SLOPE OF THE CURVE

Although the growth needle was moving faster in the mid-1990s, we
needed to change the slope of the growth curve. We still lagged some
peer companies and competitors, and the value of our stock, although
increasing, was not keeping pace with targets we had set. We also understood that it would take more time and investment to change the
company's culture and make growth a priority equivalent to profitability.

These problems and the need for a fresh approach came into focus
in 1997, when we brought together our top people in corporate headquarters, the businesses, and the divisions for a special growth conference. The conventional approach at Emerson when a problem reached
this stage was to gather the key managers and create a presentation that
would quantify the problems and define solutions and priorities in addressing them. This time, however, we decided on a different approach.

We kept it simple. Thirty of our managers were seated in a horse-
shoe arrangement, with two large boards in the front of the room. We
then went around the table, with each person speaking candidly about
our growth strategy, including what was effective and what wasn't. This
approach gave everyone an opportunity to contribute to the solution,
and it spawned a great discussion.

Four hours later we had something powerful: separate lists of things
we were doing well and things we needed to do differently (see exhibit
8-1). We were pleased to see that one list included principles and practices that we had right: the high-level emphasis on growth, the expansion into Asia, the investment, the narrowing focus on big programs,
and so on. The more important list, however, consisted of things that
we had not done, and thus it became a to-do list for us. Some steps,
such as appointing a growth champion and beefing up our marketing

EXHIBIT 8-1

1997: What we have and haven't done to improve growth

What we have done in the first years of the program
- Reached out for some large initiatives more than in the past.
- Added resources that would not have been available in the past.
- Geographic initiatives have been a success (e.g., Asia).
- Cost and quality of our products have improved to form a good basis for growth.
- Used acquisitions to change the mix to a higher-growth profile.
- Time-to-market program has improved product development.
- Overall program and resource analyses helped us understand and manage for higher growth.

What we haven't done in the first years of the program
- Created a "passion" for growth.
- Gotten sufficient creativity into our process. We are still constrained by "served market" definitions.
- Found a sufficient number of large projects and programs—business initiatives.
- Added marketing talent as we had planned.
- Resource additions have been less than we identified.
- Changed the compensation or incentive system.
- Confronted lack of brand equity problem in many products.
- Appointed a "growth champion."
- Stopped applying time and resources to assets that will never grow.
- Integrated the business strategies with growth process.
- Created technology road maps in our divisions.
- Pursued "system" integrated products, services, and buyouts that provide "solutions" for our customers.
- Improved large-account management.

capabilities, were straightforward. Implementing others, such as increasing investment in growth and stimulating more collaboration across the divisions, would be more problematic.

The group asked us to rethink our strategy of only selling components and consider moving into services and solutions. This strategy would entail coordinating approaches to customers and offering products, services, and solutions that crossed our internal boundaries. At the same time, the managers wanted us to take better advantage of our corporate capabilities, scale, and reputation, not only on the cost side but also on the growth side.

This meeting proved to be a seminal step in bringing our growth-related efforts to a level that began to approach our capability in profit planning. Our key managers were candid about our deficiencies. When they challenged us to create a passion for growth that would be equivalent to our passion for profit, it brought the significance of the initiative into clear focus. And from a practical standpoint, we had quite a list of things to do to accelerate our momentum.

In the aftermath of the 1997 growth conference we instituted a number of major changes in our organization and management process. Charlie Peters, formerly vice president for development and technology, became our corporate *growth czar* to champion growth planning, just as Jim Berges and Al Suter had championed profit planning. Peters worked with the businesses and divisions on growth strategies. He also took the lead in upgrading our skills in marketing and branding. At the same time, we reassessed our thinking about risk. We determined that if we were going to generate faster growth, we needed to reposition our portfolio for faster growth through acquisitions and divestitures.

A NEW APPROACH TO GROWTH

As we rethought our approach to growth, we received some good advice from Gary Hamel. He convinced us that in the environment we now faced, we had only two ways to grow faster: expanding our served markets and leveraging our corporate resources. Doing the first would require us to move beyond selling components to bundling them with services into solutions. We also needed to examine the possibility of creating new business models to revolutionize our industries.

Doing the second would mean doing what our managers' meeting had concluded: taking better advantage of our corporate capabilities, scale, and reputation, not only on the cost side (through revamping purchasing and supply chain management) but also on the growth side through coordinated approaches to our customers and offering them products, services, and solutions that crossed our internal boundaries.

We realized that this vision would require significant changes to Emerson's strategy, organization, and management process. These changes ranged from a relatively straightforward initiative to improve the process in the divisions for generating growth ideas, to more complex, long-term challenges such as upgrading our marketing capability, coordinating approaches to key customers across the businesses and divisions, and developing new business models.

A Process for Generating Ideas

In the early years of divisional growth conferences, the businesses and divisions contributed hundreds of ideas for growth programs. We found, however, that these were distributed unevenly across the company. Some divisions just couldn't come up with enough worthy ideas. To help them, we worked with Hamel to institute a process for generating and qualifying innovative ideas—one of the recommendations of the 1997 growth meeting.

The process begins with a one-day session involving the senior managers of the divisions and a few additional thoughtful contributors having expertise in marketing and technology. One or more representatives from corporate headquarters also attend, with perhaps an outside consultant. The participants gather in a conference room with easels and whiteboards and work through a structured list of questions (see "Seven Questions to Generate Growth Opportunities").

When we began the process, two tools came in handy to frame the discussion. One was the "mute button," which obliged individuals perceived to be dominating the conversation (such as division presidents) to remain silent for thirty minutes. A practice called "chart prohibition"

SEVEN QUESTIONS TO GENERATE GROWTH OPPORTUNITIES

1. How do you feel about growth and the progress of this division?

2. What are the impediments to growth you've experienced?

3. What are the division's core competencies?

4. What are the division's and industry's orthodoxies about competition?

5. What are the key trends unfolding in the industry?

6. Which competitors in your industry space are creating value?

7. What are the opportunities that flow from these discussions?

eliminated the use of slide presentations from planning conferences because they tended to keep the flow of ideas in well-worn channels. These meetings were intended to stimulate new thinking and not to re-play old ideas.

The new approach paid off in numerous excellent ideas. They included practical steps to integrate the sales forces of multiple divisions, new ways to deepen relationships with customers, and new solutions offerings in businesses such as process control, HVAC, and electronics.

Creating a New Brand Architecture and Identity

It seems obvious, but every great company must be skilled at understanding customers. That starts with excellence in marketing, a discipline historically undervalued at Emerson. However, our timing for addressing the issue proved fortuitous. New information technology was revolutionizing the discipline, enabling new ways to communicate with customers and enhancing the prospects of building deep, abiding relationships with them. Database marketing and integrated communications represent a quantum change, just as IT-enabled lean manufacturing processes transformed traditional manufacturing. In marketing, in fact, we discovered that we had a unique opportunity to build a state-of-the-art marketing organization and move to the front of pack.

Charlie Peters and Kathy Button Bell, a strategic marketing consultant whom we hired as vice president of corporate marketing, began to apply basic concepts and new techniques to build our capability. One of the most important steps involved a fresh examination of the Emerson brand. At the time, our brand architecture was confusing. We had a collection of divisional brands, most of which were not identified with Emerson. This diverse collection limited our ability to pursue certain initiatives with customers. At the same time, it hampered our corporate image. I had long been frustrated that Emerson did not receive the recognition it deserved as a technology leader, for example, because our achievements were closely identified with particular divisions.

But despite the good reasons to elevate the corporate brand, I was initially skeptical. For twenty-five years I had attached substantial value to acquiring dozens of companies with great brand legacies. Brands like Rosemount, Ridgid, and Liebert were widely recognized as industry leaders. I worried that amplifying the Emerson identity could compromise the identity and autonomy of our individual units.

THE EMERSON BRAND PROMISE

Emerson is where technology
and engineering come together
to create solutions for the
benefit of our customers,
driven without compromise
for a world in action.

So we approached changes to our brand architecture carefully and deliberately. Under Button Bell's leadership, we began a program to re-examine our brand using an approach that emphasized simplicity, thorough planning, quantitative analyses, and a system of follow-up. Along the way, we learned that branding, a topic we thought subjective and intangible, was amenable to the same rigor and discipline that characterized the rest of the management process.

As we proceeded, we recognized the need to formalize Emerson's brand promise. This began with a summary of input from every conceivable constituency—managers, employees, customers, analysts—about what the Emerson brand meant to them and what views they had of our future. After arduous efforts to summarize this input, three or four of us spent weeks writing, arguing, and rewriting one simple paragraph until we produced a draft all of us could accept. Then we broadened the audience to include additional top executives, including David Farr, Jim Berges, Al Suter, and Bob Staley. Our mission was to get to one fully agreeable version, one that lives today.

A related initiative—creating a new corporate logo—caused more anxiety at first but also ended in a significant change. I had stood behind our block letter *E* (at left in exhibit 8-2) for decades, and I was unsure about changing it late in my tenure. I had supporters on the board and among our management team, one of whom challenged the idea with the question, "Would America change the flag?" Button Bell pointed out, however, that Buck Persons had altered the Emerson logo several times during his eighteen-year tenure, and we were still using one formalized in the late 1960s.

EXHIBIT 8-2

Emerson's logos: From the old to the new

IEMIERSON
(1967)

EMERSON
(2000)

So how do you update your identity? I assumed that you solicited a lot of designs and hoped that one was thoughtful and a "big idea." To my great surprise and delight, the process was highly structured and objective. We used inputs from the brand promise and related it to other logos and identities of our peers and competitors. We commissioned alternative concepts and reviewed our favorites with our managers. After getting down to five alternatives, it was clear we had a good range to consider, from a simple progression of the block *E* to highly contemporary approaches that represented a significant departure for us.

As the time approached to make a decision, I preferred an alternative in the middle, acknowledging some change while also emphasizing continuity. Then we orchestrated a final test, which was revealing. We asked hundreds of people from the same constituencies we had asked about the brand promise to describe the values projected to them by each of the logo designs. The feedback supported a middle-of-the-road alternative like the one I preferred, but there was also plenty of sentiment for a more progressive choice.

In the end, we selected the most contemporary look. By then, I was convinced that our work had been rigorous and thorough and that we had followed a disciplined process of research and evaluation. Meanwhile, the businesses and divisions enthusiastically embraced the new identity. It gave our managers a platform and a kind of permission to work together across our traditional organizational boundaries.

Another key aspect of our brand architecture involved distinguishing the meanings behind our corporate-, business-, and division-level brands. It was especially important to clarify how our strong division brands would complement the business-level or platform brands in the minds of customers. Together, these eight solutions-oriented platforms were placed under the Emerson brand that was guided by our brand promise. The new identities in the form of logos and messages were tightly coordinated to reinforce that message.

One of the most important aspects of developing our new brand architecture was the enthusiasm shown by the entire organization. When we built the new brand program, we suspected that we would have to impose it in some cases where division managers might wish to protect their legacies and, most of all, their independence. To our surprise, most follow-up and control efforts were to contain groups from shifting too dramatically to the umbrella brand at the expense of our strong division-level brand equity. Although some of this response can be attributed to the thorough and innovative work led by Button Bell, it also reveals the motivation of our managers, who were eager to reinforce the Emerson brand and help us become a more balanced company.

Customers and Marketing

Through a series of actions—growth programs, a new brand architecture, a business portfolio refocused on more dynamic industries and geographies—we were positioning Emerson for better growth. Meanwhile, we had still to address the most basic dimension of successfully growing a company by improving our capabilities in marketing and in managing relationships with customers. Peters and Button Bell took on this task with the objective of making Emerson a best-practice business-to-business (B2B) marketer.

We designed a top-level education program called Industrial Strength Marketing, through which we rotated our top nine hundred managers, including sessions in Europe and Asia. Taught by faculty primarily from Northwestern University, the program not only opened our eyes to new ways of marketing but also provided a road map for change. We were exposed to the latest thoughts on customer insight and satisfaction. Our managers learned that customers create an image of companies like Emerson based on the accumulated effect of literally hundreds of touch points, and our focus had to be on how we organized and improved the most important interactions to differentiate us from our competitors. We had to transform the traditional role of sales reps from selling to consulting and advising. We also had to upgrade our knowledge of value chains and recognize the meaningful differences in perspective between OEMs and end customers.

One significant lesson of the seminar was that our timing for addressing the marketing issue was good, given our tendency to think like engineers. As noted, new capabilities such as database marketing and integrated communications were revolutionizing the discipline of marketing, enabling new ways to connect with customers and enhancing the prospect of building deep, lasting relationships with them. This trend presented us with a timely opportunity to build a state-of-the-art organization and move to the front of the pack in our industries.

A key step forward was our *marquee account* program. Initiated in the Process Management business, the program organized account teams that focused on particular global customers, putting Emerson resources in place that cut across our organizational boundaries. The purpose was to allow the customer to see Emerson as a single integrated supplier rather than a collection of independent divisions, each with a unique approach.

The payoff was huge both for our customers and for Emerson. The marquee account program gave us the potential to penetrate an account more deeply with all of our product lines. Typically, we would have strong relationships in a limited number of products or geographies but no presence in other areas. We might account for 50 percent or more of some critical segments of a particular customer's business but little or nothing in other segments. From survey research we learned that although Emerson typically was viewed as the global leader for a given customer's supply base, often we had only 10 percent or so of the total potential. From our customers' perspectives, the marquee account program gave them access to the broad range of our products, services, and solutions while also simplifying their relationship with us. For us, the upside in the first ten accounts we targeted represented hundreds of millions of dollars.

The marquee account approach produced immediate growth for Emerson. We spread the idea into the Network Power, Climate Technologies, and Professional Tools businesses and expanded the coverage to include more of our Process Management customers.

Given our product breadth and technology base, Emerson frequently stands as the most important supplier to an industry. As our relationships with customers mature, they demand greater integration with us, including more efficient ways to exchange information. Advances in information technologies allowed us to build customer portals aligned with our business platforms. We launched a series of *common customer interface* projects, which became another important initiative. The new interfaces represented yet another tangible shift away from autonomous divisions and helped make our business platforms more of a reality, even down to the level of day-to-day transactions.

Deeper and more prominent customer connections give us more opportunities to increase value to customers, ranging from providing simple order-related information to giving them access to broad technical knowledge databases and configuration tools that support customer applications. More important, both our common customer interface portals and our database marketing efforts place Emerson in more constant and meaningful contact with our customers.

Peters showed us that IT offered still greater potential to help us address the growth issue. During the first years of targeting higher growth, we were consumed by resource limitations that precluded investment in many important aspects of the program. In recent years, the Internet and lower costs of global connectivity allow our divisions to draw on the intellectual capacity of human resources throughout the world to support our customers and add value in ways unique to a global technology leader like Emerson.

ClosetMaid, for example, uses architects in the Philippines to provide design advice to retail customers who want to remodel their storage spaces. Via phone or the Internet, a customer quickly gets a customized design with details on what to buy at, say, The Home Depot. Such a model lets everyone win: customers get exactly what they want, and we sell more ClosetMaid goods through The Home Depot. Other divisions and businesses took note of ClosetMaid's success and began to use technology-based resources and Internet tools to support customers.

It takes time to upgrade a management capability like marketing and to create best practices. We test new ideas via pilot programs with a single division or customer segment before applying the concept more broadly. The ultimate value to Emerson shareholders is realized only later, when initiatives are fully exploited across the company. After the practices are piloted and understood, the next challenge is to apply the discipline of ensuring that all divisions take advantage of this skill and know-how, a challenge supported by the Emerson management process. Although the management process does not create skills, it supports their deployment, monitors applications, and measures their effectiveness.

In the customer area, we eventually applied these disciplines by developing the *customer capability model*. This tool measures each division's progress in adopting advances in customer marketing techniques and interfaces. This matrix approach assesses each division's development as it progresses through four levels (no activity, pilot programs, commitment, and completion) for the following capabilities:

1. Customer data and the development of systematic contacts

2. Customer support resources and advanced value-added activities and services

3. Customer interface and access to transactional and knowledge-based information

4. Deployment of resources for most effective back office support

Solutions

In the early phases of the growth initiative our goal was to grow by expanding our served markets. However, as we worked with outside experts a new theme began to emerge. Following the work of Lisa Fortini-Campbell, a professor at Northwestern, on customer satisfaction, we developed database marketing campaigns and started dialogues with end users, focusing on their motivations and needs. We were excited to realize that many customers viewed Emerson—with our global reach, leading-edge technology, best-cost position, and wide-ranging product scope—as an obvious source to provide solutions for their needs. Encouraged, we dug deeper to increase our understanding of these motivations and needs.

The process of understanding the customer is an example of keeping it simple. It takes energy and objectivity to research and listen, to segment a market into customer groups, and to transform their views into simple descriptions of their needs and economic trade-offs. Only after this work is done is it possible to craft a high-potential plan. Peters and Button Bell led us in making tools (such as focus groups) and quantitative techniques (such as discrete choice analysis) available to the divisions.

As we learned more about customers' perspectives and their unmet needs, we uncovered a reason our early growth programs fell short of expectations. It wasn't only the timing of our ideas relative to customers' willingness to accept them. At times, the ideas driving our growth programs evolved from our manufacturing mind-set of packaging our technologies and capabilities into solutions looking for problems. These products were not what real customers wanted or needed.

It required a change in mentality for us to develop the ability to group our products and cooperate on an integrated approach to a particular customer. We had succeeded for years by selling components, but now we faced a choice: change, or abandon our objective to achieve above-average returns. Our traditional focus on components constrained us because it denied us the opportunity to add value beyond basic manufacturing competencies. To continue to be a key contributor to

EXHIBIT 8-3

Solutions and services expand served markets: 1.25 → 2.0X

Leverage our strong technology and component position to add more value and expand served market.

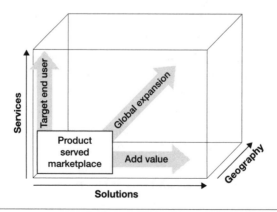

our customers' needs and success, we had to find new ways to cooperate across divisions—from joint engineering to surmounting transfer
price barriers—as well as with networks of extended partners (see exhibit 8-3).

The opportunity to provide solutions has a particularly strong fit
with our platform strategies that serve OEMs, such as makers of appliances and HVAC systems. In these industries, Emerson is often re-
garded as an excellent partner. With broad requirements for technology
development and added resources, coupled with our deeper understanding of end users, a powerful imperative is created to pull Emerson
into an OEM's innovation process.

New Business Models and Industry Reinvention

As noted in chapter 4, we recognized the tremendous potential of new
information technology to cut costs and raise productivity, and we pursued these goals intently. At the same time, we were able to apply the
savings from our cost-reduction and productivity programs to increased
investment in growth programs.

But as the demand for solutions became clearer, we began to understand the potential for entirely new approaches to serving our industries. In many instances, employing the Internet and alternative
resource scenarios not only solves customers' problems but also dramatically lowers their cost structure. Following Hamel, we term these
opportunities new business models.

Such opportunities often emerge as our most significant programs
to improve potential revenues and profits. They involve cultivating a
close relationship with end users. In climate technologies, for example,
we formed a new division, Emerson Retail Services, that is revolutionizing energy management in retail spaces such as supermarkets and
convenience stores. Other divisions are using the Internet to target
smaller OEMs that previously could not be served economically via a
direct sales force. By offering easy access to transactions in conjunction with 24/7 technical support, this technology now makes it feasible
to serve this new class of accounts.

Creating new business models is the most direct response to the
challenge Hamel presented a decade ago for us to reinvent our industries. It is the ultimate objective for businesses that master both an
understanding of their end customers and the deployment of new

information technology. The new models may produce substantial growth in revenues and earnings for a broad range of Emerson divisions.

Reorganization

The development of the corporate brand and our new strategy to sell services and solutions prompted necessary changes in our organization. At the level of the organization structure, we projected new outward-looking faces for the businesses, which we defined as growth platforms. Each bore a new *overbranded* identity under the Emerson brand (see exhibit 8-4). Thus our motors and appliance components business was presented to customers and investors as Emerson Appliance Solutions, the HVAC business as Emerson Climate Technologies, and so on.

To foster cooperation across the divisions in each business, we applied both the carrot and the stick. We preached the importance of collaboration and promoted executives who were outstanding team players. We also modified our personnel assessments to take account of performance in team and collaborative contexts (see chapter 3).

As we got better at reviewing the divisional growth plans, we learned that we had significant problems in some units, which remained too focused on profit and division autonomy. Simply stated, some managers still didn't "get" growth. After years of trying, they remained incapable of generating ideas and viable programs. Worse, some believed

EXHIBIT 8-4

Emerson brand architecture

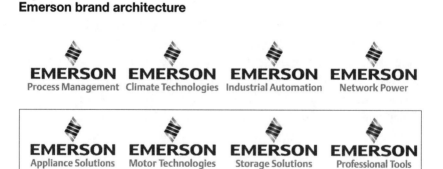

Note: The four platforms in the box are reported as the Appliance & Tools business segment.

that we weren't serious about growth and thought that they would continue to thrive as long as they generated profits.

This was a frustrating problem. It was sobering to conclude that some great people with whom we had worked closely for years would not succeed in meeting our new expectations. They were great at delivering profits but could not marry that gift with the willingness and ability to generate faster growth—even with the idea generation process and other supports we provided.

In the end, we heeded the counsel of Michael Hammer, another prominent management consultant, who pointed out that in a tough competitive environment it is costly to retain employees who cannot perform their jobs to an acceptable standard. His advice resonated at Emerson, where our philosophy is to try to help people who are willing to change and have the capacity for it. On the other hand, our belief in high standards of performance and being tough but fair with people mandates that we have low tolerance for those who don't try to change or who resist it.

Finally, the ongoing IT revolution stimulated fresh thoughts about activities we had to continue to perform ourselves, as opposed to those that could be outsourced. Conceiving of the twenty-first century as a century of networks accords well with Hamel's notion of core competencies that are essential to the long-term health and survival of individual corporations. No single corporation can possibly create and sustain all capabilities to win on a global basis with complex technical products in an interdependent world. To truly innovate, many levers are required, and companies must develop processes that allow for dependencies on others—other people who are part of the team and with whom we share the rewards of the value we create. Thus we began to see another dimension of e-commerce, one that could ultimately help the company become more intimately interconnected with suppliers, partners, and customers.

Repositioning

Beyond the plans and activities of the businesses and the divisions, the corporation as a whole carries the responsibility to allocate resources to investments that will yield the greatest long-term returns. This imperative requires making some trade-offs: short-term versus long-term, profit versus growth.

Emerson's success and reputation in the second half of the twentieth century reflected an ability to manage these trade-offs successfully, producing consistent earnings growth. As we looked ahead into the late 1990s and early 2000s, however, we understood that meeting higher investor expectations would entail taking greater risks, especially in considering acquisitions that would be dilutive. We also knew that our continued success as measured in consistent annual increases in earnings would therefore be less certain.

Our work on branding had revealed enthusiasm throughout the company for increasing cooperation across the divisions and for moving forward with our business platform strategy. This approach was the right thing to do, and we were confident that it would spur growth across the company. This encouraged us to investigate expanding into other areas with more dynamic market potential, especially considering our strong desire to shift our business mix to faster-growth markets.

In the late 1990s, it was apparent that our traditional businesses in appliance components, tools, and industrial automation would not help us reach our growth objectives because the markets were expanding too slowly. Although our process management and climate technologies businesses were growing faster, they could not by themselves generate the growth we needed. We needed to bolster these businesses while also adding another growth platform.

We chose to build from our foundation in electronic products (see chapter 6), which seemed highly promising because of the explosive growth in the number of customers in the telecommunications industry. Increasing the electronics content of our portfolio, we believed, would increase Emerson's underlying growth rate through economic cycles.

During the late 1990s, we spent approximately $3.5 billion on large acquisitions to strengthen our Process Management and Network Power businesses. At the same time, we made numerous small acquisitions to bolster our capability to offer services and solutions, a capability that was important to our platform strategy. We coupled these purchases with significant divestitures. We believed that this repositioning of the portfolio would enable us to hit our growth target.

Meanwhile, we made the company more subject to the economic cycles of the electronics business. We did not fully understand what that meant because we had never been through one of these cycles. However, we suffered the consequences with the collapse of the technology bubble in 2001. Our response to these new circumstances is covered in David Farr's epilogue (following chapter 9), but we remain convinced that our decision to increase the electronics content of our portfolio was right and that Emerson is positioned for faster long-term growth.

Assessing the Transformation: Toward a Balanced Management Process

Reflecting on the decade or so we spent immersed in the growth challenge, we can extract several lessons. This was—and probably still is—one of those areas in which, at the outset, the magnitude and extent of necessary changes could not be fathomed. We learned that applying our management process to an area in which we lacked fundamental skills simply did not work. Yet asking why the management process alone failed to fix Emerson's growth problem is the wrong question.

After several years of diligent effort, we stood back and reflected. In 1997, our team was objective about our slow progress, and everyone listened. We had made progress but not at a satisfactory rate. My instinct always is to question what we're doing, in good times and bad. When you ask meaningful questions in a culture of high performers, many people will want to contribute and bring fresh perspectives to the process.

The next few years were revealing. Certainly we started to find the keys to growth that we were missing, and we added dimensions to our program that distinguished our marketing. Emerson management, for the most part, discovered its willingness and even desire to adopt a more progressive approach that balanced growth and profit.

Have we succeeded? Time will tell. I can say only that since we embarked on this path, a majority of Emerson divisions have gained significant market share. Today's business portfolio has been reformulated through acquisition and divestiture as well as geographic investments, to the point that the base business has meaningfully higher end-market growth. And a study of the corporation's migration to business platforms, each with contemporary brands, and how they conduct business—offering solutions and services, using marquee account programs, and building common, business-level portals—shows a very different Emerson.

Have we changed our management process? Again, this is perhaps the wrong question. My feeling is that through this experience, the process has been further validated and proven to have broad applicability. These efforts have shown that the fundamentals of simplicity, challenge, follow-up, and persistence are compelling throughout a broad range of management tasks, whether they are profit-related or growth-related. What works in each context is to blend deep skills with a strong process that enhances their application. Our managers realized that it was the underlying consistency of our profitability that afforded them the time to put these new competencies in place. This capability reflects the strength and momentum of the Emerson culture and the energy required to make lasting changes of great magnitude.

There are many reasons for me to be proud of the Emerson managers with whom I served. Progress on the growth initiative certainly ranks high among them. What may be most significant is that our team achieved this progress without putting the company at significant risk. At the outset, it was not clear to me that management could add this dimension without compromising our emphasis on profit and consistency. For example, I feared that we might have to change our incentive or compensation structure to emphasize the importance of growth at the expense of profit. Those fears evaporated, however, as we began work and made headway.

In summary, growth is not replacing profit as an ultimate objective for Emerson; rather, growth is supplementing profitability. We continue to believe that profitability is a state of mind and that commitment to profitability is a necessity. Yet, as Emerson goes forward, a new set of capabilities is woven into the fabric of our culture. Although these capabilities add an important new dimension to our management process, it is important to understand that they do not replace our principles. Instead they enhance our management processes and benefit from the disciplines and rigor that have been, and always will be, important to Emerson managers.

9

Leadership Succession

*One of a leader's most important jobs
is to develop other leaders.*

—Emerson axiom

E merson has had only three CEOs in the past fifty years. The
third, David Farr, took over in October 2000 at the age of forty-
five. There is a very strong possibility, in other words, that the
company will have only three CEOs during a stretch of seven decades.

This leadership continuity is an enormous advantage for Emerson.
It reinforces the consistency we seek and limits the possibilities of our
making unnecessary changes in direction or policy. It also sets senior
executives' expectations and dampens organizational politics. When
CEOs take over at a relatively young age and serve long tenures, there
is less jockeying for position than in the senior ranks of many big corporations. Rather, the senior people at Emerson are more focused on
doing their jobs without giving much thought to whether one day they
will become CEO. Our system also breeds in the senior ranks strong
loyalty to the company and its management team and process.

The benefits of leadership continuity at Emerson make the selection of the CEO a critical matter. A mistake has bitter consequences
for any organization, but at Emerson the consequences would be magnified because we are accustomed to stable leadership and consistent

performance and we recognize the connection between them. Thus when we take up the challenge of identifying a new leader, we take particular care to get it right.

Our approach to a decision of this magnitude is illustrated in the most recent leadership transition at Emerson.

LEADERSHIP SUCCESSION IN PERSPECTIVE

When I began to plan my succession in the mid-1990s, I had a wealth of experience on which to draw. I had been CEO for more than two decades and, of course, was the result of the previous selection process. I had years of service as a director at Anheuser-Busch, SBC Communications, BP, Morgan Stanley, IBM, and elsewhere, and I had witnessed a number of executive transitions. By virtue of my position, moreover, I had regular contact with and many friends among CEOs of other major organizations who had views on succession as well as personal experience to share.

In considering the next succession at Emerson, however, I knew that we had to proceed in a way that was consistent with the company's approach to any major initiative—through careful planning and evaluation. I also reflected on what had happened decades earlier, when the board had chosen me as Buck Persons's successor.

The circumstances of my selection were unusual, and I learned important lessons from the experience. When Buck began searching for a successor, I was not a candidate. I was in my mid-thirties and already head of a successful engineering and consulting firm, Lester B. Knight & Associates (LBK). Emerson was a major client and I knew it very well, having led many consulting studies throughout the company in the 1960s and early 1970s and having served on the boards of two Emerson divisions. I also knew Buck very well. I had worked closely with him in several major assignments, including an organizational study and another on Emerson's expansion overseas.

When he reached his early sixties, Buck asked me to help him with the succession. He was still vigorous and clearly in charge, but he believed that Emerson would require new leadership to sustain its momentum. He also recognized that the selection process would require time, and he didn't want to undertake it under pressure. Most of the senior-line executives at corporate headquarters were not much younger than Buck himself, a circumstance that prompted him to look elsewhere.

One of his key concerns was that the CEO be young and energetic, with time to leave a mark. "I don't agree with the General Motors plan, where somebody finally gets on the executive committee, and if he waits long enough, he's in there [as president] for three years," he once observed. "I think you ought to give somebody a chance to really evolve his own style, and be in there long enough to give it a go."

Although Emerson had developed a cadre of excellent young general managers in the divisions, Buck believed that they lacked the breadth of experience that came from working in a variety of businesses and assignments. Thus he began to look outside the company, working with a committee of the board and with my LBK colleague Allan Gilbert and me to identify candidates having international experience, an engineering background, an understanding of cost-reduction and cost accounting procedures, and, significantly, a willingness to fit into the successful system that was Emerson.

"We must have looked at a hundred people on paper, and I must have interviewed forty-five of them," Buck later said. "In many cases, I interviewed good men who said, 'Well, Mr. Persons, I'll come in here and at the end of a year, I'll let you know how I'm going to run this business.' Invariably, I'd have to say, 'Well, we know how to run this business. We're looking for somebody who will come along and fit into this picture.'"

After we whittled down a long list to a few candidates, Buck was still dissatisfied. The more he pondered the question, the clearer it seemed that Emerson's next CEO should have the qualities he himself had manifested in 1953, when, at age forty-four, he had been selected by the board. These included energy, youth tempered by broad experience, and an outstanding track record.

Buck did not see these qualities in the right measures in the official candidates, but he perceived them in me. One day he broached the subject to me directly, asking whether I'd consider becoming his successor. I was honored, of course, but I had just acquired control of LBK and had big plans for the business. So I turned him down. I continued to think about the offer, though, and in the fall of 1972 I changed my mind. I went to see him and asked to be considered. He was delighted and shortly thereafter presented me as his choice to the board. In December 1972, I was elected vice chairman, with the expectation that I would take over as Emerson's CEO the following year.

This experience remained with me as I began thinking about recommending my successor to the board. I, too, wanted someone energetic, with a deep understanding of and appreciation for Emerson's management process, and the likelihood of a long tenure. The company was operating at a high level, and there was no need to tinker with our sources of success. I also believed in allowing ample time for the process to work. I did not want to make this decision under time pressure or merely to promote someone who was at the right age and in a big job. It would not take long to identify the most likely candidates, but I wanted to test them in a variety of ways, including in stretch assignments, to see how they would fare and who would emerge as the best choice. That process, I believed, should not be rushed.

There was still another reason to take the time to get the right answer. Two senior colleagues—Al Suter and Bob Staley—both vice chairmen, were close in age to me and likely to retire at about the same time. Thus the leadership transition would involve not only a new CEO but also a generational change and a new top management team. It was vital to stage and manage the selection process to minimize loss of the next-generation top executive talent we had labored hard to develop. In many companies, the finalists who do not get the top job decide (or are encouraged) to leave. In my view, such an outcome at Emerson would be a terrible waste. I wanted the next CEO to have the benefit of the talent and experience of the other finalists in the new management team.

LAUNCHING THE PROCESS

I began the conversation about leadership succession with the board in the mid-1990s, although there was no urgency to do so. I turned sixty in 1996 and had an evergreen employment contract. Although I had given no signals about my eventual retirement and no one on the board was asking, I knew that it would take time to make the right decision about Emerson's next leader and thus decided to initiate the process. Thereafter I discussed the matter periodically with the compensation committee of the board.

I also consulted with trusted colleagues and advisers about the process and prospective candidates. Initially this list included Al Suter and Bob Staley; Jo Ann Harmon Arnold, head of executive compensation; Bill Anderson, our chief contact at Fleishman-Hillard and a person with whom I had worked closely; and Mike Murray, a senior partner at McKinsey, who had headed many engagements for us. Later, some other people joined. I used the group as a kind of steering committee. We did not gather at the same time in the same room, however, until the very end of the process. Nonetheless, this informal steering committee, like the board's compensation committee, proved to be an invaluable resource for me throughout the selection process.

In one of the early steps, Murray helped me put together a list of the qualities it takes to run the company, which I annotated and shared with the board (see exhibit 9-1). I grouped my points into three categories—energy, leadership, and personal qualities—and the list was based heavily on my experience as CEO. Of course, the list includes qualities that are desirable in the CEO of any big company. At Emerson, though, these qualities are essential. The CEO must drive the management process, an exceptionally demanding responsibility that requires enormous energy to stay abreast of numerous commitments on a crowded calendar. The CEO must be able to preside at planning conferences and ask the right questions and demand well-supported answers. The CEO also must be able to set and observe high standards and command loyalty and respect. The eventual choice would have to be outstanding in all of these areas.

EXHIBIT 9-1

What it takes to run Emerson

Energy
- Enormous personal energy and stamina; strong bias for action

Leadership
- Strategic sense
- Ability to motivate and energize others; infectious enthusiasm to maximize the organization's potential
- Builds a strong team and gets the best from others
- Outstanding oral communications
- CEO-level presence and participation in the industry and with customers

Personal qualities
- Smart
- Self-confident but knows what he or she doesn't know; listens
- Makes hard decisions—business and people
- Passion that is visible; maniacal customer focus
- Instinctive drive for speed and impact
- Relentless pursuit of performance
- Ability to deal with ambiguity
- Understanding of how the organization works

Emerson's organization approach (see chapter 3) ensured that we had a deep pool of internal talent. Senior managers in the divisions and businesses and at corporate headquarters were excellent. Given this strength, Emerson's powerful culture and distinctive management process, and its consistent profitability, neither the board nor I saw reason to consider an outsider. Indeed, one reason we had set up the businesses in the early 1990s was to give bigger jobs to our most talented general managers, thereby grooming them, along with certain senior corporate executives, for greater responsibilities. Most of these top performers were in their forties or early fifties and were committed to the company. We hoped and expected that they would provide management continuity through the transition process.

Narrowing the Field

Our organization and HR systems gave us detailed information about all of our key executives, and, of course, they were well known to top management through our annual planning and control cycles and through their performance. What we didn't know was how our people stacked up against external standards. In the summer of 1996, we began to answer that question.

We started by identifying the top potential candidates and then tested them using a technique developed by Hay/McBer, a unit of the Hay Group specializing in leadership development. I had seen this approach used successfully at IBM and knew also that PepsiCo and many other large companies had relied on it. Mary Fontaine of Hay/McBer administered the tests and scored candidates on three dimensions: achievement (drive to accomplish), affiliation (attachments and interpersonal qualities), and power (drive to wield it).

Over the years, Hay/McBer had built a huge database of results and had identified certain patterns in the scores that were characteristic of effective CEOs. The scores were seldom consistent across the three areas, but the balance and weighting were important predictors of leadership effectiveness.

From the first round of tests and some other indicators, four leading contenders emerged. In no particular order, they were as follows:

- Bill Davis, fifty-three, a senior executive vice president in charge of the process control business and, interestingly, the

son of a former Emerson president. Bill had done an outstanding job in several posts at the Skil division, including president
and general manager, leading a turnaround of that troubled
unit. From there, he became head of the tool businesses, an
assignment in which he was intimately involved in a major restructuring, including the formation and oversight of eight
global joint ventures.

- Jim Berges, forty-eight, a bright, hard-charging executive who
  had begun his career at General Electric before joining Emerson
  in 1976 in our motors business. He soon rose to become a division president, then a group vice president, and, in 1989, the
  business leader for the industrial components and equipment
  group, distinguishing himself in every role. Three years later, he
  became our first profit czar and ran the profit planning process.

- George Tamke, forty-nine, who had joined Emerson in 1989 as
  an executive vice president after successful careers at IBM and
  Cullinet Software, where he had served as president. At Emerson, he took responsibility initially for corporate technology and
  the company's electronics businesses. He had a tremendous capacity for work and did a remarkable job in a demanding, travel-
  intensive assignment at Astec in Asia before taking charge of
  the electronics, tools, and industrial components and equipment businesses.

- David Farr, forty-one, a bright and highly energetic executive who
  had joined us in the early 1980s as a raw MBA in the corporate
  finance group. He had attracted Bill Rutledge's attention and soon
  began a rapid climb up the ladder, serving successively as director of manufacturing, vice president of planning and development, president of Ridge Tool, and group vice president of
  industrial components and equipment. During the early and
  mid-1990s, he worked with Staley and Tamke in senior positions
  in Asia, culminating in a stint as CEO of Astec in Hong Kong.

All these executives were extremely talented and held the promise
of succeeding in the top job. Our next challenge was to identify which
of the four would be the best for Emerson. To get the answer, we followed a planned process involving informal discussions, formal evaluations, and on-the-job testing in bigger jobs.

In August 1996, I invited each of the four to meet with me, and we talked informally and hypothetically about succession and what each might do as Emerson's next CEO—what would be his priorities, who would constitute the top management team, whether he contemplated any changes in our strategy, organization, and management process, and how he thought about staging the transition. This proved an interesting exercise. George came the best prepared and gave the most thoughtful answers.

During the next few months, the selection process continued to focus on these four. To help gather more information we brought in Ann Beatty, chief operating officer of Psychological Associates, an executive development firm that had worked with Emerson for many years. Ann already knew each of the four, but I asked her to work with them on issues already known to us or highlighted in the Hay/McBer instrument. She added her own evaluations and provided coaching over many months. Meanwhile, Paul McKnight, vice president of organization planning at Emerson, also became involved, setting up additional measures, including 360-degree assessments of the candidates.

While these initiatives were under way, the logjam began to break. The oldest of the candidates, Bill Davis was acutely aware that the clock was ticking, and he did not want to pass up opportunities elsewhere while waiting at Emerson. In March 1997, he came to me with news that he would be offered the top job at R. R. Donnelley, a giant printing company based in Chicago. I told Bill that we were not yet ready to make a CEO selection, and he accepted the Donnelley job.

Bill's departure triggered a series of changes in the top ranks at Emerson and opened up fresh opportunities to test the candidates in new assignments. George Tamke became president of Emerson (and a few months later, COO), and Jim Berges became vice chairman, with responsibility for three of Emerson's major businesses: motors and appliance components, electronics, and industrial components and equipment. David Farr replaced Bill as head of process management at a crucial time in the evolution of that business.

Meanwhile, another executive, Charlie Peters, forty-one, emerged as a contender for the top job. One of the brightest and most productive executives I have ever known, Charlie had worked at our Browning division while still an undergraduate in an engineering co-op program and had remained with the company since, with two years off to earn an MBA at Harvard. He, too, climbed quickly through the ranks. He spent much of his career in planning, business development, and technology management assignments at both the division and the corporate level, but he also performed well as president of our Harris Calorific division. He had an infectious enthusiasm that he communicated to peers and subordinates alike. In 1997, he became Emerson's growth czar and pursued an ambitious and important agenda to develop a corporate marketing capability, build the Emerson brand, and lead the company's initial forays into e-business.

THE FINAL ROUND

During the next few years, I watched the candidates closely and continued to discuss their progress with the board and my informal steering committee, a group now expanded to include Paul McKnight, Ann Beatty, and Mary Fontaine. Meanwhile, Emerson revamped its organization to address the growth challenge (see chapter 8). We appointed senior operating executives to head each of our major business platforms, again with the intention of having a strong management team in place when the new CEO took over.

George Tamke remained the front-runner for the top job. Responsible for Emerson's operating results, he had the biggest job, and he delivered excellent results. In May 1999, on my recommendation, the board elected George as vice chairman and co-CEO. The title was perhaps misleading because he continued to report to me and my title remained CEO, but some people inside the company and many in the business press interpreted his promotion as the indication that I had chosen my successor. However, neither the board nor I had given him that assurance. I viewed George's new job as the final hurdle, one that I hoped he would clear. I did not believe it would be a sure thing, however, and I also indicated to the other candidates that nothing was yet fixed. Indeed, two of them were promoted on the same day as George: Jim Berges became president of Emerson, and David Farr became senior executive vice president and COO. Charlie Peters had been promoted shortly before, with responsibility for our industrial components and equipment businesses added to his portfolio.

In his new job George continued to produce excellent results, but he was not connecting well with some of our managers and he was concerned that he did not have formal assurance that he would replace me. He and I discussed the overall situation, and he made the decision to leave Emerson. I agreed with that decision. Soon after, he became a principal at private investment firm Clayton, Dubilier & Rice.

George announced his resignation on February 3, 2000. We parted amicably, and he remained on the board for a period of time. Generally, the press accounts emphasized other elements in—or believed to be in—the story. Some reported that George had lost a behind-the-scenes power struggle with me, something that was far from the truth. George is a fine executive who did excellent work for Emerson and who continues to do well in the world of private investments. He and I remain friends. However, time showed that he was not the best candidate to lead Emerson, and I believe that the episode validates our deliberate process for identifying the next CEO.

And so there were three finalists. Although their profiles differed somewhat, the tests, assessments, and evaluations indicated that each possessed the qualities to succeed. Obviously this was good news, although it complicated the task of choosing among them. There was as yet no hurry—I still had an evergreen employment contract—but I believed it was time to make the decision. To do that, I wanted to gather fresh information one last time.

THE CHOICE

In July 2000, I asked each finalist to schedule in the following month a meeting with me to discuss his views of "the challenges facing the next CEO of Emerson"—a kind of replay of the sessions I had held in 1996, but this time at the end, rather than at the beginning, of the process. In particular, I wanted them to consider and answer seven questions:

1. What are the strategic issues that Emerson will face in the future? What is/are the next box(es) on the Foundation for Growth chart (see chapter 2, exhibit 2-4)?

2. How would you organize the company as CEO: Who are the key people and how would you retain them?

3. What, if anything, would you change in the Emerson management process? Why?

4. Is e-business strategically important for Emerson? If so, how do you see our organization changing to deal with e-business?

5. If you are not the next CEO, whom would you recommend, and why?

6. Should I stay on as chairman and director? If yes, what would you expect from me in this role?

7. What is your feeling re: the timing of the change?

I gave them latitude to answer these questions in any manner and in any form they wished. After I confirmed the dates of their meetings, I set up a summit meeting of my colleagues and advisers to follow. I also gave some of them an assignment to rank and compare the three candidates on a variety of dimensions that I deemed important for a CEO. This list (see exhibit 9-2) was a somewhat expanded list of qualities that I had shared with the board, merged with the list of qualities of effective leaders described in chapter 3.

EXHIBIT 9-2

Template for evaluation

Leadership (rate 1, 2, or 3)	1	2	3
Committed to success			
Tough but fair in dealing with people			
Sets high standards of excellence			
Strong sense of urgency			
Involvement			
Provides environment for innovation			
Sets proper priorities			
Pays attention to detail			
Concentrates on positives			
Has fun			
(rate 1, 2, or 3)			
Leadership			
International experience			
Technology capability			
Acquisition and joint venture capability			
Strategic thinking ability			
Customer contact ability			
People skills			
Communication skills			
Commitment to Emerson process			

My discussions with the candidates were excellent—much better than they had been during the initial round four years before—although one candidate now stood out clearly. David Farr gave me a binder that bore the title "Nothing Great Is Ever Achieved Without Enthusiasm!" Inside he had answered all the questions well and concisely. He displayed complete mastery of our strategy and organization, and he showed particular sensitivity to the need to retain key executives on the top management team. He also gave careful thought to the transition, including the board's perspective.

For some time, I had been leaning in David's direction; he had five years of experience on the ground in Asia, and he had done an exceptional job in building a more coordinated process management business, reconciling and integrating differing positions among the component makers and the systems people. He also scored the best in the informal rankings I had asked my colleagues to make. His answers to me sealed the deal. He had grown tremendously during the process, and by the summer of 2000 he was clearly ready to step up to the top job.

At the summit meeting of the steering committee—the lone occasion during the whole process when my colleagues and advisers were all together with me in the same room—I presented my recommendation and the reasons for it. The group immediately endorsed my choice but also challenged me and made helpful suggestions about the timing of the transition and the steps we needed to take to avoid losing key executives. We discussed a schedule in which we would announce the transition in November, with the transition to take effect at our annual meeting in February. We also developed a plan to enlarge responsibilities for Jim and Charlie, although the particulars would be worked out with David, whom we knew would be amenable.

I shared my recommendation and preliminary plans for the transition with the board, which immediately endorsed David. The board also approved the general outline of the transition. With the board's decision made and plans taking shape, I spoke to each of the three candidates and explained the thinking behind the choice. David, obviously, was thrilled. Although the others, naturally, were disappointed, they were more than willing to stay on in expanded roles. An important factor in their decisions, I believe, was their trust in the process.

With these steps taken, it seemed to me, the board, and my steering committee that there was no reason to delay the announcement. We accelerated the transition from February to October but kept the news a closely guarded secret until I announced it first to our top three hundred managers at our annual corporate planning conference. The news came as a surprise to the organization, but David received a thunderous ovation—led, I'm pleased to say, by Jim and Charlie.

The new team took over at the end of October. The new Office of the Chief Executive consisted of David as CEO and COO; Jim as president, with responsibility for all corporate development activities, and as business leader for Emerson Network Power; Charlie as senior executive vice president, with responsibility for e-business and integrated marketing; and Walter Galvin continuing as senior EVP and CFO. All are members of the board. As Staley and Suter stepped into retirement and I stepped back from daily responsibility, the transition to the new team proved seamless.

REFLECTIONS ON THE PROCESS

Looking back on the process of leadership selection, I'm most proud of three things. First, I believe we found the right person in David, who possessed or acquired during the process all the qualities we had identified at the outset as essential in an Emerson CEO.

Second, we retained the other two finalists, who are still pouring their considerable talents into the company. Their decision to stay speaks volumes about the professionalism and personal qualities of these outstanding executives. I cannot say enough about my confidence in them and their value to Emerson.

Third, these two outcomes are the result of an effective process, one that all parties supported and trusted. We planned and executed the process with characteristic rigor and discipline. We designed tests and experiments and then applied the learning to the next round of tests and experiments. We mined existing data but supplemented it with fresh information and then examined the amalgam from multiple angles and perspectives. We asked tough questions and demanded carefully reasoned answers. We never acted on hunches or settled for halfway analysis. Nor did we reach unwarranted conclusions, or indeed any conclusions, prematurely.

In sum, we took the time and the care to get it right. We let the process run its course—one of Emerson's guiding principles and the hallmark of a great company.

Epilogue

Restructuring is a process that never ends.

—Emerson axiom

Six months after I succeeded Chuck Knight as Emerson's CEO in October 2000, we faced a significant issue we had not expected: with a sudden and sharp drop in revenues, we had to announce the end of our forty-three-year streak of annual increases in earnings and earnings per share. (However, our forty-eight-year streak of annual increases in dividends per share, begun in 1955, still continues, given the company's strong generation of cash flow.) It was a gut-wrenching moment for the senior management team, far more than just a symbolic change, and it was driven by extraordinarily adverse economic conditions that we didn't see ending very quickly.

Yet the end of the earnings streak really had no impact on how the company is organized and managed. In fact, it created a unique opportunity for us to accelerate restructuring and become far more aggressive in our global repositioning strategy. "Speed" and "asset repositioning" became part of our everyday language as we sought to strengthen our foundation for long-term growth, profitability, and competitiveness.

The engrained management process that had sustained our consistent earnings performance for so long proved just as valuable in giving us the tools to manage in extraordinary economic times. Executed by an experienced and highly motivated Emerson management team, the process enabled us to restructure the company quickly and efficiently and emerge from the market downturn stronger than ever.

Following the end of the earnings record, we endured declining underlying sales for ten quarters, and at a rate unprecedented in Emerson's modern history. Yet despite the very challenging environment and significant cash and people investments it took to restructure the company, we continued to make money for shareholders while preparing to accelerate our growth when the global economy recovered. During this period we also outperformed our competitors and many peers on key financial measures. This operating and financial performance is testimony to the power of the Emerson management process, the strong, disciplined organization put in place before the transition, and the industry-leading business platforms built during Chuck's tenure.

Over the past couple of years investors and friends have asked me why Emerson, with our emphasis on annual planning and disciplined control processes, didn't anticipate the downturn and keep the earnings string alive. It's a fair question, and in fact one we asked ourselves a lot during 2001. We believe in learning from mistakes, and we've analyzed this economic period extensively. With the benefit of hindsight, we might have paid more attention to disturbing indicators such as the decline of the NASDAQ after April 2000, the collapse of the so-called new economy stocks, and, especially, significantly above-average growth rates in telecommunications along with industrial investment for global capacity. This growth far outpaced historical norms and could not continue indefinitely. We also would have noticed U.S. manufacturers making significant gross fixed investment in North America and parts of Europe ahead of long-term trends in demand, and some customers "double ordering" to keep their position in our production queues. At the time, though, the signals were ambiguous and people were proclaiming that the "new economy" and the Internet had permanently altered the economic fortunes of certain industries. In addition, demand continued to boom through the first four months of fiscal 2001.

Although we might have done a better job in preparing for the economic bubble that was building, the real significance of this experience is not that the management process should always keep us out of trouble—although it will do so in almost all situations—but instead that when times of extraordinary struggle inevitably appear, our process gives us a proven and solid management approach to use in working through the issues effectively and taking quick action.

THE END OF THE EARNINGS STRING

During my first two quarters on the job, Emerson recorded some of the best results in our history. In the spring of 2001, however, the monthly presidents' operating reports and other indicators revealed the onset of a sharp downturn. Orders declined rapidly and customer shipment requests were being pushed out. The bottom fell out of the telecommunications equipment market, and demand throughout our businesses worldwide began to soften and decline—an extremely unusual and unlikely occurrence. In prior downturns, the diversity of our businesses, customers, and geographical markets had cushioned us from declines in certain areas. This time, everything went down at once—and very quickly—as the bubble burst.

We kept a close eye on the situation, and, by late June, we knew we had to take business actions far beyond those already under way as our sales weakened and margins declined. It was clear that we had to reset expectations significantly and take much stronger actions to preserve our financial strength and prepare for the challenging economic times that were fast approaching. Whether we could continue the forty-three-year earnings record, however, was an open question, one that looked very challenging given trends in orders and sales.

None of us wanted to end "The Record," which was a big part of Emerson's heritage. We debated our options. We might have been able to keep the string going by, for example, delaying and cutting strategic investments or by making other changes, such as staging major facility and operational restructuring and repositioning actions over a much longer period. (It's important to consider this debate in context: it took place before the terrorist attacks on the United States on September 11, 2001, an event that sharply worsened the global economic climate and downturn. At the time, we did not appear to be facing more than a normal economic downturn after a strong growth period—although we later learned differently, especially after the September 11 tragedy.) But we didn't debate long.

As we considered our options, it became clear that keeping the earnings string alive risked eroding the long-term growth prospects of the company. To accommodate the growth and business repositioning investments of the late 1990s, we were already leveraged at levels higher than normal, and we did not believe it was prudent to increase these burdens. We also needed to protect the technology and new product programs that would carry the company forward as it continued its shift to a higher-tech business mix. Finally, we needed to press forward with investments in key emerging global markets, such as China, India, Eastern Europe, and Russia, which were quickly opening up. Preserving the earnings string conflicted strongly with our new business model and growth initiatives, so we decided, unanimously, to end it. When we later reviewed the decision with Chuck, we all agreed it was the right thing to do, given our responsibilities to shareholders and employees. The timing also was right. Given the inevitability of the necessary changes, there were strong advantages in moving fast to make it happen and get ahead of the power curve.

Clearly our management process helped us restructure the company quickly and in a well-organized way. It enabled us to act in a disciplined, coordinated manner across all businesses, as corporate executives, business leaders, and division management pulled together to identify, financially evaluate, and execute the required actions. We trusted and followed the process. We involved the board of directors, developed an action plan, supported it with extensive communications, and then executed and measured our progress.

The plans flowed out of our review of the long-term strategies for growth, profitability, and expected returns for each business and division. As noted in chapters 2 and 4, these strategies include plans and programs to be implemented over a five-year period. We agreed that our time horizon had to be less than two years to take advantage of the window that had opened and to gain a stronger competitive advantage. Then we followed the playbook already in hand and developed additional plans as needed. To pay for the initial restructuring, we took a $377 million earnings charge in 2001 and began executing.

In mid-July we announced the decision to end the earnings string. It came as a shock for many of the employees, but we did not waste time reflecting on events we couldn't change or control, and we quickly moved on. We emphasized to employees that we had embarked on a new journey together to rebalance the asset base and business makeup of the company for a new global environment. Our profit margin would suffer—although we would remain relatively profitable—but we were going to do some things differently and move faster.

Throughout these challenging times we stressed three major points. First, we wanted to get the restructuring done as quickly as possible. Second, we wanted to focus the business investments so that when the economy rebounded we could accelerate sales and earnings growth ahead of the competition. And third, we wanted to significantly improve our asset utilization as measured by free cash flow and return on total capital.

A key part of the execution plan involved communicating to the entire organization the issues we faced, the actions to be taken, our near-term and long-term goals, and our expectations of what the company would look like when we came through this restructuring period. It was important for people to know that the company was strong and financially solid and that our actions would make Emerson even stronger against our global competitors. Consequently, we began a live quarterly global Webcast to lay out the issues and actions (this, by the way, remains an effective means of communicating the current issues and directions). Second, we laid out an extensive strategic plan and communicated it at the October 2001 corporate planning conference. Moreover, each year we have followed up with employees and the board of directors on where we stand relative to these goals and objectives.

During the next two and one-half years we underwent a painful restructuring that heavily impacted global operations. We sought to increase manufacturing and engineering investments in lower-cost regions of the world and to align our total operational footprint more closely with our expanding global customer base. This meant making significantly more investment in emerging markets while focusing the right resources on core North American and Western European markets; there was no intention, nor will there be any intention, of walking away from these core markets.

Relying on the plans and disciplines of the management process, we rationalized current operations, built new facilities in low-cost locations, and accelerated some new product development and engineering programs and projects while terminating others. More than fifty plants and more than twenty thousand employees were affected. We divested ten divisions (representing $1 billion in sales) that no longer fit our long-term strategic objectives, especially our expectations for growth and return. We also completed several important acquisitions, including Avansys in China (see chapters 5 and 7) and in 2004 the Marconi DC power business in the United States.

To ensure that we had the right management team focused on the right areas, we made extensive use of our organization planning process during this period of rebalancing our physical and personnel assets. Again, we had a playbook and process that allowed us to eliminate some positions, expand the responsibilities of some executives, and re-assign still other individuals to new roles. This process was not pain-less, but it did not consume an extraordinary amount of time or become distorted by internal politics. Everyone knew that we were on a journey involving significant changes to Emerson's total cost structure and global competitive position. Our organization planning approach and tools gave us a deep understanding of the strengths and weaknesses of our key global managers, as well as their developmental needs. This foun-dation of information helped us identify the right individuals quickly and confidently.

Quick action and tough decisions paid off immediately. We re-mained highly profitable compared with our competitors and peers, and the Emerson stock price generally outperformed key competitive bench-marks after we worked through the initial market hit following the an-nouncement of the end of the earnings string. Better still, we now have a cost structure and a global engineering base that allow us to compete effectively anywhere in the world. Best of all, after economic conditions began to pick up in the late summer of 2003, we've been growing rap-idly—as is evident from our recent very strong performance.

Our management process, combined with the contributions of the entire organization, drove these favorable outcomes. Clearly, the deep understanding of goals, and the embedded knowledge throughout the company on how to execute them, paid off.

ADJUSTING THE PROCESS

The new business environment we faced mandated minor adjustments to the management process as we moved Emerson to the next level. For example, we strengthened our organization planning process by adding formal reviews at the business-leader level to ensure that the right lead-ership team was in place and that we were identifying and developing the next generation of leaders to manage the global business structure. These sessions give us a better sense of resources and evolving re-quirements as we develop growth opportunities to combine the total product offering into services and solutions for global customers and as we leverage our capabilities across business platforms.

This initiative also calls for greater involvement of our top execu-tives with customers. Although I allocate as much time to planning and organization issues as Chuck did, I freed up more time to spend with customers and to sell Emerson's capabilities. I rarely travel outside the United States without meeting with at least one marquee customer, and I normally see two or three.

Another change involved a refinement of our financial goals. Our analysis of market valuations of premium-valued companies revealed that they did a superior job of balancing sales growth, operating margin improvement, free cash flow, and return on total capital (ROTC). Emerson has few peers in the ability to improve margins steadily, but we were not as strong in the other measures. We wanted to change that, both actually and in terms of investors' expectations.

Our historical financial model behind the earnings consistency record, for example, tended to emphasize margin improvement over asset efficiency (see exhibit 2-1 in chapter 2). So we modified our fi-nancial model to create long-term value—just as Chuck had done several times over the years when new circumstances warranted. We developed a model that encouraged and rewarded our managers to pay more attention to operating capital efficiency and free cash flow (see exhibit E-1). We intensified efforts to streamline inventories and im-plement principles and techniques of lean manufacturing across the front offices and factory floors; it was all about speed and using less invested capital to achieve our sales growth. We also used ROTC to set priorities among our many investment opportunities and divisional product lines—funding those having the biggest impact on corporate financial performance and that could enhance long-term value. If they didn't or couldn't meet our financial model objectives, they went onto the "Fix-it" or "Sell-it" list (see chapter 2).

Another important change was our choice not to worry about start-ing a new earnings string. Our focus is to enhance our long-term growth and earnings profile, even if it means accepting a more volatile

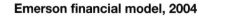

Emerson financial model, 2004

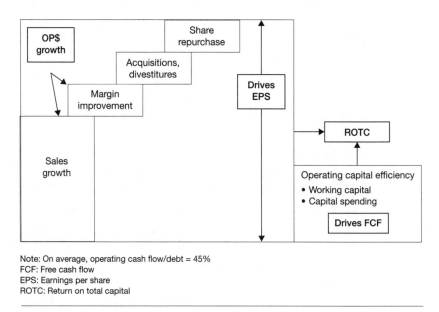

Note: On average, operating cash flow/debt = 45%
FCF: Free cash flow
EPS: Earnings per share
ROTC: Return on total capital

earnings profile. Emerson is now a different kind of company than it was decades ago, and its traditional metrics are less meaningful in the global economy of the twenty-first century. With the increasingly high-tech nature of our businesses and customer base, we have better growth prospects but also a different risk profile. We knew we were increasing our volatility when we made a series of acquisitions in the late 1990s and early 2000s, of course, but we had not yet built that consideration into our financial plan, incentives, and communications with investors.

The change is now reflected in our long-term growth and return goals, which no longer include earnings growth every quarter. We remain as dedicated as ever to delivering consistently high levels of earnings and profitability, but we've redefined what that means: not steady, incremental improvement from a high level, with all volatility dampened, but instead faster growth through the business cycles. This means accepting more variable earnings results, but at a higher long-term growth rate. We may have down stretches from time to time, but we expect to exceed historical growth rates significantly when times are good. The impact of this change is already apparent in the company's higher underlying growth rates as we rebound from the global recession.

STRENGTHENING OUR FOUNDATION

As I look back on this extraordinary time, three significant lessons stand out. First, despite the revenue decline and significant restructuring costs (nearly $1 billion over four years) we absorbed in adapting to a hostile environment, we continued to make money and generate high levels of free cash flow—enough to pay down debt levels, make acquisitions, and continue to extend our forty-eight-year record of annual increases in dividends per share.

Second, this global organization was not paralyzed by bad news nor by taking on challenging issues and targets. Following the downturn, which the September 11 tragedy made worse, we chose to accelerate the process of restructuring our global footprint, accomplishing in three years what it would have taken five or more years to accomplish in better times. And finally, keeping the top executive leaders together through the CEO transition was a huge benefit in dealing successfully with this challenge. I can't recognize or thank these individuals enough for what they accomplished. With the global economy coming back, we are well positioned to resume strong growth in sales, earnings, and free cash flow while also delivering consistently high returns.

Looking ahead, I view my job as building on the strong foundation that Chuck handed over to the new team in 2000. The company was in excellent shape, but as we all saw after the fact, we needed to reset the foundation with decisive actions—something that has happened. This management team faced the issues head-on, and I believe that the foundation for growth and profitability is even stronger after intensive work through three tough years. As we push hard to focus and improve our existing businesses, we're also looking to develop new business platforms. It takes years to form these platforms and make them into global leaders. Process Management, Climate Technologies, and Network Power each took a decade or more to emerge, and we can't afford to wait ten years for the next platforms to be developed. Therefore, we're starting now.

We developed a new scorecard (see exhibit E-2) to monitor and motivate the businesses in achieving key corporate business objectives. The scorecard consists of a matrix that arrays our businesses on the vertical axis, and our management objectives—which are tightly linked to our long-term goals—along the horizontal. These objectives consist of creating industry-transforming technology to ensure our continuing industry leadership; operating on a global scope to ensure worldwide market penetration; maintaining a contemporary customer interface to ensure that we're presenting ourselves clearly and easily to our customers as we strengthen our relationships with them; providing services and solutions to ensure that we're finding additional ways to add value to customers; and achieving capital and operating efficiency to ensure that we're taking advantage of our scale and employing our assets effectively. The number and size of the checkmarks indicate the score: two big checkmarks is best, and anything less than that indicates the need to make significant progress. The scorecard is like a map, laying out a journey that each business must invest in, develop the plans and organization to make happen, and embark upon for the company to reach our strategic goals.

Exhibit E-2 shows an example from our fall 2004 corporate planning conference. A number of businesses faced significant challenges. (Note that this is a living document and is updated every year; a current version would display different grades and checks.) The matrix isn't perfect. For example, businesses like Storage Solutions and Professional Tools have less opportunity through technology to transform their industries or to bundle products and services into solutions. Nonetheless, the scorecard clarifies our priorities and galvanizes our organization.

Incidentally, I use the scorecard in speaking to analysts and investors on the outside as well as with our management teams on the inside. All of them understand the importance of what we're focusing on, and they do react to change.

We're continuing to invest in a planned, orderly fashion in new technologies, growth programs, and businesses. With our core operations significantly restructured to be globally competitive, we now control our own destiny. Our management process remains at the heart of our success, and we have every confidence that it will continue to

EXHIBIT E-2

Emerson scorecard, fall 2004

	Industry-transforming technology	Global scope	Contemporary customer interface	Solutions and services	Capital and operating efficiency
Process Management	✓✓	✓✓	✓	✓✓	✓
Climate Technologies	✓✓	✓✓	✓	✓	✓✓
Network Power	✓✓	✓✓	✓	✓✓	✓
Appliance Solutions	✓	✓✓	✓	✓	✓✓
Storage Solutions	✓	✓	✓✓	—	✓
Motor Technologies	✓	—	✓	✓	✓✓
Professional Tools	✓	✓	✓	—	✓
Industrial Automation	✓	✓	✓	✓	✓

serve us well as we confront new challenges in the modern global economy. Emerson has a strong foundation on which to build for long-term growth, profitability, and value creation for our shareholders and customers.

—David N. Farr
Chairman and CEO
Emerson

Appendix A

Emerson Business Segments and Divisions

Network Power
    ASCO Power Technologies (automatic transfer switches)
    Astec (power supplies and electronic components)
    Emerson Network Power Systems (precision environmental control and site monitoring; uninterruptible power supplies and network protection products; power protection and voltage regulation equipment)
        Control Concepts
        Emerson Energy Systems Europe
        Emerson Energy Systems North America
        Emerson Network Power China
        Liebert Global Services
        Liebert Hiross
        Liebert North America
    Emerson Telecommunications Products (telecom and cable connectivity solutions)

Process Management
    Asset Optimization (software and service provider)
        CSI
        MDC
    Brooks Instrument (flow measurement)
    Daniel Industries (custody transfer solutions)

Fisher Regulators (gas regulators)
    China "Jeon" Gas Regulator Business
Fisher Valves (control valves and actuators)
    Valve Automation Division
Micro Motion (Coriolis mass flow)
Process Systems & Solutions (control systems and solutions for process,
power, water, and waste water applications)
    Performance Solutions
    Power & Water Solutions
    Process Systems
Rosemount (pressure and temperature transmitters; flow and level
instruments)
    Metran
    Rosemount Pressure
    Rosemount Temperature
    Saab Marine
Rosemount Analytical (gas and liquid analysis)
    Liquid Analytical
    Process Analytical

Climate Technologies

Copeland (compressors, refrigeration controls, and monitoring)
    Computer Process Controls (CPC)
    Copeland Asia Pacific
    Copeland Europe
    Copeland Refrigeration
    Copeland U.S. Air Conditioning
    Emerson Retail Services
Emerson Flow Controls (electronic flow controls)
Fusite (hermetic terminals)
Therm-O-Disc (temperature controls, sensors, and switches)
White-Rodgers (thermostats and gas control valves)

Industrial Automation

ASCO/Joucomatic (solenoid and pneumatic valves)
Branson (ultrasonic cleaning and material joining)
Buehler (material testing instruments)
Control Techniques (variable-speed drives)
EGS Electrical Group (JV electrical products)
Emerson Power Transmission (gears, bearings, reducers, cam followers)

Leroy-Somer (industrial motors, power transmission, and alternators)
  LS Fractional Motors
  LS Gears
  LS Global Alternators
  LS Integral Motors

Appliance and Tools

ClosetMaid (wire and laminate shelving systems)
  Do+Able Products
  Shanghai Jungkang
  Stack-A-Shelf
Emerson Appliance Controls (electronic timers and controls)
Emerson Motor Company (appliance, air moving, fluid, industrial, advanced, and hermetic motors)
  Automotive and Precision Motors and Drives
  Emerson Appliance Motors
  Emerson Appliance Motors Europe
  Emerson Ventilation Products
  Fluid Systems
  Heating and Air Conditioning Motors
  Hermetic Motors
  Industrial Motors
Emerson Tool Company (wet/dry vacuums, ceiling fans, and humidifiers)
  Air Comfort Products
Heating Systems (electric heating elements)
In-Sink-Erator (garbage disposers and hot water dispensers)
InterMetro (industrial-grade shelving)
Knaack (industrial storage equipment)
Ridge (professional plumbing tools)
Western Forge (hand tools)

Appendix B

The President's Operating Report—Page 5

The division president's operating report (POR) includes a single page of financial data, called the "Page 5," which is used monthly to assess the reasonableness of the individual division's current quarterly and annual expectations of sales and profit (see exhibit B-1 for an abridged hypothetical version). The sum of all Page 5s provides the same assessment for the total corporation.

The Page 5 captures and summarizes a large amount of information about division performance. As such, it is the focus of intense discussion at presidents' councils; as we say, "It draws a lot of fire."

The layout provides sixteen quarterly and four annual data points for six key lines of the profit and loss statement: current and prior month expectations for four quarters and one fiscal year, the original forecast, and the prior year's. Each month throughout the year, these data identify changes from the prior month's expectations, along with the source of these changes by individual division. Corporate and division management can then quickly follow up with appropriate actions.

If market or macroeconomic conditions change from what was forecast at the time of the financial review or if specific issues develop at individual divisions, the original forecast may become obsolete and is basically ignored throughout the year. In that case, management focuses attention on the current versus the prior month's expectations.

To test for the reasonableness of current expectations, the quarterly data provide an analysis of quarter-over-quarter comparisons—the prior quarter and the same quarter in the prior year. This allows division and corporate management to

"The Page 5" (President's operating report)

Emerson Division X
President's Operating Report
Run Date: 2/12/XX
Run Time: 10:16
Name Label: Division X

Emerson
Bridge schedule versus prior expected
Period ended January 31, 20XX

Company
Private

		Month Ago POR	Current POR Expectations	Original Forecast	Prior Year Actuals	% CY vs PY
	1st Quarter End December 31	**A**	**B**	**C**	**D**	**E**
1	Interco Sales	5,384	5,384	4,160	4,893	10.0
2	Net Sales	145,640	145,640	153,604	145,335	0.2
3	Gross Profit	36,967	36,967	41,569	38,490	(4.0)
4	% Sales	25.4%	25.4%	27.1%	26.5%	
5	S G & A	23,331	23,331	23,747	21,669	7.7
6	% Sales	16.0%	16.0%	15.5%	14.9%	
7	Operating Profit	13,636	13,636	17,822	16,821	(18.9)
8	% Sales	9.4%	9.4%	11.6%	11.6%	
9	Other (Inc)/Ded	884	884	1,227	235	276.2
10	EBIT	12,752	12,752	16,595	16,586	(23.1)
11	% Sales	8.8%	8.8%	10.8%	11.4%	
	2nd Quarter End March 31					
12	Interco Sales	5,241	5,241	4,452	4,493	16.6
13	Net Sales	152,370	149,370	152,370	144,010	3.7
14	Gross Profit	42,864	41,914	42,414	39,897	5.1
15	% Sales	28.1%	28.1%	27.8%	27.7%	
16	S G & A	24,023	23,898	23,898	22,403	6.7
17	% Sales	15.8%	16.0%	15.7%	15.6%	
18	Operating Profit	18,841	18,016	18,516	17,494	3.0
19	% Sales	12.4%	12.1%	12.2%	12.1%	
20	Other (Inc)/Ded	1,414	1,418	1,739	(155)	(1014.8)
21	EBIT	17,427	16,598	16,777	17,649	(6.0)
22	% Sales	11.4%	11.1%	11.0%	12.3%	
	3rd Quarter End June 30					
23	Interco Sales	5,968	5,968	4,608	4,292	39.0
24	Net Sales	163,053	164,000	159,090	150,440	9.0
25	Gross Profit	47,617	47,927	45,661	43,283	10.7
26	% Sales	29.2%	29.2%	28.7%	28.8%	
27	S G & A	24,271	24,396	24,396	23,331	4.6
28	% Sales	14.9%	14.9%	15.3%	15.5%	
29	Operating Profit	23,346	23,531	21,265	19,952	17.9
30	% Sales	14.3%	14.3%	13.4%	13.3%	
31	Other (Inc)/Ded	678	634	898	917	(30.9)
32	EBIT	22,668	22,897	20,367	19,035	20.3
33	% Sales	13.9%	14.0%	12.8%	12.7%	

(continued)

EXHIBIT B-1 *(continued)*

		Month Ago POR	Current POR Expectations	Original Forecast	Prior Year Actuals	% CY vs PY
	4th Quarter End September 30	**A**	**B**	**C**	**D**	**E**
34	Interco Sales	6,118	6,118	4,846	4,704	30.1
35	Net Sales	168,937	170,990	164,936	149,572	14.3
36	Gross Profit	47,525	48,165	45,825	42,504	13.3
37	% Sales	28.1%	28.2%	27.8%	28.4%	
38	S G & A	24,205	24,205	24,039	23,722	0.0
39	% Sales	14.3%	14.2%	14.6%	15.9%	
40	Operating Profit	23,320	23,960	21,786	18,782	27.6
41	% Sales	13.8%	14.0%	13.2%	12.6%	
42	Other (Inc)/Ded	504	544	661	973	(44.1)
43	EBIT	22,816	23,416	21,125	17,809	31.5
44	% Sales	13.5%	13.7%	12.8%	11.9%	
	Fiscal Year End September 30					
45	Interco Sales	22,711	22,711	18,066	18,382	23.6
46	Net Sales	630,000	630,000	630,000	589,357	6.9
47	Gross Profit	174,973	174,973	175,469	164,174	6.6
48	% Sales	27.8%	27.8%	27.9%	27.9%	
49	S G & A	95,830	95,830	96,080	91,125	5.2
50	% Sales	15.2%	15.2%	15.3%	15.5%	
51	Operating Profit	79,143	79,143	79,389	73,049	8.3
52	% Sales	12.6%	12.6%	12.6%	12.4%	
53	Other (Inc)/Ded	3,480	3,480	4,525	1,970	76.6
54	EBIT	75,663	75,663	74,864	71,079	6.4
55	% Sales	12.0%	12.0%	11.9%	12.1%	
56	Pretax	77,773	77,773	76,582	73,834	5.3
57	% Sales	12.3%	12.3%	12.2%	12.5%	(1.5)
58	Net Earnings	61,796	61,796	61,567	59,297	4.2
59	% Sales	9.8%	9.8%	9.8%	10.1%	

EBIT: Earnings before interest and taxes

identify where current expectations are unrealistic, either high or low, so that appropriate actions can be started before bad or good news shows up in the actual quarterly data.

This report quickly identifies a division that misses its sales and profit targets in the first quarter and then unrealistically increases later quarter results, or a division that exceeds first-quarter results and unrealistically lowers the later quarters. Quarter-to-quarter comparisons readily identify instances when fourth-quarter sales or profit margins (or both) increase out of line, on a year-over-year basis, compared with those experienced in prior actual quarters. Actions can then be started to reduce costs or increase later quarter expectations so that management can optimize the year's results and can be aware of those optimum numbers well in advance of year end.

Exhibit B-1 is an abridged, hypothetical Page 5 submitted in the middle of February for the close of January, during Emerson's fiscal second quarter. It details how the division's expectations for each quarter and the year now differ from its expectations at the financial review. Vertically, the form is divided into five sections, each containing a profit and loss statement. The first four rows show quarterly expectations; the final row is for the year. Within each section, column A spells out the division's expectation from the prior month, in this case from the end of December and Column B shows the current expectation by quarter. Column C illustrates the division's original forecast submitted at the financial review, and column D shows the prior year's actual results. Column E compares the current expectation to that of the prior year's actual results.

In this example, the division did not achieve its first-quarter forecast for either sales or operating profit margin. It currently expects further sales and operating profit margin misses in the second quarter. However, the division has assumed that it will realize the full-year sales and operating profit margin forecast. This would require unrealistic sales and profit margin improvement compared with that of the prior year and the current trends of the first two quarters. Looking at the data, corporate management would recognize that the division has an unrealistic current expected plan. Management would work with the division to adjust sales forecasts in the third and fourth quarters as appropriate and to immediately implement actions to bring costs down. The objective would be to develop a realistic plan to achieve the forecast operating profit margin or at least hold the prior year's operating profit margin.

Acknowledgments

The core concepts and principles in this book are those of Charles F. Knight and Emerson. Davis Dyer, a widely published business historian and coauthor of a history of Emerson published in 1990,* worked closely with Chuck to prepare this text. Most of the book illustrates the team spirit for which Emerson is justly renowned. The most common pronoun is *we*, a usage that reflects both the collaborative process of writing and, much more, Emerson's cohesive culture and the concerted efforts of a large organization in achieving high performance consistently over time.

We wish first to thank Emerson Chairman and CEO David N. Farr for his strong support and active participation in this project, including writing the Epilogue. We had virtually unlimited access to people and information at Emerson, and we are grateful to David for making that possible.

Bill Anderson of Fleishman-Hillard has been a steady and helpful presence throughout, as well as a particularly thorough and conscientious reviewer and skilled editor.

We wish also to thank a number of Emerson colleagues who contributed significantly to the content of this book. Jim Berges, Mark Bulanda, Jean-Paul Montupet, Charlie Peters, Bob Staley, Al Suter, and Jim Switzer all generated drafts and background papers on which we drew extensively.

Several other Emerson colleagues helped by contributing important information or by reading portions of the manuscript (sometimes several times) and offering numerous valuable comments: Jo Ann Harmon Arnold, Kathy Button Bell, Walter Galvin, Phil Hutchison, Ray Keefe, Randall Ledford, Paul McKnight, Scot Roemer, Tim Westman, and Wayne Withers. In addition, we benefited from comments on early drafts from two longtime directors—Dick Loynd and Gerry Lodge—

*Davis Dyer and Jeffrey L. Cruikshank, *Emerson Electric Co.: A Century of Manufacturing, 1890–1990* (St. Louis, MO: Emerson, 1990).

and from John Graham (Fleishman-Hillard), Stuart Greenbaum (Washington University), and Mike Murray (McKinsey).

Emerson executives who teach at the Emerson Leadership Program made their presentations available and answered any questions we had. These include (in addition to those already named) Craig Ashmore, Bob Cox, Larry Kremer, Ed Monser, John Rhodes, and Dennis Sollberger, as well as Ann Beatty (Psychological Associates). Phelps Jackson, Mike Rohret, William Vaughan, and Linda Wojciechowski of Emerson helped prepare the exhibits and appendixes. In addition, Olivia Burt provided administrative support during the early stages of the project.

Chuck Knight would particularly like to thank the outside Emerson directors who served during his tenure from 1973 to 2000 for their contributions and support. These include (in addition to individuals already named) David R. Calhoun Jr., George T. Pfleger, Joseph A. Frates, Gen. Bernard A. Schriever, USAF (Ret.), Robert H. McRoberts, Maurice R. Chambers, Gene K. Beare, Vernon R. Loucks Jr., Eugene F. Williams Jr., Louis J. Conti, Ramsay D. Potts, William M. Van Cleve, August A. Busch III, Robert B. Horton, David C. Farrell, Edward E. Whitacre Jr., Rozanne L. Ridgway, and Arthur F. Golden.

Chuck also expresses appreciation to a number of senior executives who served as directors or advisory directors during this period, including (in addition to those already named) J. Joe Adorjan, John M. Berra, Thomas E. Bettcher, Laurance L. Browning Jr., John W. Burge Jr., William L. Davis Jr., William L. Davis III, Charles A. Dill, Vincent T. Gorguze, Charles Hansen, James F. Hardymon, E. Lawrence Keyes, James J. Lindemann, Robert J. Novello, F. W. Ouweleen, Charles O. Planting, John C. Rohrbaugh, William A. Rutledge, Patrick J. Sly, George W. Tamke, Jan K. Ver Hagen, and John C. Wilson.

Chuck also wishes to thank colleagues who joined him in top management over the years who are too numerous to name here but several must be called out including (in addition to those already named) Ike Evans, Hal Faught, David Gifford, Allan Gilbert, Vern Heath, Claude Henry, and Ernie Lovelady.

Chuck would be remiss in failing to single out Les Heikkila, who joined Emerson in 1974 and built from scratch a premier corporate aviation department. Over these years he logged thirty-two thousand hours in the air, during half of which Chuck was his passenger.

Countless others in management, administration, and the hourly ranks helped make Emerson's achievements possible. It's impossible, of course, to credit all of them here, but it has been a privilege to work alongside them for these many years.

Chuck's father had a saying about setting personal priorities, starting first with health, second with family, and third with career. He noted the need to organize the first two so that you can focus on the third. Chuck's successful career rests on strong family bonds, with special, heartfelt thanks due to his wife, Joanne;

children Lester, Anne, Steve, and Jennifer and their spouses; and the Knights' twelve grandchildren.

Finally, this book is dedicated to the memory of W. R. "Buck" Persons, Emerson's chairman and chief executive officer between 1954 and 1973. When Buck arrived, Emerson was a small, troubled company with uncertain prospects. Nineteen years later, he left behind a strong, diversified, and well-managed organization, with key components of the management process beginning to emerge. It is no accident that Emerson's strong performance began on his watch.

Index

A.B. Chance, 51
AC/DC Electronics, 43
acquisitions
  average internal rate of return (IRR) on, 143–144
  benefits of, 143
  commitment to planning, 147–148
  compatibility with Emerson management process, 153–154
  contribution of management process, 148
  deal-making process, 155, 156, 157
  disciplined approach, 148–149
  due diligence and, 150–152, 157
  in Europe, 168–169
  people factor, 149–150
  post-deal integration, 158
  return to large deals, 145
  sponsorship requirement, 146–147
  strategic fit requirement, 152–153
  strong management team requirement, 153
  technology leadership and, 129
  top management involvement and, 146
  valuation, 154–155, 157
action-orientation at Emerson
  benefits of approach, 68–69
  color-coded chart use, 62, 63, 64
  communication emphasis, 57–59
  compensation policies, 65–66, 67, 68
  corporate organization, 54–55
  culture elements, 61
  key elements, 55
  management development and, 64–65
  management process and, 9
  organization review, 60, 62, 63
  principles for personnel development, 60
  staff size and, 56
Adorjan, J. Joe, 40, 145, 242
Advanced Design Center, 131, 132
Allen-Bradley, 149
Anderson, Bill, 210, 241
APO team, 112
Arnold, Jo Ann Harmon, 68, 210, 241
ASCO Valve, 47, 139, 173
Ashmore, Craig, 107, 242
Asia
  division-led penetration, 175–176, 177
  early initiatives, 172–173
  focus on China, 131–132, 141, 173–175
  management process application, 178–179
  materials procurement efforts, 112
  planning approach, 175
  sales results, 178
  strategic advantages gained, 176, 178

Asset Optimization Services, 138
Astec, 44, 79–80, 129, 139, 173
attributes of effective leaders
  acknowledging possibility of failure,
    82–83
  attention to detail, 81–82
  being tough but fair, 75–78
  commitment to success, 70–71
  focus on positives, 78–80
  have fun, 85
  personal involvement, 83–85
  priorities setting, 71, 74
  sense of urgency, 80–81
  setting high standards, 74–75
  summary, 72–73
Avansys, 44, 129, 140, 178
awards program, 133–134

Battelle Research Institute, 131
Beare, Gene K., 242
Beatty, Ann, 214, 215, 242
Beckmann, Jennifer Knight, 243
Berges, Jim, 74, 96, 97, 186, 213, 214,
    215, 241
Berman, Phyllis, 76
Berra, John, 37, 71, 78, 137, 242
Best Cost Producer strategy, 12,
    92–93, 166
Bettcher, Thomas E., 242
board of directors (BOD)
  role in control cycle, 37
  role in planning, 28–29
  technology expertise, 123–124
BOD. See board of directors (BOD)
brand management. See marketing
Branson, 47
Brooks Instrument, 40
Browning, Laurance L. Jr., 242
BSR International PLC, 44, 79
Bulanda, Mark, 241
Burge, John W. Jr., 242

Burt, Olivia, 242
Busch, August A. III, 242
Button Bell, Kathy, 65, 193, 196, 200,
    241

Calhoun, David R. Jr., 242
Caterpillar, 48, 172
CESET, 168, 169
Chambers, Maurice R. "Dude," 78, 242
chief technology officer (CTO),
    127–128
China, 131–132, 141, 173–175
Christophersen, Henning, 171
Clairson, 47
climate profile score, 58, 59
ClosetMaid, 47, 198
color-coded chart, 62, 63, 64
common customer interface projects,
    198
communicative management, 57–59
compensation policies, 65–66, 67, 68
Conti, Louis J., 242
control cycle
  benefits of approach, 38–39
  BOD's role in, 37–38
  division management board, 36
  financial review, 34
  monthly operating reports, 34–36
  OCE's role in, 36–37
  overview, 35
  presidents' councils, 36
  role in shaping strategy, 39–40
  waterfall chart, 36
Control magazine, 139
Control Techniques, 169, 171
Copeland Corporation, 42–43, 81,
    129, 135–136, 168, 173, 178
corporate planning conference (CPC),
    26–28
Cortinovis, Steve, 105, 172
Cox, Bob, 82, 242

Craftsman, 45
CTO (chief technology officer), 127
culture, company, 15–17, 19, 61. *See also* profit focus
customer capability model, 199
customers and growth. *See* marketing

Davidson, Anne Knight, 243
Davis, William L. Jr., 242
Davis, William (Bill) L. III, 212, 214, 242
depreciation in profit waterfall, 103
Design Engineering Center, 133
digital process control, 137–138
Dill, Charlie, 165, 242
divestitures, 158–159
divisions
    communications plan, 58
    design reviews, 132–133
    expected performance in creating value, 18–19
    globalization, 164–165
    management board, 36
    planning conferences (*see* planning conferences, division level)
    profit and growth planning, 20–21
    profit reviews, 21–22, 99–100
    SIP and, 126–127
Dremel, 45
Drucker, Peter, 7

Eastern Europe, 105–106, 170–171
e-business, 116–118, 180–181
Edison Welding Institute, 131
Electrolux, 46
Emerson
    annual returns, 1, 2
    average profitability, 87, 88
    business segments and divisions, 19, 233–235

company at a glance, 3
core beliefs and values, 4–6
decision to end earnings string, 223–226
management process (*see* management process)
organization structure, 19
outlook for the future, 229–230, *231*
2001 market downturn results, 221–222
Emerson Appliance Solutions, 49–50
Emerson Climate Technologies, 41–43, 135
Emerson Electric China Holdings, 174
Emerson Industrial Automation, 47–49
Emerson Motor Technologies, 49–50
Emerson Network Power, 43–45, 135, 139–142
Emerson Power Transmission, 47
Emerson Process Management, 40–41, 135, 137
Emerson Professional Tools, 45–47
Emerson Storage Solutions, 47
Emerson Technology Council, 128
employee recognition, 133–134
Ericsson, 44
Ericsson Energy Systems, 169
ESCO, 52
Europe
    acquisitions in, 168–169
    creation of advisory council, 171
    expansion into Eastern Europe, 170–171
    planning process applied to, 170
    sales results, 167, *168*
    strategic advantages gained, 171–172

European Advisory Council, 171
Evans, Ike, 242
executing plans
   control of (*see* control cycle)
   Emerson Appliance Solutions,
      49–50
   Emerson Climate Technologies,
      41–43
   Emerson Industrial Automation,
      47–49
   Emerson Motor Technologies,
      49–50
   Emerson Network Power, 43–45
   Emerson Process Management,
      40–41
   Emerson Professional Tools,
      45–47
   Emerson Storage Solutions, 47
   exit decision examples, 50–52
   factors in success, 32–33
   reasons for plan failures, 32
   role in shaping strategy, 39–40

Farr, David, 24, 34, 65, 79, 137, 174,
      213, 214, 215, 218, 241
Farrell, David C., 242
Faught, Hal, 127, 242
F.G. Wilson, 48, 169, 172
Fieldbus Foundation, 71
financial review
   control cycle, 34
   planning model, 17–18, 227
Fisher, 129, 137
Fisher Controls, 41, 81–82
Fisher Electronics, 51
Fleishman-Hillard, 55
Fontaine, Mary, 212, 215
Forbes, 75, 77
Fortini-Campbell, Lisa, 199
franchise strategy, 43
Frates, Joseph A., 242

Galvin, Walter, 34, 65, 75, 97, 241
Gifford, David, 242
Gilbert, Allan, 209, 242
globalization
   Asian performance (*see* Asia)
   division-level involvement,
      164–165
   e-business opportunities, 180–181
   European performance (*see* Europe)
   export-led strategy, 164
   footings expansion, 165
   future prospects, 181–182
   growth outside the United States,
      161, *162*
   international sales, 163
   international sales goals, 165
   Latin America and, 180
   management process effectiveness,
      166–167, 178–179
   Middle East and, 180
Golden, Arthur F., 242
Gorguze, Vincent T., 242
Graham, John, 242
Greenbaum, Stuart, 242
growth at Emerson
   assessment of growth efforts,
      205–206
   brand development (*see* marketing)
   business models creation,
      201–202
   challenges presented by slow econ-
      omy, 183–184
   growth programs, 187
   idea generation process, 192–193
   investors' expectations for, 185
   lessons learned from first phase,
      188–189
   recommendations for achieving de-
      sired level, 185
   refocusing of conferences, 186–187
   reorganization, 202–203
   repositioning, 203–205

roadmap for second phase, 189–191
  vision for, 191

Haier, 49, 178
Hamel, Gary, 185, 186, 191, 201
Hammer, Michael, 203
Hansen, Charles, 242
Hardymon, Jim, 34, 242
Hay/McBer, 212
Heath, Vern, 242
Heikkila, Les, 242
Henry, Claude, 242
Hiross, 169
Home Depot, The, 46
Horton, Sir Robert B., 171, 242
Huawei, 44, 176
human resources, 54–55. *See also* personnel development
Hutchison, Phil, 57, 241

India, 133
Industrial Controls division, 43
Industrial Strength Marketing, 196–197
inflation in profit waterfall, 102
In-Sink-Erator, 45, 47
intellectual property, 128
InterMetro, 47
international growth. *See* globalization

Jackson, Phelps, 242
Japan, 147
Joucomatic, 168, 171

Kato Engineering, 48, 172
Keefe, Ray, 65, 114, 241
Keyes, Larry, 33–34, 242
Knaack, 47

Knight, Joanne, 76, 242
Knight, Lester B., 72
Knight, Lester B. III, 243
Knight, Steven P., 243
Kremer, Larry, 65, 108–112, 242

Latin America, 180
LBK (Lester B. Knight & Associates), 208
leadership
  attributes of (*see* attributes of effective leaders)
  benefits of action-orientation, 68–69
  environment at Emerson, 69–70
  keys to, 10
leadership succession
  benefits of continuity, 207–208
  CEO selection process beginnings, 208
  desired CEO qualities, 209–210, *211*
  final evaluations, 216–219
  preliminary steps, 210–212
  process success, 219–220
lean manufacturing, 114–116
Ledford, Randall, 65, 127, 241
Leroy-Somer, 48, 129, 130, 135, 169, 171
Lester B. Knight & Associates (LBK), 208
leverage in profit waterfall, 103
Liebert, 43, 139, 173
Lindemann, James J., 242
Lodge, Gerry, 28, 124, 241
Loeb, Marshall, 69
loose-tight controls concept, 83–84
Loucks, Vern, 124, 242
Lovelady, Ernie, 242
Lowe's, 46
Loynd, Dick, 29, 124, 241

MagneTek Alternators, 48, 172

Major, John, 171

management compensation (*see* personnel development)

management process
    acquisitions and (*see* acquisitions)
    action-orientation and (*see* action-orientation at Emerson)
    adjustment to new business environment, 226–229
    applied to Asia, 178–179
    applied to international operations, 166–167, 178–179
    applied to restructuring, 224–226
    commitment to planning, 8
    definition of management's job, 6–7
    effectiveness of, 11–13
    evolving nature of, 10–11
    follow-up and control system, 8–9
    leadership environment, 10
    operational excellence, 9–10
    planning component (*see* planning)
    simplicity and, 7–8

manager chart, 62, 63, 64

Marconi DC, 226

marketing
    brand promise, 194
    common customer interface projects, 198
    customer capability model, 199
    management education program, 196–197
    marquee account program, 197
    new brand architecture, 193–194, 196
    new logo adoption, 194–195
    value in understanding the customer, 199–201

marquee account program, 197

Material Characterization Center, 131, 132

Material Information Network (MIN), 111–114. *See also* materials procurement

materials procurement
    conflicts with divisions, 112
    efforts in Asia, 112
    main elements, 111
    preliminary consolidation, 108–111
    reverse auction concept, 113–114

McKnight, Paul, 60, 214, 215, 241

McRoberts, Robert H., 242

Mexico, 95, 105

Michaels, James, 75

Micro Motion, 40, 129

Middle East, 180

Monsanto, 41, 81

Monser, Ed, 33, 80, 107, 242

Montupet, Jean-Paul, 98, 174, 241

Motor Technology Center, 130, 135

Muir, Earl, 81

Murray, Mike, 210, 211, 242

Nortel, 44

Novello, Bob, 81, 136, 242

office of the chief executive (OCE)
    control cycle and, 36–37
    succession decision and (*see* leadership succession)

Okura Intex Ltd., 147

operational excellence at Emerson
    average profitability, 87, 88
    Best Cost Producer strategy, 92–93
    cost reduction mentality, 89–90
    e-business, 116–118
    expansion into Eastern Europe, 105–106
    expansion into Mexico, 105

lean manufacturing, 114–116
materials procurement (*see* materials procurement)
Mexican plants' successes, 95
outsourcing, 117–118
philosophy of profitability, 87–88
plant relocation decisions, 94–95
profit planning (*see* profit focus)
quality improvement program, 93–94
rise in competition, 90–92
salary cost containment, 104
summary, 118–119
wage cost containment, 104, 107
organization planning, 60–64
organization reviews, 60–62
organization room, 62–64
outsourcing use, 117–118
Ouweleen, F. W., 242

patents, 128
pay for results (*see* personnel development)
Peltier, Dick, 81
personnel development
color-coded chart use, 62, 63, 64
compensation policies, 65–66, 67, 68
leadership environment at Emerson, 69–70
management development and action-orientation, 64–65
marketing management education program, 196–197
organization review, 60, 62, 63
principles of, 60
Persons, Buck, ix, x, 208, 243
Peters, Charlie, 65, 82, 116, 191, 193, 196, 200, 214, 215, 241
Pfleger, George T., 242

planning
benefits of approach, 29–30
BOD's role, 28–29
business segments, 19
calendar, 19–20
conferences (*see* planning conferences, division level)
corporate planning, 26–29
cycle overview, 20
execution of the plan (*see* executing plans)
exit decision examples, 50–52
expected performance by unit, 18–19
financial model, 17–18, 227
as philosophy and practice, 15–17
profit and growth in divisions, 20–21
profit reviews, division level, 21–22
results examples, 30–31
role in shaping strategy, 39–40
strategy reviews, business level, 25–26
tracking the plan (*see* control cycle)
planning conferences, division level
benefits of, 23
CEO's role, 24
critical nature of, 25
mood in, 23–24
objective of, 22
output of, 24
refocusing for growth, 186–187
time horizon used, 22–23
Planting, Charles O., 242
PlantWeb, 41, 137–139
PLASET, 169
Potts, Ramsay D., 242
Poulan chainsaws, 45
presidents' councils, 36
presidents' operating reports (PORs), 34–36, 237–240

profit focus
  average profitability at Emerson, 87,
    88
  containment action examples,
    103–104
  division-level profit review, 99–100
  factors influencing margin erosion,
    96–97
  flaw in traditional planning ap-
    proach, 98
  philosophy of profitability, 87–88
  profit and growth planning in divi-
    sions, 20–21
  profit reviews in divisions, 21–22,
    99–100
  "profit waterfall" analysis tool,
    97–99
  "profit waterfall" example, 100, *101*,
    102–103
Provox, 137
Psychological Associates, 214

Qilong, Wang, 131

reverse auction concept, 113–114
Rhodes, John, 242
Ridge Tool, 45, 47, 161, 164
Ridgid, 46
Ridgway, Rozanne L., 242
Robert Bosch GmbH, 46
Roemer, Scot, 241
Rohrbaugh, John C., 242
Rohret, Mike, 242
Rosemount Inc., 40, 52, 80, 129, 130,
    137, 165, 172, 173
Rutledge, Bill, 34, 77–78, 242

sales gap chart, 184
Sarbanes-Oxley Act, 148

Schriever, Gen. Bernard, USAF (Ret.),
    29, 123–124, 242
scroll compressor, 42–43, 135–136,
    178
Seals, D., 93
Sears, 46
SIP (Strategic Investment Program),
    83, 126–127
Skil, 45, 154
Slovakia, 105
Sly, Patrick J., 242
Software Center of Excellence, 131
Solid State Center, 130
Sollberger, Dennis, 242
Stack-A-Shelf, 47
Staley, Bob, 84, 125, 166–167, 175,
    210, 241
Stern, Joel, 28
Strategic Investment Program (SIP),
    83, 126–127
strategy reviews, business level,
    25–26
Suter, Al, 34, 90, 107, 210, 241
swarm engineering, 117, 140,
    141–142
Switched Reluctance Drives Ltd.
    (SRDL), 129, 130
Switzer, Jim, 241

Tamke, George, 79, 213, 214, 242
technology leadership
  awards program, 133–134
  board of directors expertise,
    123–124
  competitive advantage and,
    122–123
  design reviews, division level,
    132–133
  funding commitment, 124–125
  network of expertise, 130–131
  network power strategy, 139–142

new product programs, 125–126
PlantWeb control system, 137–139
results of efforts, 134–135
scroll compressor development,
    135–136
strategic investment program (SIP),
    126–127
technical links outside the U.S.,
    131–132
through acquisitions, 129
through internal initiatives,
    129–130
technology road mapping, 127
Therm-O-Disc (T-O-D), 91
Thurow, Lester, 167
Time, 70

unions, 57

Van Cleve, William M., 242
variable-speed motors, 83
Vaughan, William, 242
Ver Hagen, Jan K., 242
Vermont American, 46, 47
Vuma, 105–106

Waigel, Theo, 171
waterfall, profit, 36, 97–99, 100, *101*,
    102–103
Weed Eater, 45
Westman, Tim, 241
Whirlpool, 90, 91
Whitacre, Edward E. Jr., 242
Williams, Eugene F. Jr., 242
Wilson, John, 34, 242
Withers, Wayne, 241
Wojciechowski, Linda, 242

About the Authors

Charles F. Knight is Chairman Emeritus of Emerson. He was the company's CEO for twenty-seven years (ending in 2000), and Chairman for thirty years (ending in 2004). As CEO, he spearheaded Emerson's evolution from a primarily domestic producer to a technology-based global manufacturer. The company's record of increased earnings per share and increased dividends for each year of his term as CEO is among the longest for consistent performance in U.S. business. Mr. Knight has been recognized frequently for his management expertise and serves or has served on the boards of directors of a number of leading global companies, including Anheuser-Busch; Baxter International; BP; Caterpillar; Emerson; IBM; Morgan Stanley; and SBC Communications.

Davis Dyer is president and a founding director of The Winthrop Group, Inc., a Cambridge, Massachusetts–based firm specializing in the documentation and use of organizational experience, and a faculty member at Monitor University, part of The Monitor Company Group, LLP. He is author or coauthor of many publications, including *Rising Tide: Lessons from 165 Years of Brand Building at Procter & Gamble* (2004, with Frederick Dalzell and Rowena Olegario) and *Changing Fortunes: Remaking the Industrial Corporation* (2002, with Nitin Nohria and Frederick Dalzell).